Strategic Decision Making for Successful Planning

Strategic Decision Making for Successful Planning

Solving Problems for Great Results

CJ Rhoads
William Roth

A PRODUCTIVITY PRESS BOOK

First Published 2022
by Routledge
605 Third Avenue, New York, NY 10158

and by Routledge
2 Park Square, Milton Park, Abingdon, Oxon, OX14 4RN

Routledge is an imprint of the Taylor & Francis Group, an informa business

© 2022 CJ Rhoads

The right of CJ Rhoads to be identified as author of this work has been asserted by her in accordance with sections 77 and 78 of the Copyright, Designs and Patents Act 1988.

All rights reserved. No part of this book may be reprinted or reproduced or utilized in any form or by any electronic, mechanical, or other means, now known or hereafter invented, including photocopying and recording, or in any information storage or retrieval system, without permission in writing from the publishers.

Trademark notice: Product or corporate names may be trademarks or registered trademarks, and are used only for identification and explanation without intent to infringe.

ISBN: 978-1-032-05552-7 (hbk)
ISBN: 978-1-032-05550-3 (pbk)
ISBN: 978-1-003-19806-2 (ebk)

DOI: 10.4324/9781003198062

Typeset in Garamond
by Deanta Global Publishing Services, Chennai, India

To my many mentors
Currently the count is 34
Too many to name here

You have helped me, cleaned me,
propped me up
And treated me like a precious jewel.

You scrubbed the dirty rock that was me
Until, with your help, my talents showed through.

Collectively you taught me that I could do anything,
So I thought I could.
And I did.

CJ Rhoads

To Eric Trist
My teacher and friend.
One of the founders of the systems approach
To management theory.
A man who remains to me
an ongoing model for
completeness and humility. With thanks.

William Roth

Contents

List of Figures xi
List of Tables xiii
Preface xv
Acknowledgments xix
Authors xxiii

1 Creating the Optimum Culture 1
  The Challenge 1
  The Optimum Reward System 4
  Beginning with the Basics 5
    Physiological Needs 6
    Safety Needs 7
    Love and Belonging 8
    Esteem 9
    Self-Actualization 10
  How Do We Get There? 11
  Onward and Upward 12
  Summary Chapter 1 Questions 14

2 Shaping the Optimum Attitude, Perspective, and Method 15
  The Optimum Attitude for Change 15
  Interactive Is the Future 18
    The Optimum Perspective for Change 20
    The Optimum Vehicle for Change 24
    Once Again, Who's In Charge? 27
  The Next Step 29
  Summary Chapter 2 Questions 30

3 Picking the Optimum Techniques and Tools 31
Techniques for Individuals 31
    Individual Techniques Using Word Games 32
    Individual Techniques Using Attribute Manipulation 34
    Individual Techniques Using Elaboration 36
    Individual Techniques Using Analogy Making 40
    Evaluation of Techniques Used to Enhance Individual Problem Solving Ability 42
General Group Techniques 44
    General Group Techniques That Focus on the Generation of Ideas 44
    General Group Techniques That Focus on Defining Priorities 50
    Evaluation of General Group Techniques 59
Holistic Techniques 60
    Holistic to Identify Problems 61
    Holistic Techniques Used to Discover Solutions 66
Evaluation of Holistic Techniques 77
Tools for Measuring Productivity 78
    Check Sheet 78
    Statistical Control Chart 79
    Histogram 80
    Pareto Diagram 80
    Scatter Diagram 81
Measuring Productivity Summary 82
Putting It All Together 82
Summary Chapter 3 Questions 83

4 Choosing the Optimum Analytics 85
What Is Analytics? 85
Why Do We Need Business Analytics? 88
Big Data 88
    Benefits and Pitfalls of Big Data 88
    Where Does Big Data Come From? 90
Knowledge Management 92
    Difficulties with Human Knowledge 93
    Natural Language Processing 94
    Identifying the Context of Business Data 95
    Dirty Data and GIGO 96
Tools of the Trade 97

	How to Tell If It's Good Data	99
	Preparing Data	102
	Foundational Tasks of Analytics	103
	Four Type of Analytics	104
	Steps of Analytics	104
	Which Analytical Tools to Use	105
	Descriptive Statistics	106
	Data Visualization	106
	Regression Analysis	106
	Group Differences	110
	Multivariate Analysis	111
	Summary Chapter 4 Questions	113
5	**Mapping the Optimum Approach**	**115**
	On the Optimum Track with Just a Few Adjustments	115
	The Best Model from a Macro Perspective	118
	Into the Trenches	120
	Corporate-Wide versus Individual Facility	122
	Succeeding at Decision Making	123
	Summary Chapter 5 Questions	124
6	**Overview of the Ideal Decision Making Model**	**125**
	Introduction	125
	Understanding the Decision to Be Made	126
	Step 1: Document the Decision to Be Made in the Charter	126
	Step 2: Identify the Scope of the Decision	128
	Step 3: Collect Initial Data and Survey the Customers and Stakeholders	128
	Understanding the Process	129
	Step 4: Define and Diagram the Process in Order to Understand Current Circumstances	129
	Step 5: Establish the Process Performance Measures and Targets	131
	Understanding the Causes	134
	Step 6: Diagram the Causes and Effects	134
	Step 7: Collect Data on Causes	134
	Understanding the Numbers, Solutions, and the Future	135
	Step 8: Analyze Data	135
	Step 9: Develop and Consider Possible Options	136
	Step 10: Measure Success or Failure	136
	Summary Chapter 6 Questions	138

7 Integrated Case Study: Jan's Technology Services 139
The Company 139
Changing Conditions 140
Quality Comes to JTS 141
Establishing a Strategy 142
The Balanced Scorecard 147
    Setting Priorities 153
    Implementation 153
    Initial Training 154
The Ten-Step Ideal Decision Making Model (IDMM) Begins 156
    Step 1: Document the Decision to Be Made in a Charter 156
    Step 2: Identify the Scope of the Decision 157
    Step 3: Review Data on Customers and Stakeholders 161
    Step 4: Define and Diagram the Process 165
    Step 5: Establish the Process Performance Measures and Targets 167
    Step 6: Diagram the Causes and Effects 172
    Step 7: Collect Data on Causes 176
    Step 8: Analyze Data 176
    Step 9: Develop and Consider Possible Options 177
    Step 10: Check: Measure Success or Failure 199
Summary Chapter 7 Questions 213

References 215

Index 221

List of Figures

Figure 1.1	Maslow's Hierarchy of Needs	6
Figure 3.1	Example of Fishbone Diagram for Root Cause Analysis	54
Figure 3.2	Flowchart Diagram for Insurance Claim Process	62
Figure 3.3	Search Conference Stages	73
Figure 3.4	Service Blueprinting Example	76
Figure 3.5	Statistical Control Chart Example	78
Figure 3.6	Histogram Example	79
Figure 3.7	Pareto Diagram Example	80
Figure 3.8	Scatter Diagram Example	81
Figure 4.1	The Boy Hit the Boy with the Girl with the Hammer	95
Figure 4.2	Average Healthcare Cost Per Capita and Percent of GDP	107
Figure 4.3	A Tableau Data Visualization of Health Expense by Country	108
Figure 4.4	A Tableau Example of Data Visualization Sales by Category	109
Figure 4.5	Comparison of a Strong Correlation (left) to No Correlation (right)	109
Figure 7.1	Ideal Decision Making Model	155
Figure 7.2	Rules of the Road	156
Figure 7.3	Check Sheet: Support Calls for Two Weeks	158
Figure 7.4	Pareto Diagram of Support Calls	159

Figure 7.5	Historical Average Days for Support Call Resolution	161
Figure 7.6	Pareto Diagram of Customer Concerns	163
Figure 7.7	Macro-Level Flowchart of Bug Fix Request	167
Figure 7.8	Micro-Level Flowchart of Bug Fix Request	168
Figure 7.9	Flowchart with Process Points Indicated	171
Figure 7.10	Fishbone Diagram: Major Bones	173
Figure 7.11	Fishbone Diagram: People Bone	173
Figure 7.12	Fishbone Diagram: Subpart of People Bone	174
Figure 7.13	Fishbone Subpart of People Bone with Root Causes (Cloud)	175
Figure 7.14	Relationships between Incomplete Info and Long Delay	177
Figure 7.15	Solutions Selection Matrix. Scale of 1–10	180
Figure 7.16	Pareto Diagram of Support Calls	201
Figure 7.17	Pareto Diagram Comparing Before and After	202
Figure 7.18	Number of Days to Resolution	202
Figure 7.19	Flowchart for New Process	205

List of Tables

Table 3.1	Sliding Column Method Example	35
Table 3.2	Morphological Forced Connection Example	37
Table 3.3	Flowchart List Example	63
Table 3.4	Breaking the Ice Technique Example	66
Table 3.5	Listing Example of Force Field Analysis	67
Table 4.1	Magic Quadrant of Business Intelligence/Analytics Software	98
Table 7.1	Strategic Objective Table	146
Table 7.2	Items in JTS Balanced Scorecard	152
Table 7.3	Cost–Benefit Analysis	191
Table 7.4	Restraining and Driving Forces	192
Table 7.5	Action Plan	193

Preface

Decision making has been going on since the beginning of time. It is traditionally one of the major chores in all facets of our lives. As the centuries have passed, the art of decision making has necessarily evolved. It has evolved because the decisions we must make have become increasingly sophisticated and the problems we encounter increasingly complex. The number of variables involved has grown. The range of potential solutions has expanded. The web, or "mess", of interrelated problems to which ours belongs, and which affect ours, has spread.

Today, in the world of work, due to the increasing level of competition, the cost of incorrect solutions is rapidly growing. More effective decision making, therefore, is critical to success. As a result, society has turned decision making into a science complete with schools of thought on how best to shape the workplace culture so that it will encourage effective efforts, on how best to shape vehicles to facilitate these efforts, on what the best decision making tools and techniques are, and, finally, on how best to fit the critical pieces of decision making efforts together.

Strategic Decision Making for Successful Planning was written as a study of these pieces—culture, vehicles, tools, and techniques—and as an exploration of their relationships. The book was written from a holistic multi-dimensional perspective.

In Chapter 1, we begin by addressing the issue of workplace *culture*. We focus initially on the development of a reward system that will facilitate effective decision making. We do so because we believe that an organization's reward system does more to shape its culture than anything else. We use Abraham Maslow's *hierarchy of needs* as a frame of reference for our argument.

Chapter 2 begins by introducing four different *attitudes* toward decision making—reactive, inactive, hyperactive, and preactive—all of which treat problems as a threat. It then defines an alternative, the interactive attitude, which helps turn problems into opportunities as well.

Next, the chapter addresses *perspective*, which helps shape both culture and attitude. It identifies the origins and characteristics of the holistic perspective and talks about how this perspective facilitates decision making. Finally, Chapter 2 identifies two decision making vehicles to solve problems—task forces and autonomous work groups. It discusses the strengths and weaknesses of each and how they can be combined.

Chapter 3 gets down to the nitty-gritty and looks at the *techniques and tools* available for decision making efforts. The chapter identifies four broad categories—individual, group, holistic, and productivity measuring—into which all techniques and tools can be fit. It spells out in detail the steps in 43 of them and then identifies situations where each can be used effectively and how they can be combined.

Chapter 4 talks about *analytics* and where it fits into the decision making process. In previous decades, business leaders could only make guesses as to what was really going on. These days, the ability to gather real data has enabled the use of information to provide a more solid basis upon which to make decisions.

Chapter 5 talks about *approach*, about how to start organization change efforts so that they can generate the necessary culture, maintain the optimum attitude, build the most appropriate vehicle, and properly utilize the optimum tools and techniques. It addresses the issue of training and discusses whether it should be introduced up front or on the job and how training in problem solving efforts should be organized. It gives an example of how the necessary training was effectively introduced in one corporation.

Chapter 6 introduces a model for holistic decision making efforts, the *Ideal Decision Making Model*. This model is spelled out, step by step, for readers.

Finally, Chapter 7 presents a comprehensive case study involving a technology firm that sells technology services. The major problem addressed is the lack of necessary information flowing between management and employees and between company and customers. The case study explores in-depth the trials and tribulations of attempting to change the culture of an organization by attempting to introduce the Ideal Decision Making Model and the necessary teams, techniques, and tools.

The major obstruction in this case study, as in most, is the differing perspectives of various employees. We show what can be done to deal with these differences and what can be done to draw employees together into a comprehensive, successful strategic decision making effort.

Why You Should Read This Book

Strategic Decision Making is not a new topic. Many books have been written on it. Few, however, have "hit the mark."

While there are many books on decision making, problem solving, and planning, they tend to fall into one of two camps: lightweight guides that simply outline the process or provide tips and techniques, or academic tomes that delve into the human process of planning, problem solving, and decision making. This is because they have lacked the necessary focus and the full range of necessary ingredients. Approaching strategic decision making theoretically may be easier than providing practical steps and applications for the often-messy process of making strategic change happen. Easier, but not as helpful.

What is unique about *Strategic Decision Making for Successful Planning* is that it is based on a strong academic foundation, but does not get bogged down in the human-planning or psychological process of solving problems. This book does not provide pie-in-the-sky creative solutions, nor a five-year process for making strategic decisions, solving problems, and planning for the future. This book is the optimum balance between practical and academic; this book has been written by highly experienced people with one foot in the practical real-life work of strategic decision making and the other foot in the academic world of education and credible sourcing. This book is useful as a textbook, while targeted for real-life.

Features of the Book

This book has the following distinct features:

1. The importance of culture in strategic decision making
2. Various techniques and tools for planning and problem solving
3. The issues in strategic decision making from macro to micro
4. The role of analytics in strategic decision making
5. The Ideal Decision Making Model
6. An integrated case study that demonstrates different aspects presented in the book
7. End of chapter questions for the reader to pose to themselves after completing the reading

Acknowledgments

As I've said before, and will say again: anyone who has their name on the cover of a book knows that no book is written solely by the author. A good book cannot exist without an entire team of people working on it, and it is only by convention and convenience (not to mention space) that not all of those names appear on the cover.

Firstly, this book would not have happened if Bill Roth had not urged me to contact Kristine Mednansky at Taylor and Francis in 2015 to publish my book on Telehealth. Kristine was wonderful then, so when she called me to ask me to update one of the books that Bill had written for them before he passed away, how could I say anything but yes? And, of course, Carly Cassano and Andrew Corrigan managed the production project very well, ensuring that the book got published in time for me to use it as a textbook in one of the graduate courses I teach at Kutztown University, PA. Additionally, it was through Linda and Ted Thomas of the Pagoda Writers Group that Bill and I started doing projects and books together.

I must also thank James Ryder and Frank Voehl who worked with Bill on the original text. Though they did not work on this version of the book, the foundation that they laid in the last two chapters of the book was well utilized.

This book is also due, in part, to the determined and intelligent help of my "team"; a disparate group of people, many of them my students, who helped me with the hard labor of viewing, reviewing, discussing, arguing, revising, and redoing all of the work imbedded within these pages. They are: Timothy Coyle, Kimberly Duhamel-Murray, Seth Ecker, Blase Garracht, Lynn Loaiza, Sheldon Rone, Dan Chen See, and Mohammad Ibrahim B.

Many of the tools, techniques, and projects I worked on with my clients appear in these pages, though none with their real names. In any case, my own knowledge is always expanded greatly by those whom I have served, for I learn much from them in the course of our activities together. I'd especially like to extend my heartfelt thanks to Lee Baker, Peter Baker, David Bosler, David Dries, Bob Goodman, Michael Guido, Joanne Just, Conrad Karlson, Andy Klee, Pat Krick, Harriet Layton, Jane Palmer, Samantha Reimert, LuAnn Seyler, Patrick Sullivan, Anthony Triano, and Linda Wade.

I would also like to thank the former faculty and staff of the College of Business (in alphabetical order) who all helped me with encouragement and support over many years: Okan Akcay, Dan Benson, Pat Blatt, Henry Check, Donna DeLong, Arifeen Daneshyar, Mark Dinger, Ken Ehrensal, Philip Evans, Robert Everett, Stacey Gambler, Tom Grant, Keshav Gupta, David Haas, John Hamrick, Ray Heimbach, Roger Hibbs, Eileen Hogan, Arian Hungaski, Fidel Ikem, John Kruglinski, Patricia Patrick, Elisabeth Rogol, Paul Sable, Norman Sigmond, and David Wagaman. Of course, I also need to thank the current faculty and staff at Kutztown who have also encouraged and supported me: Paige Brookins, Anne Carroll, Gary Chao, Alfred Esposto, Ashwini Gangadharan, Carolyn Gardner, Qin Geng, Emma Hao, Gregory Kaufinger, Mahfuzul Khondaker, Su Kong, Jonathan Kramer, Rajeev Kumar, Liao Liao Li, Mostafa Maksy, Therese Maskulka, Victor Massad, Kimberly O'Neill, Shawn Riley, George Rogol, Abdul Sraiheen, Donna Steslow, Qian Sun, and John Walker. My fellow faculty at Kutztown University are all incredibly important to me, and there is not a one who has not helped me tremendously over the years.

Furthermore, many of my colleagues at Hi-TECH Connections, MBNA, and First USA as well as my own businesses were instrumental in developing my ability to plan strategically. Of course none of this would be possible without my many mentors over the years (in alphabetical order): Fred Beste, Mike Bolton, David Bosler, Jack Bradt, Tom Casey, Betsy Chapman, Martin Cheatle, Jim Collins, Vanessa DiMauro, Jonathan Dreazen, Francois Dumas, Marsha Egan, Dale Falcinelli, Steve Higgins, Roger Jahnke, George Lipper, John Lucht, John MacNamara, Brenda Moretti, Nancy Magee, Ray Melcher, Sally Milbury-Steen, Maggie Newman, Pete Musser, Josephine Painter, Joe Puglisi, Leo Robb, Robert Rubin, Lee Scheele, Glen Snelbecker, Steve Sperling, Alan Weiss, Kevin Wren, and Yang Yang. Though the amount of time I spent with each varied, each one has given me a gift that has turned out to be of extreme value in my never-ending quest to improve myself.

No list would be complete without my fabulous family; my mother Judith Liffick, and my father Martin Devlin and his wife Jeri, along with my brothers and sisters Jeffrey Devlin, T. Max Devlin, Eileen Piccolo, and Denise Rankin. I also wish to thank Sister Mary Morley and Sister Pat Dotzauer as well—who provided the LBI getaway that formed the backdrop of many hours of my writing.

Again, as always, this book is the beneficiary of the largess of my friends, family, students, and colleagues who must put up with my absences when I'm focused on a book deadline. I thank you all.

–CJ Rhoads

Authors

Christine "CJ" Rhoads is currently a full professor at Kutztown University and worked on many projects with Bill Roth. She shared his love of writing and convinced him to come and join the Pagoda Writers, a support group for local writers in Berks County, PA. When she was asked by the publisher to help rewrite Bill's earlier works for the modern business world, she was honored to help out.

Dr. Rhoads is the Founder and CEO of HPL Consortium, Inc., developing technology tools to help people achieve health, attain prosperity, and develop leadership. She is also the Managing Director of HPL 501c3 Institute, the non-profit partner to HPL that provides help and support to other groups and causes for the same purpose. She speaks and writes about entrepreneurship, business strategy, and leadership development.

In 2009, she was honored as one of Pennsylvania's Best 50 Women in Business; in 2011, she received the Athena Leadership Award; in 2013 was named one of most Influential Women in Lehigh Valley Business; in 2014 was named Top Researcher of the Year; and in 2017 was awarded the Distinguished Alumni Achievement Award by Kutztown University College Of Education. She has written over 200 articles and nine books, among them *Telehealth in Rural Hospitals: Lessons Learned from Pennsylvania* by CRC Press as well as *Managing Enterprise Information Technology* by HPL Publications.

William "Bill" Roth was a full professor at Kutztown University in Kutztown, PA, when he passed away relatively suddenly in 2016. Previously, he had taught at Allentown College of St. Francis de Sales in the Lehigh Valley of Pennsylvania. He had previously published four quality-related books, including *The Evolution of Management Theory: Past, Present, Future* with St. Lucie Press. He has also published a large number of articles in leading journals and a series of novels about his early years.

Dr. Roth earned his Ph.D. in management sciences from the Wharton School, University of Pennsylvania, PA. He consulted in quality, organization design, and strategic planning for some 20 years. In the late '90s, he had taken the lead in designing a comprehensive quality training program called "Beyond TQM: The Systems Approach to Quality Improvement," sponsored by the AQP which was widely offered nationwide through a network of colleges and universities. He was an active member of the ASQC Education Division Strategic Planning Committee.

Chapter 1

Creating the Optimum Culture

The Challenge

The world of business is becoming increasingly turbulent. Change is occurring more so at a geometric (1, 2, 4, 16) than an arithmetic (1, 2, 3, 4) rate. It has been estimated, for example, that more new technology has appeared in the last 20 years than in the rest of human history combined. At the same time, the level of competition is rising rapidly as strong new players enter the arena. Partnerships of different kinds are springing up between companies offering the same product, between companies offering complementary products, between companies on different continents, and between companies with very different cultures.

At least partially as a result of these advances in technology and our rapidly expanding perspective, facets of operations which were once relatively straightforward are growing more complex. Management systems are in a state of crisis. The top-down, hierarchical, "make no decisions without my okay," channeled mode of operation has been out of fashion for a very long time (though management egos generally being what they are, the command-and-control methods seem to hang on and on despite the research that shows they are not nearly as effective as modern methods of management). The need for ever-increasing speed and accuracy requires us to flatten the chains of command and to break down the walls between functions.

One of the management responsibilities being most strongly challenged is decision making and problem solving. Increasingly we are hearing calls to push decision making and problem solving authority downward, to encourage the solution of problems on the lowest possible level.

DOI: 10.4324/9781003198062-1

Decades ago, when Frederick Taylor's Scientific Management theories were in vogue, the emphasis was on simplifying jobs to the point where lower level employees did not have to think. Human potential was ignored, and employees were treated like simple, mindless, replaceable machines who were to do what they were told rather than try to contribute or improve the process. But this methodology eventually became fraught with problems as technology and services advanced beyond the cookie-cutter assembly-line approach to production (Cutterbuck 1979; Dickson 1977; Elliot 1990; Emery 1976; George 1968; Guiliano 1982; Gunn 1982; Roth 1993b).

Eventually it became apparent that top managers did not always have the time or knowledge necessary to make all the decisions for the growing number and variety of issues and problems encountered. For optimum operations, employees needed to think for themselves and take corrective action instead of simply complaining and seeking a solution from management.

In addition to the growing complexity of operations, a second factor reinforcing this trend is changes in the workplace itself. Technology has made old-style, centralized, office-based operations somewhat obsolete. Telecommuting and utilizing videoconferencing and other technologies have been demonstrated to be very effective. It makes no sense in terms of time, expense, efficiency, or the environment to force employees to travel long distances in order to meet the same job responsibilities they could perform just as well or better at home. But telecommuting made it difficult for authoritative bosses who like to watch their people to make sure they were working.

Despite our realization that change is inevitable and ultimately beneficial, we, as a culture, have always had difficulty moving away from an outdated mindset. We continue to operate "the way we've always done it" because that is familiar and comfortable. Frederick Taylor's Scientific Management was in vogue for a very long time, and spawned an endless search for the most efficient means of monitoring employee activities. But this reactive approach to an increasingly complex issue is causing our quality of life, both at home and in the workplace, to suffer (Ackoff 1975; Chems 1975; Durmaine 1994; Fenwick 1978).

Eventually, of course, things will, indeed, change. It is inevitable. The most instinctual desire beyond survival which has driven civilization historically has been the desire to improve the quality of life for both individuals and for society as a whole. From this perspective, we have done well in terms of achieving our objectives and have come a long way in a relatively short period of time.

Our present difficulty in accepting advantageous change, therefore, is not new. Rather, it is normal. It is a coping mechanism to protect us from the unknown. It is reflected in individuals with power trying to hang onto the status quo because they are comfortable with it and not secure enough to accept change, no matter how obvious the need and benefits. It is another one of the stumbling blocks that have littered the pathway of progress but which will eventually be swept away by the irresistible forces of social evolution, like all the others before it.

As this happens, the workplace, management systems, decision making and problem solving are becoming increasingly decentralized. The nature of work itself is changing radically and we will, hopefully, begin as a culture to remember its development-related purpose.

A large-scale education effort is one of the support systems we must organize if we are to make the desired transition as smooth as possible. Two things will be key if such an education effort is to be effective. The first is that top-level management must be helped to rethink its concepts of organizational attitude and organizational design so that it encompasses strategic decision making. The second is that employees on all levels must concentrate on improving their decision making skills.

In terms of the top-level management rethinking exercise, those involved must be willing to look beyond what has brought success in the past and shift into the new world paradigm. They must move beyond the need for an organizational structure carved in stone with rigid lines of communication and authority. They must become more flexible and willing to risk creative new arrangements. They must become more pragmatic and be willing to go with what works in terms of decision making. They must honestly and openly address the following issues:

1. Which employees should be responsible for making which decisions?
2. Which employees should be responsible for addressing which problems?
3. Who should have access to what information in order to effectively make good decisions?
4. What is the best way to integrate the results of individual and group efforts?
5. What is the best way to make sure that such a participative approach is effective in terms of the long-term objectives of the organization?

These are among the issues that will be addressed in this book. This is no easy challenge. These are tough issues that affect every facet of an operation. They cannot be addressed in the most effective manner until the necessary changes in organizational culture have occurred.

The Optimum Reward System

Perhaps the toughest of the challenges we are talking about, and the most threatening of the necessary changes, will involve the reward system. It must be reshaped. The reward system is the cornerstone of all operations. More than any other system, it determines the culture of the organization and frequently its structure and processes. It affects such things as the way employees on all levels interact with each other and with employees on other levels, the size of departments, the willingness of employees to take risks, and the way information is guarded or shared.

If a reward system pits managers against each other and creates an adversarial relationship between management and the workforce, the shift to the type of cooperative atmosphere necessary for more effective decision making will not occur. Each group will sub-optimize in favor of its own self-interest, to the detriment of the system as a whole. That is human nature.

People are not natively altruistic, generally. The major priority during their work lives is not to satisfy customers (in-house or external), bosses, or owners. Rather, the major priority is to shape a job in that way which will best satisfy their own needs and desires.

Unless the company also enjoys success, of course, such satisfaction will not occur. Customers, bosses, and owners (or "stakeholders" as systems professionals call them) are indeed important, but the most important stakeholder (in the eyes of the individual employee) is the individual employee himself or herself. That is as it should be in any pragmatic society. That is the realization upon which the free enterprise system was built.

Most of the models upon which the current quality improvement movement depends, for example, make the customer the most important target. This has happened because our quantitatively oriented business community favors measurement and numbers. Customer satisfaction is one of the factors that we are set up to measure in an improvement process. It is the most important strategic factor in the organization's continued success.

We also make the customer the most important target because focusing on improving customer relations is much more fruitful in terms of public relations and marketing.

However, if we focus on the customer to the exclusion of the employees, we have confused the ends with the means, the results with the producers. Customer satisfaction is a *result* produced by *committed employees*. The focus, therefore, in organization improvement efforts should be to get employees effectively involved and do what is necessary to develop the necessary level of commitment.

This can be accomplished by incorporating satisfaction of employee needs into the model. But to which employee needs and desires should we be paying attention? Which ones are important? Which ones are the company's responsibility? If everyone wants to drive a new company-provided car, should we feel obliged to satisfy that desire? Must we, in essence, be willing to "give away the store" (Wilkerson 1995; Roth 1989c)?

The evidence refutes such fears. In poorly run organizations, where management is out to get the most from employees while giving the least, the employees will indeed take the company for everything they can. In companies like this, such fears are realistic. They are, however, also largely the result of management's attitude.

In organizations that show true concern and respect for employees, such standoffs do not usually occur. Workers want to be there, and understand that they are part of a team. They are willing to make sacrifices of time, effort, and even money if such sacrifices are necessary to the survival and healthy growth of the organization, as long as everyone else, from top to bottom, has the same attitude.

When the team and the organization do well, the employees want to enjoy the victory, along with their coworkers, and be rewarded fairly for their contribution.

Beginning with the Basics

What employees define as their needs, in a respectful atmosphere, is reasonable and, in fact, differs little from what they define as their needs in private life. The nature of basic human needs has been questioned throughout the history of mankind, and the answer has changed little over the centuries. Psychologist Abraham Maslow described the range of these needs thoroughly in the middle of the last century (Maslow) in a hierarchy (as seen in Figure 1.1*). His definition, which incorporates the work of many others,

---

* Image by Saul Mcleod, used with permission.

6 ■ *Strategic Decision Making for Successful Planning*

Figure 1.1 Maslow's Hierarchy of Needs. (Source: Image by Saul Mcleod, used with permission.)

seems complete, has not been greatly improved upon despite the number of years that have passed, and can be related back to the workplace with relative ease.

Physiological Needs

On his first foundational level, Maslow places physiological needs (those necessary to physical survival). These include food, water, shelter, and an environment capable of sustaining life. These needs are obviously the most basic. When one of the requisite inputs is missing, the penalty for not replenishing it is death. The quest for life may often supersede all other needs.

In the workplace, physiological needs can be framed in terms of salary, i.e., earning enough money to be able to afford the necessary food, liquids, and environmental needs. As people stopped growing their own food and building their own homes and began to work for others who headed companies that manufactured goods to be sold in sometimes distant marketplaces, salary became the primary focus.

Although the industrial revolution spurred the growth of wealth, the results were not always rosy at all levels. For example, during the early Industrial Revolution in England, it was estimated that an average weekly factory wage allowed the purchase of only three days of food for a family of four. Today, many single working mothers or fathers in low-level jobs do not earn enough to adequately satisfy the physiological needs of their families and must depend upon public assistance to do so.

In the modern-day workplace, therefore, despite seemingly tremendous wealth, adequate salary remains the major issue for most. People must earn enough money before they can even consider addressing the other needs in Maslow's hierarchy. If the source of adequate income disappears, emphasis must revert immediately to it, no matter how far up the hierarchy we have progressed.

Safety Needs

Safety needs are on Maslow's second level. They include security, protection from physical injury, freedom from fear, and so on.

Security at home frequently depends upon security at work. In today's workplace, job security has become a major and very controversial topic.

Some firms identify job security as their number one priority. They promise employees they will do everything possible to ensure it. According to their way of thinking, job security is a critical ingredient of long-term improvement of the bottom line. On the other hand, some firms boldly declare that no one's job is secure. The company's major responsibility is to earn money for its owners. The company, therefore, does whatever is necessary to improve the bottom line.

The latter group has defined downsizing (or the attempt at a politically correct term, "rightsizing") as a valuable tactic to quickly produce numbers that "look good." In reality, however, downsizing wreaks havoc with employee morale as well as productivity (which is tied to employee morale), although a number of defenders would loudly dispute this statement noting that if the company goes out of business then no one has a job (Roth 1993a; Rubach 1995; Hackman 1977).

Quite simply and in line with Maslow's reasoning, people do not work as well for, and are loath to commit to, employers or projects once it is made clear that the bosses feel no allegiance to the employees, no matter how good their performance might be. If employees think that management sees them as expendable, they will think of management as untrustworthy.

In addition, temporary workers (or "temps") are becoming increasingly popular as a way to cut costs. Their pay scale can be kept relatively low, no benefits are currently required, and temps can be dismissed relatively easily.

The following scenario is becoming increasingly familiar. First, a company downsizes in order to cut costs, which batters the morale of both survivors and those released. Then, management realizes that the company is chronically understaffed and brings in temps as an alternative to rehiring. This deals another blow to the permanent work force, as people wonder who will be replaced next. The temps, who understand the climate and know what their real role is, do not feel very secure either. Top management, on the other hand, which is far removed from the pain, frustration, and fear and which is unaware of or unconcerned about Maslow's hierarchy, is pleased because the bottom line looks good, at least for the short term.

Despite a number of articles protesting the practice of downsizing, in the United States especially, companies continue to utilize this demeaning process. While the skill and education levels of employees are steadily increasing, management's respect for employees seems to be decreasing. And downsizing doesn't really help the long-term numbers. Indeed, in the long term, downsizing leads to bankruptcy (Zorn et al. 2017).

In Japan and Europe, apparently business leaders tend to downsize less often; usually only as a last resort. In Japan, in fact, when things do not go well, it is often the executives and managers who take the blame and penalize themselves by cutting their own salaries. Sometimes they even resign rather than penalize the workers who have faithfully followed their lead. It would be a disgrace to do otherwise (Ouchi 1981).

The fact is that there is a very large gray area between getting rid of employees to make the numbers look good and doing what is necessary to keep a business afloat in bad times. In a company where the management has proven time and time again that they care about their employees, the necessity for layoffs can be understood by the employees. Instead of causing a rift between management and employees, bad times can enable both employees and management to pull together to save the company.

Physical safety, the second consideration in this category, is another major on-the-job concern of employees on all levels. Nobody wants to get hurt. When accidents do happen, focus is frequently forced back to the basic survival/physiological need level. In terms of workplace safety, the United States is doing pretty well, partially because companies have come to realize that injured workers can cost them a great deal and partially because of government regulation. But in all cases, when the company makes decisions that cause employees to get hurt, they resent it. And when companies make decisions to safeguard the health and wellbeing of employees, they appreciate it.

Love and Belonging

Maslow's third level, after physical survival (pay) and security/safety needs have been satisfied, has to do with belongingness. The need for belongingness, which begins in infancy, is well documented in the scientific literature (Randel et al.). Children who feel rejected by parents and other key figures in their lives never really recover. They might learn to cope with the emotions involved so that they can function almost normally, but the scars remain.

The need for belongingness persists throughout our school years, during which we form peer groups. It also persists into our working lives, where we frequently get as much done while socializing over coffee, in the cafeteria, or on the phone as we do at our desks.

Some companies realize this and encourage an open, trusting atmosphere. A whole class of consultants spends time conducting exercises to open channels, improve communication, and take the mistrust out of relationships between departments. Off-site retreats and nature-based training programs are two of the techniques that have been used for years to encourage cross-functional cooperation, teamwork, and the development of authentic leadership (van Droffelaar and Jacobs; Stayer).

Another movement that has proven successful is the quality improvement movement (often called TQM for Total Quality Management or Six Sigma) (Rodgers et al. 2021). A comprehensive quality effort centers on employees forming teams in order to work together to make improvements in products, manufacturing processes, management systems, and the work environment itself. Effective team building is based on trust, empowerment, and respect, which are also keys to generating a sense of belonging (Main 1994; Roth 1989b).

Esteem

Maslow's next level covers the need for esteem. People need to feel that they are making a contribution which they themselves can respect. In most cases, such self-respect results from the impression one's contribution makes on others—family, friends, peers, co-workers, bosses. Society understands this need. It works to build esteem in the young through school programs, scouting programs, teams, and clubs which work to ensure that everyone who tries is a winner and is rewarded.

Things tend to become murkier when we enter the world of work, where the traditional reward system is highly competitive and focuses on individual achievement. Because of this often competitive/conflictive atmosphere, the ploy is frequently to promote one's own accomplishments while denigrating those of others, which fosters envy and suspicion instead of respect.

In this type of atmosphere, employees obviously are less willing to share their ideas. Doing so puts them at risk. The result of joint exercises, therefore, is rarely respect and the desired end product—self-esteem. Businesses must do what they can to encourage a reward system that is cumulative and aggregate to avoid problems of self-esteem in individuals.

Self-Actualization

On the highest level of Maslow's hierarchy is the need for self-actualization. This involves people's desire to gain the opportunity and inputs necessary to realize their positive potential as human beings. The desire for self-actualization is the driving force behind societal evolution.

In the workplace, self-actualization may seem impossible for lower-level employees. Jobs frequently involve hours of dull, repetitive, non-developmental work performed in order to earn the input/money which, hopefully, will allow the employees to do what they want during nonworking hours. But even the lowest level job can provide motivation for employees, and many professional level and "assistance" professions are important for self-actualization (Bożek).

Unfortunately, the number of nonworking hours available for such developmental activities appears to be decreasing. While it increased steadily from the middle of the Industrial Revolution through the 1950s, in the United States at least, the weekly number of working hours the average family currently spends working just to maintain a suitable standard of life is growing.

There are, however, several bright spots. One is that the number of jobs that are developmentally challenging is increasing. Teaching is an example. Education is rapidly becoming a life-long process for most of us, and the number of opportunities to teach has increased. The teaching process has also changed drastically by becoming more innovative, creative, and global as online educational opportunities increase. Technology will become a major tool, making our classes richer and more interesting.

Research and consulting are also growing fields that are becoming more challenging. Some believe that a majority of jobs will eventually be held by consultants rather than traditional full-time employees. More efficient technology has been replacing humans in factory and clerical jobs for decades. This frees employees to move about more easily, to focus on improvement-related projects, and to incorporate education and research into their activities.

It is also believed that an increasing number of people will begin to shift back and forth between industrial and teaching jobs on a regular basis, combining the challenges of a "real-world" sector with those of the education sector and providing more developmental opportunities.

How Do We Get There?

We are not all getting what we want as employees in the workplace. What is stopping us in almost every case can be traced back at least partially to a reward system which is antithetical to the necessary changes, which breeds disrespect and distrust, which makes tight controls over employee activities necessary, which by its very nature is contradictory to a team approach, and which discourages the open sharing of information, ideas, and opinions.

The traditional reward system has never been very efficient in terms of guiding and encouraging the positive expenditure of employee energy. Too much "negative energy" has been wasted defending oneself or neutralizing possible threats. The problem has been that we have had nothing to compare it to.

But now that is changing. Other players in the world market are introducing reward systems which improve productivity and profitability in ways that only the most gridlocked management corps can ignore. Quite simply, instead of conflict and win-lose competition, they are encouraging cooperation and a win-win atmosphere.

At the same time, a growing amount of research on the subject shows that a majority of employees would prefer an arrangement which reinforces the team approach; open sharing of information, ideas, and opinions, etc. (Garbers and Konradt).

The reward system of the future is becoming increasingly well defined. It is a system that encourages the highest level of commitment in all employees and encourages them to use their full range of potential most effectively to increase productivity.

Such a system will obviously include certain well-defined characteristics. First, everyone's take will necessarily be tied to the bottom line in such a way that it will increase in good years and decrease in bad. The most frequently cited example of the bottom-line-based salary system is Lincoln Electric, where 50% or more of everyone's yearly reward can come as part of their bonus package, which is tied directly to the overall success of the company. Lincoln Electric has consistently been one of the most successful companies in the United States. No one quits and no one is laid off. Everyone feels they belong, and everyone feels they contribute toward the goal (Mink, Morrow, and Shindell).

Second, everybody will know what everybody else earns. This will eliminate game playing and deception. It will also help bring salaries into line.

Third, a team approach to rewards will be used, preferably at multiple levels—department, division, and organization. Emphasis on individual performance will decrease. Emphasis on contribution to team efforts will increase. This should reduce the amount of negative energy expended and the amount of politicking that goes on.

If such a system is instituted properly, it should shift the emphasis from outperforming co-workers to encouraging the fullest possible realization of each other's work-related potential.

This may sound simple, and it is. It has been proven to work in a growing number of companies.

In terms of Maslow's hierarchy of needs, starting at the first level with physiological needs, the pay scale under such a system would obviously become more reasonable, and employees would be more likely to look out for each other's interests.

In terms of Maslow's second-level safety needs, decisions that affect job security would no longer result from the whim of a CEO or the votes of a few top-level executives. Decisions impacting safety would, instead, be understood and accepted by the work force, because the various alternatives would be explored participatively.

The team approach upon which such a reward system is based would obviously enhance feelings of belonging, Maslow's third-level need. The contributions of team members would be applauded because they would now benefit everyone, thus also enhancing self-esteem, Maslow's fourth-level need.

Finally, all of this would help satisfy the need for self-actualization, which lies at the fifth and highest level of Maslow's hierarchy.

Onward and Upward

In summary, organizational decision making as a means to produce the best results must be a participative activity. When it is, the richness of the contribution made by employees will depend upon their level of commitment to the cause. People naturally want to commit to the organizations for which they work. It adds purpose to their lives.

As mentioned, people are not altruistic. They need to know that they will benefit in some acceptable way for their efforts. The benefits they seek from work have to be spelled out. The reward system must offer the benefits, but it must tie them to the success of problem solving efforts in order to encourage both commitment and effectiveness. This is the ideal situation, and it is certainly not out of reach. It is just different, and anything different, no matter how obviously superior, takes some getting used to.

We hope that by nudging the culture in the right direction, by improving our decision making process and our approach to problem solving, and by gradually introducing a more cooperative and profitable atmosphere, we will encourage top-level management to eventually address the issue of rewards.

What kind of organization-wide attitude toward problem solving will be most useful? How should we alter organizational perspective and structures to most effectively take advantage of employee expertise in terms of the activities involved? These are some of the issues that are addressed in the next chapter.

Summary Chapter 1 Questions

- What factors are influencing the need for organizations to change their decision making methods?
- Why is the nature of work becoming increasingly decentralized?
- What are the five decision making issues which need to be addressed openly and honestly?
- What does the reward system have to do with the challenges of a changing workplace?
- Which is more important, the customer or the employee? Why?
- What is Maslow's hierarchy and why is it important to company culture?
- What are the three characteristics of a well-defined reward system?

Chapter 2

Shaping the Optimum Attitude, Perspective, and Method

The Optimum Attitude for Change

Decision making is the essence of any business operation. It is also the most interesting part of such operations. New businesses must deal with problems concerning funding, location, advertising, suppliers, licenses, taxes, technology, record keeping, competition, insurance, transportation, staffing, and organization. Ongoing businesses must solve a constantly expanding array of problems generated by social and technical forces which daily grow more numerous and complex. They must also deal with the problem of defining the organization's future, a problem which is never completely solved.

One factor that strongly affects an organization's success in decision making is its attitude toward problem solving. Several different ways of reacting to problem solving situations have evolved.

The most unrealistic, but by no means least popular, is to simply ignore them. Russell Ackoff (Ackoff 1971; Ackoff 1972; Ackoff 1974, 1978, 1981a; Ackoff 1981b; Ackoff 1994), who, along with Peter Drucker ((Drucker 1987, 2001)) and W. Edwards Deming (Aguayo 1990), is considered one of the trinity of modern-day management theory, calls this the *inactive* attitude or approach to planning/problem solving in his book *Redesigning the Future*.

DOI: 10.4324/9781003198062-2

Organizations that have gridlocked themselves with boundary building and turf-protection stratagems tend to adopt this attitude. Nobody wants to take a chance.

Top-level management in such organizations, however, while putting itself in position to take the lead in all problem solving efforts, does not always have the time or the range of expertise necessary to do so effectively. As a result, many solutions never materialize, many are slow in coming to an effort to avoid making a mistake, and too often, those that do eventually arrive are not well thought out.

The inactive attitude is frequently found in companies where the reward system pits employees against each other. The problem solving skills of most employees in such organizations, due to lack of usage, are limited. As the environment and markets become more turbulent and competitive, the chance of such companies surviving decreases rapidly.

A second planning attitude that can be related to problem solving has been labeled by Ackoff as *reactive*. The objective of companies practicing reactive problem solving is to limit the number of problems employees have to deal with by establishing rules for every possible situation. This attitude is frequently found in hierarchical organizations with firmly entrenched bureaucracies. Workers are not encouraged to think. Their chief responsibility is to learn the rules and to follow them.

The frantic rate of change experienced in the modern-day environment makes this approach extremely time consuming and often futile. Many such rules are obsolete before they have been written. This happenstance approach causes confusion, creates an atmosphere of confrontation, and ultimately, perhaps, increases the severity of those problems which do eventually surface, working their way through the closely knit fabric of control.

Organizations with a reactive attitude cling to tried-and-true ways of doing things and are suspicious of innovation and creativity, no matter how great the apparent need. To their leaders, new approaches are not worth risking. The problem solving skills possessed by employees in such companies are usually well learned and proven, but limited to a dangerous degree. Organizations with a reactive attitude, however, strongly believe that such skills are sufficient. Because all the acceptable solutions have already been worked out, problem solving sessions are mainly spent defining the most appropriate match, with upper-level management (because of its greater experience and in order to ensure that control is maintained) again functioning as the final judge.

Organizations that practice reactive problem solving tend to be old and large and to have a traditional reward system. The all-encompassing maze of rules has evolved, at least partially, as an attempt to limit the infighting such a reward system fosters by providing a final authority.

A third problem solving attitude (added with tongue in cheek) is *hyperactive*. This attitude calls for quick, aggressive attention to problems which always seem to be in a crisis stage—call a meeting, form a task force, concentrate employee expertise on attempts to find an immediate and usually short-term answer, and then return to business as usual until the next crisis arises or is generated.

This attitude usually results from the management style of an extremely ambitious, aggressive boss who wants to be in the spotlight and enjoys the feeling of power that such situations bring. A lot of the problems which quickly turn into crises are actually created by such bosses. They also, of course, make the final decision based in large part on their own frequently hidden agenda. Loyal employees are expected to agree and implement solutions delivered by their leaders without question.

Hyperactive problem solving efforts are totally orchestrated, so that the skill level of everyone but the boss is unimportant. Employees just need to know how to appear to be intensely involved, how to nod their heads emphatically, and how to make periodic, short, innocuous, supportive comments.

The next attitude identified by Ackoff which can be applied to problem solving is *preactive*. A majority of organizations at least aspire to this one. It is very much in vogue. Preactive problem solvers try to predict problems they will have to face in the future and prepare solutions in advance. They do this to get a jump on both the problem and their competition. Forecasting and a range of problem solving techniques, many of which are discussed in this book, are used. Consultants and internal experts are relied upon heavily to contribute to the process.

The preactive attitude considers employee input important, but feels that it should be carefully monitored and channeled. Employees are told what to work on. Once they have outlined alternatives within the carefully defined parameters of their project, the alternatives are presented to a boss, who is responsible for the final decision.

Preactive problem solving occurs in companies which still sport traditional reward systems, have not yet questioned them, but are beginning to realize the value of and need for employee input and commitment and are looking for ways to encourage it. Many of them are altering their organizational design with this goal in mind. By so doing, they have taken the first step along the pathway to comprehensive change.

Interactive Is the Future

One thing the four attitudes thus far discussed—inactive, reactive, hyperactive, and preactive—have in common is that they treat the problem as an interloper, a factor alien to the operation, one which should be ignored, restricted as thoroughly as possible, confronted forcefully once it has successfully penetrated organization defenses, or prepared for in advance. In any case, problems are treated as the enemy.

A fifth attitude, the *interactive* attitude, takes a different perspective. It views problems as having a positive as well as negative side. It views them as opportunities as well as obstructions. With this in mind, the fifth attitude defines problem solving as an integral, ongoing part of any healthy operation rather than a nuisance at best and a waste of time and resources or a serious obstacle at worst. It defines problem solving as a pastime critical to positive organization and individual development.

Interactive problem solving stems from the growing realization that organizations are capable of designing their own futures in order to avoid problems, rather than waiting for them to occur and reacting or even trying to predict them.

For organizations to successfully cultivate this attitude in terms of problem solving, they must have a clear vision of their purpose which is accepted by all employees. This is also called the *hedgehog concept*, a term coined by Jim Collins (Collins and Porras), the unique value proposition of the organization.

Employees must also have a clear understanding of the role each of the functions and individuals within the organization must play in terms of that purpose. Such organizations must be capable of learning constantly from their environment and adapting.

It is no longer the company that comes up with the best one-shot solution that wins; rather, it is the company that is able to keep its vision in tune with an increasingly turbulent environment and is able to constantly readjust flexible structure and processes in order to avoid falling behind.

Such a scenario, of course, calls for radical changes which will affect every facet of an operation. To succeed, three basic organizational characteristics must evolve:

1. All employees must be encouraged to identify problems and work on their solutions. Participation must be present in the broadest sense of the term.
2. The interactive attitude and resultant activities must become part of the culture, a key part of daily operational activities.
3. These interactive activities must span the entire organization, extend into the environment, and be well integrated.

Interactive problem solving is the future. At this point in time, however, not many companies are practicing it. Though "interactive" has become a buzzword in good currency, "talking the talk," in this case, is much easier than "walking the walk." Our traditional workplace culture precludes at least two of the three necessary organizational characteristics defined above.

The first pitfall has to do with participation. Allowing employees to truly participate takes a great deal of trust. Most managers, even if they want to, are unwilling to trust their staff to the necessary degree for a range of reasons, including pressure from above, their training, and fear of losing control.

The second pitfall is that developing a well-integrated, comprehensive network of problem solving activities requires breaking down walls, ceasing internal competition, and overcoming suspicion between functions. In most cases, this will not happen until we rethink our reward system.

What we currently have in the workplace, then, instead of an approach to problem solving, is an aggregate of competing opinions from which decision makers are forced to choose. These opinions, of course, usually result from the perspective of their source.

For example, in a business situation, a young employee operating a machine or filing records might say that the repetitious, unchallenging nature of the job is the problem underlying a relatively low productivity level which is not rising. The employee's older foreman or office manager might say that the problem is that young people today no longer take pride in their work. The director of personnel might see the problem as one of improper staffing patterns. The company president might decide that the problem is due at least partially to the fact that employees have been kept in jobs which can be done more efficiently by technology. Finally, a consultant called in might offer the opinion that the problem results from a lack of proper training for managers.

Which opinion is correct in this situation? Which defines the real problem? Should they all be considered correct? Do they all actually define parts of the same problem?

If this last possibility proves true, how can such a many-headed hydra be attacked and dealt with effectively? In most cases, while the various opinions might be listened to, management's decision will be of the "either-or" type. Management will first try its luck with the "either" solution, but will find that it does not really solve the problem. Then management will drop the "either" solution entirely and will switch to the "or" solution, but the "or" solution will, of course, generate results that are not much better.

The Optimum Perspective for Change

What is the real issue, then? What underlies all this confusion and the inability of organizations to put together a system capable of dealing interactively with problems? The real issue keeping us from achieving a good, long-term solution in this situation and many like it is, as we have said, perspective, which shapes attitude and is, therefore, critical to culture. The key to understanding this conclusion, however, is the realization that what we are talking about is management's macro rather than its micro perspective.

What does that mean? Quite simply, it means that we, as a business culture, continue to think analytically when the time has come to start thinking holistically as well. Again, what does that mean? In order to explain, we have to go back into history, several hundred years to be exact. Since the Renaissance and the beginnings of what we call "modem science," the emphasis has been on analysis. "Analysis" means that scientists have broken down the object or event under investigation in an attempt to identify all its component parts. Once the parts have been identified, the investigator has carefully studied them. The belief has been that by thoroughly understanding the nature of the parts of the system, scientists could understand the nature of the system itself.

This approach was critical to the development of the physical sciences. For some disciplines, it was, in fact, the only feasible pathway. For example, because of the limitations of early technology and theory, astronomers were incapable of formulating an accurate overview of the solar system galaxy, and universe. They had to piece the vision of the universe together from a very limited series of observations delineating often random bits of the puzzle.

In terms of the workplace, this approach has been most useful with strictly mechanical systems. The wheel and axle, the lever, and the inclined plane have been identified as the basic design elements of all machines. Different combinations of these basic elements have made different manufacturing processes possible. Modifications of each element plus the design of more elaborate combinations have made a greater variety of increasingly sophisticated mechanical systems available.

In view of the above, all one has traditionally needed in order to understand such a system has been a definition of the elements involved, an explanation of modifications to these elements, and an explanation of how the elements involved have been combined.

The moment, however, that the human operator became a factor in the formula, problems arose. Initially, attempts were made to define the operator as just another mechanical part of the system. Such a role facilitated evaluation of the employee's performance through analysis—identify the employee's various needs and then formulate ways to manipulate these needs in order to make the human "machine" more productive.

Many started from this perspective (e.g., Frederick Taylor [Taylor] searched for the "one best way." Frank Gilbreth [Gilbreth and Gilbreth; Gilbreth and Emerson] introduced the concept of motion studies, Henry Gantt [Gantt] developed the Gantt chart, and Harrington Emerson [Emerson] emphasized standardization), and many managers and consultants still do.

With social (human) systems, however, it was eventually found that this approach did not work as well as with purely technical systems. Social systems were much more complex, and the "parts" involved (especially when emotions came into play) were constantly changing. Also, human participants, it turned out, did not especially appreciate being treated like machine parts and reacted accordingly.

Another reason this approach could not work, as scientists eventually realized, was that all systems, and especially social systems, are more than simply the sum of their parts. In terms of social systems, any sports fan, for example, knows that a team is more than an aggregate of individual players. The team has a tradition, a style of play, an attitude, and fans, all of which contribute to its performance.

A third reason the analytic approach did not work as well with social systems and the social side of sociotechnical systems was that they are part of a larger system or environment which cannot successfully be ignored. The larger system helps shape the behavior of the embedded system. In order to fully understand the embedded system, therefore, we must also understand the containing system. In order to unravel the operation and interaction of a floor full of junior executives, we must take into consideration the pressures exerted by their bosses.

This need is becoming increasingly obvious for technical systems as well. As they become more powerful and consume growing quantities of our natural resources, the role of technical systems in the containing environment is being scrutinized more intently. For example, environmental issues are of increasing importance in decisions concerning the way we as a nation generate, distribute, and consume energy.

This more holistic way of looking at organizations was labeled, not surprisingly, the "systems" approach. A system is a set of interrelated parts that work together to reach a common goal, objective, or ideal which has either been defined for the parts by others (as with machine parts) or has been defined by the parts themselves (as with any team). Three types of systems exist in the workplace—social systems, technical systems, and sociotechnical systems (E. Trist, Higgins, G. W., Murray, H., and Pollock, A. B.; E. Trist).

A *social* system is a set of two or more individuals who interact. Any work force or segment of a work force with a common purpose is a social system. An entire factory or office staff is a social system. Assembly-line workers, computer operators, salespeople, secretaries, internal consultants, middle managers, boards of directors, and janitorial staffs are all more specifically defined social subsystems which together comprise the larger system.

Each individual worker belongs to more than one social system in an organization. An employee can be part of a social subsystem of assembly-line workers or secretaries responsible to a foreman or to an office manager. At the same time, this employee can be part of a team responsible to an executive for achieving certain production quotas and quality standards. Finally, the employee can be part of an organization responsible to customers and investors.

A *technical* system is a set of two or more techniques and/or tools that interact to produce a certain quantity and quality of goods and services. "Techniques" include the expertise (usually gained through training) necessary for the production of a certain item, whether material (shoes) or nonmaterial (information). "Tools" are implements used to facilitate techniques—a cobbler uses knives and needles to shape and sew together shoes much as a junior executive uses a computer to generate reports.

A *sociotechnical* system is a set of one or more individuals and one or more techniques interacting to produce a certain quantity and quality of goods or services that facilitate achievement of a goal, objective, or ideal defined by the individuals who control that system, sometimes with the help of techniques and/or tools.

Social, technical, and sociotechnical systems are always embedded in a larger system. For example, the sociotechnical system that puts together left front doors in an automobile assembly plant is contained by a larger sociotechnical system that assembles car bodies. This sociotechnical system, in turn, is part of a system that produces entire automobiles which, in turn, is part of a company that manufactures and distributes them. The company system, in turn, is part of a society which uses automobiles for transportation, and so on.

The *holistic* approach shifts the emphasis from understanding the parts as thoroughly as possible to understanding the relationships *between* these parts on all levels and understanding the system-wide dynamics created by these relationships. The holistic approach is considered an update of the *systems approach*, which was the first approach to recognize that it is best to approach decisions when viewing the entire environment as a whole ("Strategic Management in Corrections Tool Workbook, Management and Behavioral Science Center"; Von Bertalanffy). As West Churchman says in *The Systems Approach* (1968, p. 11) (Churchman), this approach leads to identification of "the most effective organization of your system (its parts, relationships and system-wide dynamics) in terms of fulfilling its role in (the) containing system."

The holistic approach obviously necessitates movement away from analysis and toward synthesis. Instead of always looking inward and breaking things down, systems thinkers begin looking more so at the whole and examining a relationship in terms of that whole and in terms of the larger whole of which it is a part.

To further clarify the distinction between the traditional analytical approach and the holistic approach, suppose two consultants were called into a company to address the same problem—bad labor-management relations. The analytical consultant would focus immediately on the "pieces" by spending as much time as possible with as many individual employees on both sides of the issue in order to solicit their views. He or she would try to discover who the troublemakers were and who to work with, train, or get rid of so that the remaining "pieces" might fit better.

The holistic consultant, in contrast, would focus on the glue that holds the pieces together—the communication process, access to information, the reward process, the training process, the evaluation process, the punishment process, etc. According to this consultant, bad relations result mainly from weaknesses in the way these processes were set up. His or her approach would be to get the process optimum, and a majority of the personal problems and bad attitudes will correct themselves.

This shift from an inward to an outward orientation broadens our perspective tremendously. During the long reign of the analytical approach, emphasis was focused on "what" and "how." We asked *what* the system was supposed to achieve in terms of short-term goals and *how* the pieces of the system should be organized in order to achieve those goals in the most efficient manner. We asked *what* models of sailboats or televisions or hairbrushes the company should gear up to produce in order to maximize sales and *how* bonus systems should be organized so that individual salespeople could achieve or surpass their sales quotas.

The holistic approach with its outward perspective encourages us to address the question of "why" as well. We are beginning to ask *why* something is being produced and consumed in terms of the needs and desires of all those individuals and social systems that affect or are affected by the processes involved. We are wondering, for example, whether the current boom in computer technology is, in the long run, going to be totally advantageous to society or whether, in fact, one end result might be a great deal of suffering and social turmoil.

We have realized that our joint sociotechnical systems, in both the private and work sectors, have become so powerful and so interdependent that even a minor shift in emphasis or a minor miscalculation in one can set off a far-reaching chain reaction of repercussions. As a result of this new awareness, the "why" question has become much more important.

The Optimum Vehicle for Change

What does an organization look like when it has adapted an interactive attitude toward problem solving, has begun thinking systemically, and has decided that synthesis and the "why" question are just as important as analysis and the "what" and "how" questions? What is its structure, and what are its processes in terms of problem solving? Which is the major activity of its social system now that technology is handling most of the grunt work?

Let's start with structure. As mentioned, interactive problem solving is, by definition, participative, ongoing, organization-wide, and integrated. This means that everyone who is going to be affected by solutions must, in some way, be encouraged to contribute on an ongoing basis. It does not mean conducting a survey to gather a total cross-section of opinions and then discussing each opinion individually whenever an issue arises. Rather, it means that a vehicle must be put in place which allows representatives of stakeholder groups to examine, question, and contribute to tentative solutions generated by a sponsoring group or team.

What should the vehicle look like? There are several alternatives. We will start with the least sophisticated. The most familiar version to working people is the task force, a hand-picked group of employees, usually including both middle managers and hourly employees, who work on a specific problem defined and assigned by upper-level management. Participants come up with either a set of alternative solutions or one solution which they consider the best and present it to upper management, which makes the final decision. The task force then disbands.

Integration often does not exist between the efforts of different task forces. They can pop up and disappear all over an organization at the whim of managers. They are popular in the competition/conflict-driven workplaces with an inactive, reactive, hyperactive, or preactive attitude because management stays in charge—assigning the problem to be addressed, participating in and often leading the exercise, and making the final decision.

Task forces also appear in organizations with an interactive attitude, but their role is different. In order to make the most effective use of employee expertise at all levels, interactive organizations build their problem solving approach around one of two vehicles. The first and less sophisticated of these is the improvement team network. This network is the core piece of successful quality efforts. It is composed, initially at least, of separate hourly and management teams that span the organization. The teams in the network represent all functions and meet regularly, usually on a weekly or bi-weekly basis. The purpose of the task force is, however, determined by management. This is the quality improvement team.

Quality improvement teams identify their own projects. Their efforts are closely integrated by a web of facilitators trained by a head facilitator who reports directly to the organization or unit leader. In order to maintain the necessary momentum and control, all quality teams must obey a set of ground rules agreed to by all participants at the beginning of the process.

One key ground rule is that team members have access to anyone in the organization for required information or decisions. Another is that when such a request is made, the responder has a limited period of time in which to respond. If a response in not forthcoming, the head facilitator, and then the organization leader, is called upon to encourage it.

A third critical ground rule is that anyone who will be affected by a proposed solution must have knowledge of it and a chance to contribute before the team begins implementation. Obviously, any change in products, services, processes, management systems, or the work environment designed by an hourly team will affect the manager. The manager, therefore, eventually becomes a player and can have decisive input, because all final decisions are reached through consensus (Roth 1991b; Roth 1991a).

The differences between the task force directed by management and the task force directed by the quality improvement teams are considerable. First, quality improvement teams, both hourly and management, are truly empowered. They are allowed by management to pick their own projects and to define their own solutions without the guidance of superiors. This gives real ownership and shows a greater level of respect. The key is that team members invite the manager to participate when his or her input is eventually needed, rather than the process being aimed and led by a manager from the start.

Task forces are effectively created in this scenario when a problem is addressed which spans several functions or several teams. Task forces can also be created by top-level management around projects it considers important that are not being addressed. The difference is that when the assigned problem is adequately dealt with, the task force disbands, while quality improvement teams remain in place and begin working on another item from their list (perhaps continuing the efforts of the task force).

The two vehicles, quality improvement teams and task forces, can exist side by side and complement each other in an interactive environment. They cannot, however, always co-exist in a preactive environment due to the fact that the level of empowerment proposed for team members would not be acceptable.

The quality improvement team approach can and has been mounted in organizations with traditional reward systems. If it succeeds and the company's profits increase as a result, one of the teams will eventually make the design of a fairer and more realistic reward system one of its projects. Such an initiative has been known to spell the rapid demise of team efforts. It has also, however, been known to trigger a successful transition to the new cooperative mentality we are all ultimately seeking.

In some cases where a team approach has survived and thrived long enough for the ground rules to be absorbed into the corporate psyche, the teams stop meeting formally and their work is absorbed into the daily production unit process so that something more akin to autonomous work groups evolves from the quality improvement team.

Interactive organizations that use autonomous work groups divide their operation into functions. They then give a managerless team of workers control over each function. Members of this group are responsible for producing an agreed upon number of items, be it cabinets, car doors, ads, sales, formulas, etc. They decide how to do so. They decide which group member will complete which task and when to rotate tasks. They do the job skills training and pick new group members when someone leaves. Managers take on the role of a facilitator rather than a decision maker. They provide resources and expertise to the groups only upon request.

To be a true autonomous work group all members would be paid the same. This is obviously different from the quality improvement team network setup. While the latter eventually evolves toward the point where a more equitable reward system is designed, autonomous work groups start with such a system in place.

Task forces can again exist side by side with quality improvement teams (and/or autonomous work groups if the teams have evolved into them). All three of these types of groups complement each other.

Once Again, Who's In Charge?

In interactive organizations, all participants are allowed, by the ground rules, to define problems they consider important. This does not mean that a team or work group will choose to work on one individual's idea, at least at first. It does mean, however, that the idea will, at some point, receive attention.

A second process issue that middle managers in particular want to address when they form teams is who, exactly, is responsible for what decisions concerning what problems. In inactive, reactive, hyperactive, and often preactive organizations, again, no one is quite sure. At the same time, for a variety of reasons, people are afraid to ask. As a result, things tend to be pushed upward.

This might be good for the self-esteem of top-level managers, but it is not very effective in terms of time, the quality of solutions, and generating employee commitment.

In truly interactive organizations, as we have said, decision making authority is pushed downward to the lowest possible level, instead of upward. While managers, as stakeholders, provide input, employees do not turn to them automatically for all the answers. Emphasis is on involving those who will be affected the most by the solutions.

After problem identification and solution come the definition of action steps and implementation. In organizations with the first four attitudes, once a solution is agreed upon it is placed on management's desk, where it might sit forever, be changed arbitrarily, or be implemented piecemeal. Management oversees and shapes implementation.

In an interactive organization, implementation is the responsibility of the sponsoring team or work group. The logic behind this shift is simple. The employees who lead the effort to generate the solution understand it best. It is their idea. Therefore, they will be more persistent in getting their ideas implemented. Also, because there are more team members than there are top-level managers, things will happen faster.

For the same reasons, teams and work groups in interactive organizations are also responsible for monitoring results of the improvement effort and fine tuning, when necessary.

EXAMPLE OF QUALITY IMPROVEMENT TEAM

An administrator's team was formed as part of a quality improvement process instituted by the Allentown, Pennsylvania city government. Members were not satisfied with the in-house phone directory. It had been reorganized by consultants two years before, but was difficult to use. Some of the headings were misleading, there was no answer at some of the phone numbers listed, some of the numbers listed were incorrect, and callers were often transferred several times before reaching the party they were calling.

The secretaries took on the project of reorganizing the directory. They started from scratch. Representatives from each department listed the information their people could provide and the numbers to call. The team then broke the book down into simple, well-defined categories.

Finally, they developed a quick access list of the most frequently used numbers for each department and printed it on a separate sheet to be placed next to each phone.

The secretaries developed a draft of their revised listing and distributed it for a test run. Only two months later, team members, with feedback from all departments, fine-tuned the directory and printed it.

The Next Step

Now that we have defined the attitude, the types of vehicles, and the general process characteristics which best facilitate problem solving, it is time to move on to the problem solving activity itself. Do we just turn team and work group members loose and let them do their own thing? Do we say, "Hey, you're picking your own problems. Now you figure out how to address them." Or do we train participants?

If we decide that training is a good idea, what do we teach our employees? There are many problem solving techniques floating around and being sold. How do we decide which one to use or which will produce the most effective results in our specific situation? How do we even gain an accurate overview of what is available?

These are some of the questions that will be addressed in the next chapter.

Summary Chapter 2 Questions

- What are the five different ways of reacting to problem solving situations?
- How does an organization successfully cultivate an interactive problem solving attitude?
- What are the three basic organizational characteristics that must evolve?
- What is the difference between a macro and micro perspective, and how does it influence long-term solutions to problems?
- Why does the analytical approach often fail in social systems?
- What is the social system, and how does it apply to management organizations?
- What is a technical system, and how does it relate to management?
- How does a sociotechnical system differ from either social systems or technical systems?
- What is the relationship between a holistic approach and a systems approach?
- What are the differences between task forces, quality improvement teams, and autonomous work groups?

Chapter 3

Picking the Optimum Techniques and Tools

Decision making has various techniques and tools. The techniques can be divided into three categories based on use:

1. Used to improve the creativity and/or to enhance the problem identification and decision making skills of the individual
2. Used to improve the creativity and/or to enhance the problem identification and decision making ability of groups
3. Used to work with problem networks or "messes" (as systems scientists call them)

In this chapter, we shall identify a comprehensive cross-section of techniques in all three categories, describe how they work, and judge their effectiveness. These tools came from a variety of sources (Andersen 1980; Dickson 1969; Ewing 1977; Hayes 1981; Jackson 1975; Newell 1972). Then we will discuss the tools that are generally used to measure productivity.

Techniques for Individuals

All of the techniques discussed here can be utilized by individuals in a group as well as by solitary problem solvers. Emphasis, however, is on overcoming self-imposed individual constraints.

DOI: 10.4324/9781003198062-3

Most of the techniques described have to do with the manipulation of something. Human thought processes tend to fall into habitual patterns. A specific type of stimulus brings a specific type of response. By changing the way a potential solution is formulated, we can sometimes break out of our self-imposed ruts and develop a new perspective. By reorienting our thought patterns or adding new ones, we can modify our vision of reality, sometimes in useful ways.

To help accomplish the above objective, the techniques presented in this section are divided into four subcategories: word games, attribute manipulation, elaborations, and analogy making. Examples of each are provided.

Individual Techniques Using Word Games

The techniques using word games include Word Manipulation, Lateral Thinking, and Forced Connections. All of these techniques "play" with words to spur creative thinking.

Word Manipulation

This category includes several techniques that focus on the manipulation of both the way words are put together and the words themselves in order to give sentences or phrases new meaning. They can be introduced in at least two ways:

1. State the problem or potential solution verbally or symbolically, and then reorganize the words or symbols in the statement to suggest different approaches or alternative solutions. Take, for example, the following problem statement:

    Assembly-line workers don't listen to their supervisors.

    This statement can be changed to read:

    Supervisors don't listen to assembly-line workers.

    This transition leads problem solvers to more carefully explore the attitudes and motivations of the supervisors making the accusation.

2. Substitute similar or more specific words for those in a problem or potential solution statement. In the preceding example, the statement might be altered to read:

    Assembly-line workers don't respect their supervisors.

or

Assembly-line workers often can't hear what their supervisors are saying above the noise.

The first modification offers a reason for their not listening. The second suggests the nature of potential solutions.

Lateral Thinking

In his book entitled *Lateral Thinking,* Edward DeBono (DeBono 1971) discusses the need to challenge all verbal assumptions, recurring themes, clichés, and recurring obstacles. Perhaps his most sophisticated offering is an exercise that encourages practitioners to relate to the issue through a number of concepts developed through free association, hopefully inspiring new insights.

The issue at hand might be inadequate employee input into the planning process. The first step in the lateral thinking technique is to randomly name an object, animal, or color, picking any alternative that comes to mind. Let's use "dog" as an example. The second step is to list down the left side of a sheet of paper as many attributes and concepts that can be thought of which are related to "dog." The last step is to transform each characteristic or concept into a decision making approach.

A dog might be characteristically "friendly." An approach to solving the problem of inadequate employee input which takes this characteristic into consideration might be for those running the process to improve relationships with all participants. A dog might also be considered to be a "protector." The related approach would be to ensure the optimum of all stakeholders to contribute to the decision making process without harassment or fear of retribution.

Forced Connections

Forced Connections is a technique similar to Lateral Thinking and is used mainly to address technical system problems. For example, in attempting to define a new transportation system, we might ask what the result would be if the attributes of a car were joined to those of a train. Answers might include "a car that can go anywhere roads exist without being driven" or "a train that does not need track."

This technique can also be used to address social system problems. For example, the problem might be a bad relationship between the sales force and the investment department of an insurance firm. The question addressed might be: "What would happen if the attributes of the two units were combined?" Answers would help identify areas where the units complement each other, as well as areas where they conflict. The questioner might also discover possible compromises, as well as syntheses that would strengthen both operations.

Individual Techniques Using Attribute Manipulation

Previously defined attributes of a decision or potential solution can be organized in order to suggest alternative approaches. This can be done by matching, combining, grouping, ordering, elaborating upon, dissecting, challenging, viewing from another perspective, and so on. The techniques discussed here are Matrix, Sliding Column Method, Definition of Grouping Similarities, Solution Preference Identification, Morphological Analysis, and Morphological Forced Connection.

Matrix

One traditional means of identifying alternatives is cross-classification. A Matrix is a tool used to facilitate the cross-classification process. It helps define the results of forced relationships between problem or potential solution attributes which have been divided into two or three categories. A matrix is designed to ensure that every possible combination is identified. The tool was developed originally to help make technical decisions. It can, however, also be used to deal with decisions in social systems.

Sliding Column Method

Another cross-matching technique is S. J. Parnes' Sliding Column Method. When using this technique, individuals again categorize and list desired or required solution attributes.

If the problem is employees complaining about the hours they work, the categories of potential solution attributes might include working hours, overtime policy, or self-scheduling. The categorized lists are then laid side by side and shifted up and down to allow different fits. The variety of

Table 3.1 Sliding Column Method Example

Working Hours	Overtime Policy	Self-Scheduling
Shorter	Employee choice	Weekend work
Fixed shifts	Cut down on	Work at home

combinations created by this shifting should suggest alternatives. Table 3.1 shows one example.

One fit might be shorter working hours/cut down on overtime/work at home, and a second fit might be fixed shifts/employee choice/weekend work.

Definition of Grouping Similarities

Practitioners of the Definition of Grouping Similarities technique list attributes of the decision or potential solutions, group the ones that seem similar, and then try to define what makes those assigned to each group similar to one another and different from the attributes assigned to other groups. This helps them to better understand the true nature of the decision. It also helps them to better define the relationship between the various attributes.

Solution Preference Identification

Practitioners of the Solution Preference Identification technique list potential solutions in order of preference and then try to identify what their preferences are based on. This technique helps decision makers better define the nature of the desired final solution.

Morphological Analysis

Morphological Analysis, developed by F. Zwicky (Zwicky 1969), is an expanded version of the Sliding Column Method. The process begins with the practitioner thinking of as many attributes of potential solutions as possible and listing them. Once the list is complete, the attributes are combined in every way possible. The final step is to design solutions around every individual grouping of attributes.

For example, if the problem is lack of an appropriate incentive system for managers, the four potential solution attributes listed might be more money, more free time, educational opportunities, and promotions. Possible combinations of these four potential solution attributes include:

1. More free time to moonlight and make more money
2. Financing for job-related and/or nonjob-related education
3. Promotions that include raises
4. Free time to take courses
5. Promotion to a position that allows more free time
6. The promise of a promotion if certain educational goals are achieved
7. Free time to take advantage of educational opportunities paid for by the firm
8. A promotion and salary increase if certain educational goals are achieved
9. A promotion that offers more free time and a salary increase
10. Free time to take advantage of education opportunities which can lead to a promotion

The intent is that one of these groupings will produce an acceptable novel solution.

Morphological Forced Connection

Morphological Forced Connection, a modification of Morphological Analysis, was presented by Dan Koberg and Jim Bagnall (Koberg 1974). In this technique, the attributes possessed by potential solutions are defined, but instead of immediately combining the results, practitioners list as many alternatives as they can think of beneath each attribute. For example, if the attributes are more money, educational opportunities, promotions, and more free time, the alternative lists might read like Table 3.2.

Practitioners then combine alternatives from the different lists to define novel problem solutions.

Refer to the case study presented in Chapter 7 for an example of how a team found this process useful in resolving an early dilemma in Step 1 of its Ideal Decision Making Model.

Individual Techniques Using Elaboration

This subcategory includes various checklists. A checklist is a list of possible conceptual manipulations that are in some way relevant to the

Table 3.2 Morphological Forced Connection Example

More Money	Educational Opportunities
Stock options	Night courses at school
Bonuses	Day course in-house
Profit sharing	Self-study programs
Promotions	**More Free Time**
Opportunity for lateral movement	Longer weekends
Opportunity to develop new operations and grow with them	Longer lunches
Opportunity to develop a dual advancement track	Longer vacations

problem being addressed (Adams). This section discusses Osborn Checklist, Manipulative Verbs Technique, Interaction Associates Checklist, Expert Consultant, Problems-Within-Problems, Seek-the-Larger-Network, and Ask Why At Least Five Times.

Osborn Checklist

Alex Osborn (Osborn) offers perhaps the best-known general-purpose checklist. Manipulations suggested in his offering relate to both technical and social systems. They include:

- Put to other uses? New ways to use it? Other uses if modified?
- Adapt? What else is like this? What other ideas does this suggest? Does it offer parallels? What could I copy? Whom could I emulate?
- Modify? New twists? Change meaning, color, motion, odor, form, shape, etc.?
- Magnify? What to add? More time? Greater frequency? Stronger? Larger? Thicker? Extra value? Additional ingredient? Exaggerate? Multiply?
- Minify? What to substitute? Smaller? Condensed? Miniature? Omit? Streamline? Split up? Understate?
- Substitute? Who else instead? What else instead? Other ingredient? Other material? Other process? Other power? Other place? Other approach? Other tone of voice?
- Rearrange? Interchange components? Other pattern? Other layout? Other sequence? Transpose cause and effect? Change pace? Change schedule?

- Reverse? Transpose positive and negative? How about opposites? Turn it backward? Turn it upside down? Reverse roles? Change shoes? Turn tables? Turn the other cheek?
- Combine? How about a blend, an alloy, an assortment, an ensemble? Combine units? Combine purposes? Combine appeals? Combine ideas?

Manipulative Verbs Technique

The checklist developed by Koberg and Bagnall is composed of what they call Manipulative Verbs. Many of the suggested actions are more exotic than those called for by Osborn. They include:

Multiply	Dissect	Soften	Stretch
Divide	Distort	Fluff-up	Extrude
Eliminate	Rotate	By-pass	Repel
Subdue	Flatten	Add	Protect
Invert	Squeeze	Subtract	Segregate
Separate	Complement	Lighten	Integrate
Transpose	Submerge	Repeat	Symbolize
Unify	Freeze	Thicken	Abstract

Interaction Associates Checklist

The Interaction Associates Checklist is extensive. It includes 67 idea manipulations or "strategies." Each is accompanied by a description of powers and limitations and by an exercise which shows how the strategy can most effectively be used. The list includes the following actions:

Build up	Select	Exemplify	Symbolize
Eliminate	Plan	Compare	Simulate
Work forward	Predict	Relate	Test
Work backward	Assume	Commit	Play
Associate	Question	Defer	Manipulate
Classify	Interpret	Leap in	Copy

Generalize	Adapt	Hold back	Systemize
Focus	Reduce	Combine	Record
Release	Exaggerate	Separate	Retrieve
Force	Understate	Change	Search
Relax	Incubate	Vary	Hypothesize
Dream	Display	Cycle	Guess
Imagine	Organize	Repeat	Define
Purge	List	Verbalize	Transform
Transform	Check	Visualize	Substitute
Translate	Diagram	Memorize	Randomize
Expand	Chart	Recall	

Expert Consultant

Another elaborative technique is the Expert Consultant technique. As a means of developing a different perspective, exercise participants think of a person they know and respect who might approach the problem they are attempting to solve differently because of different personality characteristics and/or experiences. They then "become" that person and attempt to address the problem as they think he or she would, developing the ideas and approaches they think he or she might use.

Problems-within-Problems

The next offering is a pair of elaborative techniques which encourage reorientation. The Problems-Within-Problems approach dissects the problem network addressed in an attempt to discover the subproblems of which the network is composed. The goal is that an understanding of these subproblems will help practitioners better define the original problem network and suggest possible solutions for decision making.

Seek-the-Larger-Network

The Seek-the-Larger-Network alternative is the opposite of the Problems-Within-Problems technique. This technique attempts to define the larger network of which the immediate problem is a part. Suppose that the immediate problem is that a department lacks access to all the information required to do its job properly. Instead of attacking this problem directly, you would investigate the degree to which the entire division enjoys access to information. What you learn at the higher level might change your perspective concerning the local situation. It probably will also suggest a more elaborate set of solution steps.

If possible, it is advantageous to combine the Problems-Within-Problems and Seek-the-Larger-Network techniques in order to simultaneously look both inward and outward during the exercise. This, of course, is the holistic approach and allows the participants to develop the most holistic definition of the problem network.

Ask Why at Least Five Times

One final technique which helps an employee reach and define the real problem, instead of simply attacking symptoms, is to Ask Why At Least Five Times, a technique used by Taichi Ohno at Toyota. Suppose the original problem is that the department secretary is not transferring incoming calls to salespeople in a department quickly enough. Instead of telling the secretary to start doing the job or else, ask "why." When you find out that the secretary is away from the front desk a lot, ask "why" again. When you find out that the secretary is delivering messages personally because intradepartmental phone lines are continuously busy or salespeople are away from their desks, ask "why" again. When you find out that the phone system has no voice mail feature, ask "why" again. When you find out that management planned to purchase such a service but has not yet done so, ask "why" again. Obviously, there can be more than five "whys" involved in this exercise.

Individual Techniques Using Analogy Making

All analogies are based on the inference that if two or more things agree in some respect(s), they will probably agree in others. This area discusses Relationship Analogies, Attribute Analogy System, and Synectics.

Relationship Analogies

Problem solvers using the Relationship Analogies technique list analogies that define the relationship of key elements in a problem situation. If the problem is management-labor relations, a worker might say that he or she has experienced a "slave to master," "victim to mugger," or "dictator to subject" relationship. The managers, on the other hand, might say that they have been party to a "parent to youngster," "teacher to pupil," or "truant officer to delinquent" relationship.

Once listed, these descriptions can be discussed with others to decide which or what combination is most accurate. The next step would be to develop a list of analogies to describe what the relationship ought to be ideally.

Attribute Analogy System

The Attribute Analogy System was developed by Koberg and Bagnall. After identifying the critical attributes possessed by an object, technical system, social system, or sociotechnical system, instead of listing alternatives beneath each one as in Morphological Forced Connection, participants list analogies. For example, if the problem is to improve efficiency in the media relations department, key attribute categories could be workload, skills involved, experience level, and incentive system. The workload might be heavy but sporadic. An analogy would be "compressed to waste time" or "hurry up and wait."

Ideas resulting from these analogies might include hiring more personnel to work shorter hours, using temps, rescheduling input to even out the workflow, and developing additional duties for personnel in the department.

Synectics

The last technique presented here is William Gordon's Synectics. It seems that no two reviews explain this technique in the same way. There are two possible explanations for this. One is that the technique is too complex for anyone but the founder to understand. The second is that Gordon purposely incorporated this vagueness in order to enhance the technique's flexibility.

Synectics uses analogies, metaphors, and similes to define relationships between things. Four approaches are possible. The first is to develop "direct analogies." The purpose is to discover how the problem network being discussed is similar to other things. Suppose the problem is a rapidly growing market of which a young company wants to take advantage. An analogy might be a hive of bees that has just discovered a bathtub full of honey. What similarities might exist in the reactions of the two organizations?

The second approach, the development of "personal analogies," involves a type of role-playing. The person(s) using this approach must become the company, as a physical entity or a body. As the company, the person must gather certain things from his or her environment in order to grow. He or she must also provide certain goods and services. How does a person best utilize his or her body parts in order to accomplish this objective?

The third approach, called "compressed conflict," involves identifying the essence of the problem as a functional description of the desired outcome in which conflicts or paradoxes are condensed. This essence is then formulated as an analogical question which generally captures the uniqueness of the situation. After the question has been formulated, a metaphor is sought to address it.

Ackoff and Vergara use an example in "Creativity in Problem Solving and Planning" that includes two people in the same room (Ackoff 1981b). One wants to read in a quiet setting while the other wants to listen to loud music. An analogical question which captures the uniqueness of the situation is: "How can a loud silence be produced?" An appropriate metaphor might be: "A bullet that embeds itself in one body cannot strike another." The metaphor suggests that the music lover use headphones.

The last approach described is the "fantastic analogy." Users must allow their imaginations to ramble unrestrained, to concoct the most bizarre solutions possible. Suppose you are a young organization faced with the enviable task of having to meet the demands of a rapidly growing market. You must pretend that you are a wizard capable of producing any type of organization you desire with a snap of your fingers. What would you produce to meet this challenge? What would the organization's attributes be?

Synectics has been used mainly in group settings. It is included here because its emphasis is on releasing the power of the individual mind and imagination, rather than deriving the most from group interaction.

Evaluation of Techniques Used to Enhance Individual Problem Solving Ability

Now let's evaluate the problem solving techniques for individuals in terms of strengths and weaknesses. Each technique, for example, is designed to encourage boldness and originality. At the same time, none fully utilizes the intelligence and imagination of participants. Also, by definition, from a holistic perspective none encourages all participants to play an active role or encourages the inclusion of representatives from all stakeholder groups.

None of these techniques is sophisticated enough to include a mechanism for defining the network or "mess" of which the problem addressed is a part. The Ask Why Five Times technique could conceivably do so but is too loosely structured to guarantee that happening.

In the word game subcategory, a strength of Lateral Thinking is that it allows unlimited shifts in direction. The participant simply has to pick another random "object, animal, or color" and start again. In the Attribute Manipulation subcategory, more structure exists. Due to the fact, however, that the attribute lists used can always be expanded, flexibility is open-ended.

Checklist techniques in the elaboration subcategory also combine structure with an ultimately limited but large degree of flexibility. The Expert Consultant technique allows the user to fire and hire at will. The Problems-Within-Problems technique obviously has limits, as does its partner, Seek-the-Outer-Limits, which moves "outward" instead of "inward." These limits, however, will probably never be reached in most cases. In the analogy making subcategory, the only limits are those of imagination.

An obvious major weakness of all individual techniques is that they do not include an apparatus for encouraging feedback to others who might be affected by the results. When such feedback does occur, it generally concerns only one small element of the problem network. It also usually occurs in a random way, which does not ensure that all stakeholders are reached.

Further strengths include the fact that all of the techniques discussed are designed to maintain interest. Also, they all allow and encourage timely solutions. Because they are "one-shot" exercises that focus on a specific problem network piece, however, they do not encourage continuity of effort. Finally, they have no effect on implementation, unless the problem addressed is itself one of implementation.

In summary then, the general strengths of the individual-oriented problem solving techniques are that they:

1. Encourage boldness and originality
2. Encourage flexibility and allow shifts in the direction of thought concerning the specific problem being addressed, while at the same time providing the necessary structure
3. Maintain interest over the course of the exercise
4. Allow timely solutions

The major weaknesses of these same techniques are that they:

1. Do not fully utilize the intelligence and imagination of the individuals involved
2. Do not take into account group dynamics of the stakeholder group involved
3. Focus on too small a segment of the problem network of "mess" and, therefore, do not encourage continuity
4. Do not encourage the development of an appropriate vehicle for implementation of solutions achieved

General Group Techniques

In the modem world of work, the individual is rarely equipped or qualified to solve problems in the most effective manner (although some executives who hang onto the "boss" mentality would strongly disagree). At the same time, the pressures experienced by a group, both internally and from external sources, are more numerous than those experienced by an individual.

The dynamics between group members themselves often create a degree of pressure. When a group effort is undertaken, outsiders who will be affected by outcomes might also feel threatened. As a result, these outsiders might try to influence or even thwart the activities of those directly involved.

Group decision making techniques, therefore, must generally be more sophisticated in order to deal with these additional pressures and challenges and to encourage maximum quality input. At the same time, they must ensure that "the whole is more than the sum of its parts," i.e., that the solutions generated are more than an aggregate of individual contributions. In essence, they must be designed to generate a focused, participative, well-integrated effort.

The general group techniques have been divided into three subcategories: (1) techniques designed specifically to generate ideas, (2) techniques that group and/or rank ideas as well, and, finally, (3) techniques that use competition to define the relative value of the ideas generated.

General Group Techniques That Focus on the Generation of Ideas

The purpose of these techniques is to create a cooperative atmosphere where participants involved in a group process support and feed freely off each other's attempts to generate useful ideas. The efforts of each group member help the others achieve their desired objectives. There are four techniques in this section: Brainstorming, Operational Creativity, Storyboard, and Problem Setting.

Brainstorming

Brainstorming, developed by Alex Osborn, is probably the simplest and best-known group technique. It was designed to generate as many ideas as possible related to the problem addressed. The belief behind this technique is that the greater the number of associations produced, the less stereotypical and more creative they will be.

Four rules are presented to the participants of a Brainstorming exercise in order to create the desired cooperative atmosphere:

1. They must suspend judgment on all input, no matter what is suggested. Judgmental comments, especially criticism, must be withheld.
2. They must generate as many suggestions as possible without worrying about the quality of the suggestions. This will help stimulate originality.
3. Once the process has started, they must keep up the momentum by offering anything that comes into their heads.
4. They must build on ideas already produced by themselves and others, twisting them and turning them around in order to use them in any way possible.

> Present Brainstorming rules to participants.
> Write initial statement of the problem to be addressed on a flipchart or blackboard.
> Solicit different versions of this problem statement from participants and write them down.
> Have participants select the most appropriate version through discussion and vote if necessary.
> Solicit solution-related ideas from participants, adhering to the rules, and write them down.

After providing several warm-up problems to allow participants to develop a "feel" for the process and the group, the facilitator presents an integral statement of the problem at hand. Different versions of this statement are solicited and written on a blackboard or flipchart to encourage as great a variety of perspectives as possible. When no more suggested versions are forthcoming, participants choose that which is most appropriate in terms of both identifying the problem and inspiring solutions.

The next step is the generation of solution-related ideas by group members. The facilitator lists these ideas and encourages adherence to the four previously defined process rules. The facilitator is the only one allowed to question contributions and does so solely as a means of clarification.

To help generate a wider variety of ideas, participants can incorporate techniques for individuals into the process at different process stages. During the stage when the most appropriate problem statement is being formulated, they can use techniques that rearrange ideas or substitute similar or more specific words. During the stage in which the spectrum of ideas generated is expanded, they can use Lateral Thinking, Forced Connections, Morphological Analysis, or the Expert Consultant technique.

Operational Creativity

An alternative to Brainstorming is William Gordon's Operational Creativity. Gordon developed this technique to deal with the weakness of Brainstorming. Participants in a Brainstorming session begin defining solutions and solution characteristics immediately. Gordon believed that this approach was too direct in that it does not encourage an adequate effort on the part of group members to explore all possible alternatives. Gordon thought that the results of such an effort would be relatively superficial.

An Operational Creativity session begins with only the group facilitator knowing the exact nature of the problem to be addressed. Instead of stating it, however, the facilitator asks and then writes on a board or flipchart the most general question he or she can think of that retains the essence of the problem. For example, if the problem is a faulty interdepartmental communication system, the question might be: "What are the different ways of passing information found in both the natural and mechanical worlds?"

The four rules of Brainstorming are then explained. During the following idea-generating session, responses are listed on a flipchart. When no more responses are forthcoming, the facilitator tears the sheet of paper off the flipchart, tapes it to a wall, and begins again with a more specific question. The facilitator might ask: "How have and can these ways of communicating be fit to human social systems?"

1. Present the same rules used in Brainstorming to participants.
2. The facilitator asks the most general question possible that retains the essence of the problem addressed.
3. Brainstorming responses are listed until no more are forthcoming.
4. The facilitator then asks a more specific question which comes closer to the essence of the problem addressed, and participants respond.
5. The facilitator continues to ask increasingly specific questions, listing response, until the actual problem at hand is addressed.

Later questions grow increasingly specific until eventually the problem at hand is addressed. Gordon finds this roundabout approach more interesting and stimulating and believes the output generated by participants to be much richer.

Storyboard

The Storyboard technique combines Brainstorming with a studio system for developing film plots. The facilitator brings along a flipchart, a corkboard, thumbtacks, and a supply of five-by-eight-inch cards. The corkboard is hung in view of all participants. (Refer to the case study presented in Chapter 7 for an example of the use of the Storyboard.)

The facilitator begins by describing the problem to be addressed. Participants then name potential solution categories. For example, suppose the problem is: "What should we do with the personnel who are part of an operation being shut down?" The categories might include reorientation, relocation, release, retraining, and retirement. Each category is printed on a card and the cards are pinned up at the top of the corkboard.

1. The facilitator offers an initial version of the problem to be addressed.
2. Participants name potential solution categories which are printed on five-by-eight-inch cards and are pinned up across the top of a corkboard.
3. The facilitator asks idea-generating questions concerning each category.
4. Participants write individual answers on five-by-eight-inch cards and turn them in.
5. Answers are grouped according to common themes and pinned up under the most appropriate category card.

6. The facilitator asks further idea-generating questions based on these initial answers.
7. The idea groups in each category are ordered by group consensus vote.
8. The three most popular ideas in each category are then expanded upon by the group leader asking further idea-generating questions.

The facilitator then asks an idea-generating question concerning each category. For the first, it might be: "How can these employees be reoriented in a way that will profit the company?" Participants write their ideas on cards, one idea per card. The cards are collected, read aloud without naming the contributor and without criticism, grouped according to common themes, and pinned on the board under the proper category card. Depending upon what he or she sees, the facilitator asks related questions to generate more ideas.

When the process has been completed for each category, the groupings are discussed and ranked by vote. At this point, several things can occur: (1) categories or groupings can be deleted if none of the ideas contained are popular enough, (2) new categories or groupings can be formed with various idea combinations, or (3) ideas can be shifted to an entirely new category or grouping. Ideas can also be pinned up under two groupings.

If the most popular idea grouping in the "reorientation" category advances the concept of "allowing those being released to attempt to develop a new, related business," the facilitator might begin the second round of questions by asking: "What kind of support should the company provide for such a project?" He or she would frame similar questions for the three most popular groupings in each category to help define their practicality. The ensuing answers in all instances would then be called out, discussed, and listed on a flipchart sheet bearing the grouping concept as a title. When completed, these sheets would be torn off the chart and taped to a wall.

Once the three top idea groupings in each category have been expanded upon, the 15 "finalists" in our sample case would again be ranked by vote. The Storyboard technique can utilize various individual techniques during the idea-generating part of the session.

Problem Setting

The Problem Setting technique focuses on developing a full and accurate problem definition for the decision to be made. It encourages group members to generate the fullest possible range of ideas concerning both problem producers and problem consequences. It helps those taking part to better understand each other's viewpoints and develop a consensus. Such elaboration and consensus, in turn, help suggest more comprehensive and universally acceptable solutions.

1. The facilitator writes an initial version of the problem to be addressed on a flipchart or blackboard.
2. Participants brainstorm to identify producers, which are listed to the right of the problem.
3. Participants brainstorm to identify possible consequences and/or changes that might occur if the problem is solved. These are listed to the left of the problem.
4. Possible relationships between the individual factors in the two or three lists are explored, and lines are drawn to connect them.
5. These relationships are numerically weighted, and the various weights are written on the connecting lines.

The group facilitator of a Problem Setting exercise writes an initial version of the problem or decision to be made in the middle of a flipchart sheet. Group members then suggest possible "producers"—items that might produce the problem or influence the decision. These are listed to the right of the problem. Brainstorming as well as various other individual techniques can be used to define these producers.

Once the initial list is recorded, the group facilitator can expand it by asking participants to define "second-level" producers. For example, if the problem is declining productivity, an originally defined producer might be lack of worker commitment. When asked to suggest "second-level" producers responsible for this lack of worker commitment, participants might offer boring work, lack of appropriate incentives, or bad management attitude.

During the second phase of the problem setting exercise, group members are required to suggest possible consequences or, as an alternative, the changes they think might occur in their individual situations if the decision made solved the problem. These suggestions are listed by the group facilitator to the left of the problem. For example, a possible consequence of declining productivity might be layoffs. One change that might occur if the problem were solved could be salary raises. A third approach would be to list both consequences and changes, allowing participants to view and compare their two possible futures.

The third phase of the problem setting exercise includes an exploration by group members of the relationships that exist between individual factors in the three lists. Lines can be drawn to connect related factors. Comparative numerical weights can be assigned to these relationships and written above the connecting lines as a means of defining the central issues. This third phase could be considered a sophisticated form of preferential listing or establishing priorities. The accompanying discussion will also help identify areas where adequate information is lacking.

Refer to the case study presented in Chapter 7 for an example of how a team employed some of these techniques to define its problem and write a problem statement.

General Group Techniques That Focus on Defining Priorities

The last two techniques discussed in the previous subcategory include grouping and/or ranking. Idea generation, however, rather than idea grouping or idea ranking was their central objective. Their strength was the raw number of ideas they could produce. In contrast, the strengths of the techniques described in this subcategory are: (1) their ability to facilitate the building of a useful series of ideas concerning a specific problem and/or (2) their ability to define the group's opinion concerning the relative merit of an idea.

The purpose of the techniques described in this subcategory, therefore, is to again create a cooperative atmosphere, but this time one in which participants in a problem solving process support and feed freely off each other's efforts so as to successfully group and order useful ideas. The efforts of each group member help the others achieve their desired objective.

The TKJ technique (described next) is an elaboration of the individual technique that uses grouping. The Nominal Group technique is an elaboration of preferential listing. The Cause And Effect or Fishbone Diagram and Modified Delphi techniques, in turn, combine the strengths of both the TKJ and Nominal Group techniques.

TKJ

TKJ is a technique developed by Kawakita Jiro (a Japanese anthropologist). TKJ stands for Team Kawakita Jiro (sometimes referred to as the KJ Method or the Affinity Diagram) and is a systematic, creative, and participatory method of problem solving and decision making.

TKJ is led by a facilitator. The required props are a flipchart or blackboard and a supply of five-by-eight-inch cards. Alternatively, if everyone has access to a computer during the meeting, software simulating putting index cards on a board might be utilized*. As a first step, the facilitator describes and then writes on the board or chart an initial version of the problem to be addressed. Participants then individually list problem- or solution-related facts on separate cards. These facts must be important and objectively verifiable.

1. The group facilitator writes an initial version of the problem to be addressed on a flipchart or blackboard.
2. Participants list important and objectively verifiable problem or solution-related facts on five-by-eight-inch cards.
3. The cards are collected and redistributed so that no participant receives his or her own.
4. A randomly chosen participant reads aloud a fact from one of his or her cards. The fact is recorded on the flipchart or blackboard by the group facilitator.
5. Other participants read related facts aloud from their cards. These are added to the list headed by the initial fact.
6. When one round has been completed, another is begun with the reading of another fact by another randomly chosen participant.
7. Other participants again read aloud related facts which are added to that list.
8. When all facts have been assigned to a set, participants choose a name for each set that reflects its essence and write the name on a card. If more than one alternative is generated, the choice can be made by vote.
9. Set names are then distributed and the process is repeated. Someone randomly chosen reads a set name, and others add related set names to the list. Someone else reads another set name, and so on.
10. The cycle continues until only one all-inclusive set name card remains.

---

* This will be the case throughout the book; software simulations can be utilized for Zoom or other web conference calls instead of physical index cards and boards.

The goal is to synthesize all the different perspectives into a definition acceptable to all process participants. It can be used both to elaborate on the nature of a problem and the potential solutions to the problem.

For example, suppose the initial version of the problem for a computer firm is falling sales in the Philadelphia area. Relevant facts that are objectively verifiable might include: (1) salespeople are not covering all possible targets, (2) another computer firm is focusing its marketing resources on the Philadelphia area, (3) a new complex of information-based industries is growing just outside the city limits, (4) the sales force in this area has recently been cut, and (5) the marketing budget for this region is relatively low in terms of expected sales.

As a second step, the fact cards are collected and redistributed so that no participant receives his or her own. The facilitator then randomly picks a participant and asks that person to read one of his or her facts out loud. Others are encouraged to offer facts related to this initial one from their cards, thus building a set. For example, if fact 3 from our example concerning the computer firm in Philadelphia is read first, facts 1 and 4 might fit with it into one set. Then the facilitator picks another participant to read a fact out loud. Again, others with related facts on their cards add them to build a set. This process continues until all of the facts have been incorporated into one of the sets.

The next step is for participants to choose a name for each set that reflects its essence. This name is written on a new card. Set names are then distributed and the process is repeated with them. The facilitator picks a participant to read one of his or her set names. Then others add related set names to build a set name set, and so on. This type of synthetic group activity continues until one all-inclusive set name card containing one all-inclusive problem definition or solution is obtained.

Nominal Group

The Nominal Group technique is in many ways similar to TKJ. Its focus, however, is on establishing priorities rather than synthesizing. The technique was developed by Andrew Van De Ven and Andre Delbecq. Their purpose was to encourage the useful participation of all group members in a problem solving situation. The nominal group technique requires that participants contribute ideas, but in a way that initially nullifies the constraints of challenge and possible domination by others. At the same time, it provides a system for critiquing and selecting between ideas, which again limits confrontation and encourages well-considered contributions.

1. The facilitator writes an initial version of the problem to be addressed on a flipchart or blackboard.
2. Participants write their ideas concerning solutions on a piece of paper.
3. Each participant reads aloud one idea, which is written down, and then the second after other group members have contributed, until all ideas are recorded on the flipchart or blackboard.
4. The ideas are briefly discussed and clarified.
5. Participants then rank the ideas and turn their results in to the facilitator.
6. Votes are recorded on the flipchart or blackboard and voting pattern inconsistencies discussed.
7. A final individual listing of top priorities are made by participants, turned in, and recorded on the flipchart or blackboard.

The process begins with an impartial facilitator posing to the group a question that indicates the nature of the problem to be defined or solved. The question must be carefully designed. It is a good idea to pretest it. Participants are told to silently list their ideas concerning answers on a piece of paper. Each group member then reads one of his or her ideas aloud. The ideas are recorded, still without discussion, on a flipchart. When one round is completed, a second is begun, and so on, until all ideas are recorded.

Each idea is then briefly discussed and clarified if necessary. Participants can voice agreement or disagreement at this point, but drawn out debates are not allowed. The next step is for participants to silently write the ideas they think are most important or worthwhile on individual five-by-eight-inch cards. Then, participants order these cards and turn them in to the facilitator, who records the votes on the flipchart. When this tabulation is completed, the results are discussed and voting pattern inconsistencies are examined. Following the discussion, priorities are finalized by another session of writing priorities on five-by-eight-inch cards.

Fishbone Diagram

The Fishbone Diagram (also known as the Cause and Effect Diagram) is one of the simplest techniques available for identifying and organizing the causes of a problem in terms of sequence or priority. It was developed by Kaoru Ishikawa and is usually grouped with statistical productivity measuring techniques because it complements them so well.

The Fishbone Diagram technique is based on a pictorial representation of the issue addressed. The representation is in the shape of a fish skeleton as can be seen in Figure 3.1. The head of the fish is the problem or decision to be made or the desired improvement. The spine is the major cause of the problem or the major step necessary to accomplish the desired improvement. The bones running off the spine are contributing factors to the major producer or supporting steps to the major step. Smaller bones might also angle off the main bones to represent subfactors or substeps. Even smaller bones might angle off those, and so on.

If there is more than one major cause, it is necessary to create more than one skeleton with the same head but different spines. It is also possible that one of the bones/factors might eventually replace the spine as the major cause or step. This change could result from participants' increased understanding of the situation.

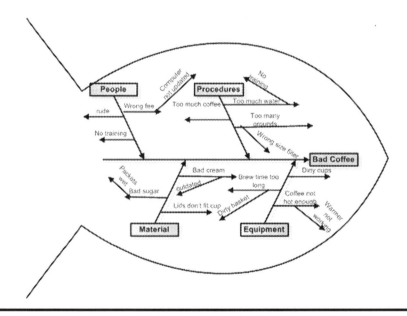

Figure 3.1 Example of Fishbone Diagram for Root Cause Analysis.

The Fishbone Diagram can be used to show sequence. The bone closest to the head represents the first factor. It can also be used to show priority. The closer to the head a bone lies, the higher its priority as a cause.

Suppose the problem is low productivity. The spine of the Fishbone Diagram might initially be inappropriate use of technology. The bones that extend from the spine could include lack of maintenance on existing equipment, lack of corporate reinvestment in technology, lack of research into technological improvements and new technologies, lack of appropriate long-range technological planning, and lack of a vehicle that allows employees to suggest ways to improve current technology.

Angle bones off the bone representing lack of research might include lack of facilities for research, lack of funds for research, and lack of staff for research.

Participants might also decide that the spine for the problem of low productivity should actually be "lack of appropriate long-range planning" and that a bone angling off this spine should be labeled "inappropriate use of technology." Thus, a new Fishbone Diagram would evolve, using many of the same causes but arranging them differently.

Modified Delphi

The Modified Delphi technique for smaller groups is another means of gathering related information to clarify the nature of a problem and to suggest comprehensive solutions. It can be considered a synthesis of the TKJ and Nominal Group techniques in that it does two things: (1) groups characteristics and (2) ranks groupings. Its uniqueness is that participants do not meet each other until the mid-point of the process, if at all.

Again, the exercise begins with a facilitator presenting the problem to be addressed in the form of a question. Participants privately list problem-related factors they consider relevant to or part of the solution on a sheet of paper. The facilitator collects and synthesizes these individual lists, culling out or combining repetitious items.

The resulting master list is then presented to group members, who privately divide the factors into classifications on a second sheet of paper. The results are again collected, organized, and redistributed so that participants can decide either privately or through discussion which categories are repetitious and which are the most relevant. It is preferable that decisions are reached through consensus; if this is not possible, the majority rules.

1. A facilitator presents the problem to be addressed to participants.
2. Participants privately list problem-related factor or answers.
3. The lists are gathered by the facilitator and combined into one nonrepetitive list which is distributed to the participants.
4. Participants privately divide the items in this "master" list into categories.
5. The results are collected, combined, and redistributed. The combining in this case can be done either by the group leader or by participants in the group.
6. Participants privately rank the categories decided upon.
7. The results are recorded and discussed in a group session.

The final step is for group members to privately order the categories according to their own feelings on a third sheet of paper. These lists of priorities are collected by the leader and totaled. The results can then be written on a flipchart and discussed. If, during this phase, the facilitator feels that opinion is shifting significantly, he or she can repeat the part of the exercise in which priorities are established.

General Group Techniques That Introduce Competition

All of the group techniques discussed thus far are designed to encourage cooperation. Some establish rules that outlaw competition or conflict. Others simply do not allow any judgmental interaction to occur. Groups that use these techniques might eventually rank ideas, but in a nonaggressive manner.

In this subcategory, however, two radically different techniques are introduced. They actually incorporate competition as a means of: (1) encouraging greater effort by process participants and (2) defining more accurately the relative strengths of the alternative solutions generated.

The theory behind this approach is that a competitive atmosphere makes participants try harder. It stimulates more originality and a greater degree of discernment in problem solving efforts than does cooperation. The question of whether or not such a theory is, in fact, supported by experimental evidence remains unanswered. Some experiments show that a competitive atmosphere does make participants try harder, while others indicate that cooperation is the best alternative. It is likely that the personality types of the participants play a major role in the outcome (Gharajedaghi 1984; Roth 1982).

The two methods discussed are Dialectic and Swapping.

Dialectic

The first technique that incorporates competition is Dialectic. Developed by West Churchman (Churchman), it is used mainly to identify the assumptions on which the most holistic, effective solution can be based in a group decision making situation. The key participant is a decision maker who must be acceptable to everyone else involved.

1. A decision maker forms two or more teams from exercise participants and provides each with a statement and relevant information about the decision to be made.
2. The teams are assigned conflicting sides of the issue, generate answers representing these sides, and present them to the group as a whole.
3. The decision maker (or a third team with the decision maker acting as referee) creates a synthesis and defends it before the teams representing conflicting sides.

The first step in the process is for the decision maker to form two or more teams from the group participants. The decision maker supplies the teams with the same statement and, when possible, with relevant information. The teams then formulate individual solutions. The decision maker can also predefine the objectives and/or approaches of the different teams. For example, if the decision is about whether or not an oil company should buy a shipping line, one team would be instructed to support the purchase and the other to oppose it.

In this example, the two teams would probably generate most of their own information. Also, the decision maker would probably be a collection of top-level executives, or a board of directors, rather than a single individual.

The dialectic can also be used as a follow-up to other group techniques. A problem solving exercise could begin with Brainstorming, Storyboard, TKJ, or Modified Delphi. In cases where more than one attractive alternative materializes, the group would be introduced to define the most appropriate choice. Obviously, the various alternatives would have supporters who would be assigned to the appropriate teams.

After all arguments have been heard, the decision maker in a Dialectic exercise traditionally creates a synthesis, developing his or her own set of assumptions from which an effective solution can be generated.

A modification to the process would be for a third or fourth team to act as the synthesizer. Once this additional team has defined its assumptions, it would be asked to defend them before the two or three original teams. The decision maker would referee this final exchange and settle any disagreements that threatened ultimate consensus.

Swapping

The second technique in this category, a modification of the Dialectic developed by Roth, is called Swapping. It is most valuable in situations where participants in a decision making exercise have generated two extremely different and/or irreconcilable alternatives or sets of assumptions upon which an option is to be based.

The breakdown of conflicting opinions is usually according to frame of reference. For example, the decision facing a beer manufacturer and distributor might be how best to dispel a nasty rumor about product ingredients started by a rival company. Representatives from the finance department, with cost foremost in their minds, might believe that the best and cheapest solution is personal contact (e.g., salespeople should take the time necessary to personally deny the rumor and calm any fears key clients might have). Representatives from the sales department, on the other hand, concerned about the added workload and the uncertainty of such an approach, might strongly support a more expensive advertising campaign.

Once the arguments have been fully developed and a state of impasse reached, the Swapping technique is brought into play. A referee is assigned, and the swap is made. The two sets of combatants are instructed to develop a 30-minute or longer presentation of the *opposition's* argument, adding at least two new supportive points or solution ideas.

1. Participants are divided into teams based upon their opposing solutions to the problem to be addressed.
2. A referee is assigned.
3. The teams are instructed to develop a 30-minute or longer presentation of the opposition's argument, adding at least two new points or solution ideas.
4. The referee decides whether or not the presentations are adequate.
5. If they are not, the referee can force the teams to reorganize and re-present as many times as he or she thinks necessary.

6. Each presentation acceptable to the referee is critiqued by the other teams.
7. Once all teams have made acceptable presentations, another attempt is made to achieve a solution that is acceptable to all sides.

They must put themselves in the shoes of their opponents. In order to facilitate development of the necessary mindset, they are given access to any information requested, unless the referee deems it irrelevant.

If the referee decides that a presentation is insincere or does not adequately address the proposed solution, he or she can force the team to reorganize and re-present as many times as necessary. When the referee finally approves the team offerings, each presentation is critiqued by the other teams. Finally, another attempt is made to achieve synthesis.

This approach has the following strengths: (1) it is educational and broadens the perspective of participants in problem solving exercises; (2) because of the different frames of reference introduced, the opposition's solution might be strengthened; and (3) because of the broadened perspectives of all participants, an acceptable synthesis might now be possible, whereas before it was not.

A possible weakness of the approach is that participants might not take it seriously. In such cases, whether or not top-level management supports the referee in his or her decisions may be the determining factor.

Evaluation of General Group Techniques

The general group techniques defined here begin with the least sophisticated and progress to the most sophisticated. We began with those designed simply to generate the greatest number of ideas concerning a problem or desired improvement and proceeded to the second level, techniques which generate ideas and identify common themes that run through them. The third level included techniques which generate ideas, identify themes, and then define the relative value of those themes through ranking. The fourth set introduced the element of competition in order to excite efforts and, in swapping, to help clarify the opposition's viewpoint.

All of the general group techniques encourage boldness and originality. They go much further toward utilizing the intelligence and imagination of participants than do the individual techniques discussed earlier. They encourage all participants to play an active role in the decision making process and allow the inclusion of representatives from all stakeholder groups, although, with the possible exception of the Modified Delphi technique, they do not generally require it.

Again, most of these techniques are problem specific and do not force participants to pay attention to the problem network or "mess" of which the problem addressed is a part. One exception might be the Fishbone Diagram, which allows and can encourage the necessary exploration. Due to this same focus on an individual problem, very few of the general group techniques can be considered truly flexible. All provide continuous feedback and, with the possible exception of the Modified Delphi technique, all provide timely decisions.

Because these techniques are problem specific and are used in "one-shot" exercises, they do not encourage continuity of effort. Neither do they provide a vehicle for implementation of results.

In summary, the strengths of the general group techniques are that they:

1. Encourage boldness and originality
2. Utilize the intelligence and imagination of participants
3. Encourage participants to play an active role
4. Take group dynamics into account
5. Encourage flexibility in terms of the problem addressed
6. Maintain interest over the course of the exercise
7. Allow timely solutions

Their weaknesses are that they:

1. Do not force the participation of representatives from all stakeholder groups
2. Focus on a small segment of the problem network and, therefore, do not encourage flexibility or continuity in terms of the network as a whole
3. Do not encourage development of an appropriate vehicle for the implementation of solutions

Holistic Techniques

The techniques described in this section are used mainly in situations where problems are known to exist but have been defined only in the most general terms. They are also used in situations where organizations are trying to identify/address a suspected network of problems rather than focus initially on one or several problems. Their similarity is that they all adopt a holistic perspective in terms of the issues addressed. Instead of simply being compatible with the previously defined individual and group techniques, they quite frequently absorb and enhance the other techniques.

Two basic types of holistic techniques are presented. The first type is used solely to help identify the problems in a network, and includes the Flowchart, Two Words, and Breaking the Ice techniques. The second type's purpose is to discover solutions to problem networks. It include the Force Field Analysis, Idealized Design, Modified Idealized Design, and Search Conference techniques. One of the techniques discussed, Search Conference, addresses both identifying the problem and discovering a solution.

Holistic to Identify Problems

The three techniques discussed here are holistic oriented because they try to view the entire situation and environment from end to end: Flowchart, Two Words, and Breaking the Ice. They are mainly used to identify problems.

Flowchart

This first systemic tool is used to generate a frame of reference within which a network of organization-, unit-, or system-wide problems can be more easily identified. A Flowchart can be a diagram, especially when a manufacturing process is being charted. Often, however, it is a straightforward, comprehensive list of steps involved in a process. The trick is not to leave anything out. Once the list is complete, participants look for problem areas within the defined process steps and within the gaps between these steps. They then develop clear definitions of the problems involved and use other techniques to deal with them.

The Flowchart is useful in understanding the process as well as identifying areas for measurement. It is important that each step identify *who* is involved, *how* they receive input, and *what* they do with it, as specifically as possible. Instead of simply saying "claim is received," for example, we need to specify that the "customer calls in the claim to the call center rep."

An example of a Flowchart diagram can be found in Figure 3.2 concerning an insurance claim process. The issue that is identified by the Flowchart was a choke-point at the insurance verifier leaving a long period of time when the claim number was unknown, causing a great deal of rework and frustrated customers who could not wait for the claim number to get medical treatment.

62 ■ *Strategic Decision Making for Successful Planning*

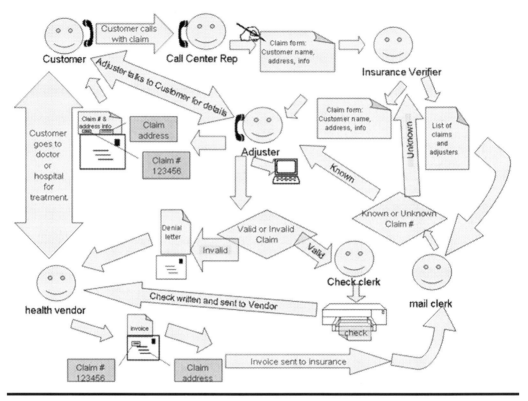

Figure 3.2 Flowchart Diagram for Insurance Claim Process.

The list in Table 3.3 provides an example of a Flowchart list developed by the work services unit affiliated with a rehabilitation center. The unit tries to employ people with disabilities, frequently those who have spent time in the rehabilitation center, to complete relatively simple tasks which they are capable of completing, such as packing pieces into boxes or changing labels on equipment. The unit accepts a wide variety of jobs from a constantly shifting range of companies. Obviously, it needs to remain extremely flexible while at the same time maintaining control.

The Flowchart list was developed jointly by the functional managers and the work services director. The group opted to start with the procurement process and to chart the entire operation through to shipping. Only that segment of the Flowchart exercise dealing with procurement is presented in the list.

Table 3.3 Flowchart List Example

1. Project Manager (PM) reviews nature of work requested by potential client
   Do we have necessary expertise?
   What are the customers' requirements?
   - Quality
   - Turnaround time
   - Date customer could make components available
2. PM does time study and methodology study for job
   Determines of need for "fixtures"
3. PM discusses project with Production Department (PD)
   Establish tentative schedule
   Consider labor hours available
   Consider need to hire additional personnel
4. PM develops bid price; presentation of written bid and terms to customer
5. PM receives notification of acceptance of bid from customer
6. PD confirms production schedule and required turnaround time
7. PM recruits additional manpower when necessary
8. PD constructs fixtures, if necessary
9. PM makes arrangements for incoming materials
10. Shipping Department (SD) receives incoming materials
11. If discrepancies noted, SD notify PM to resolve
12. PM compares incoming materials to samples
13. PM makes sure enough pieces are available to complete actual order
14. PM uses actual materials, verifies time study, reviews price and methodology
15. PM issues production order and purchase order for any necessary equipment
16. PM writes step-by-step procedures
17. PM assigns and enters job step codes into process control system
18. PM enters production order and any purchase orders involved into process control system
19. PM gives production department copies of all written information (receiving information, step codes, purchase orders, time studies, etc.)

Two Words

The Two Words technique was used at Paul Revere Insurance Group and is described by Pat Townsend (Townsend and Gebhardt; Townsend and Gebhardt) in his book *Commit to Quality*. The process begins with the unit involved as a whole describing what it does in just two words, one verb and one noun. Offerings are written on a flipchart and then discussed and debated until a consensus is reached.

The unit is then broken down by function. Representatives from each function write on three-by-five-inch cards all the things they do in just two words, one verb and one noun. Once this part of the exercise is completed, the cards for each function are laid out on a large table or on the floor and are linked to see what the relationships are, whether or not the tasks complement each other, and where they might overlap.

If any of the cards do not fit into the chains formed, the participants ask: "Why not?" The possibility that they might actually belong in another function is explored, as well as the possibility that they are not necessary.

Breaking the Ice

The Breaking the Ice technique was developed and is used extensively by Roth. It borrows heavily from Fred Emery's (F. Emery) search conference, which is discussed at the end of this chapter. Breaking the Ice is used with groups or teams that represent one function. It cannot be used with cross-functional teams for reasons that will become apparent.

Breaking the Ice begins with a facilitator asking participants to identify trends in the general community which affect their ability to do their jobs the way they want to do them. This technique allows the participants to get to know each other by talking about something that is not threatening. It gives them a chance to warm up to the situation rather than staring suspiciously at the facilitator. All contributions are listed on flipchart sheets, which are taped up in order on a wall.

After these contributions have been discussed and the participants are a little more comfortable with both the process and the facilitator, the next challenge thrown out is: "Now let's identify trends in our organization which affect your ability to do your job the way you want to do it."

An obvious modern-day example of such a trend would be downsizing. Another would be the willingness or unwillingness of managers to communicate with each other and with employees. There are two parts to this question—organization-wide trends and trends within a function/department. The facilitator starts with organization-wide trends, but the team usually moves without prompting into function/departmental trends.

After these trends are listed and discussed, the facilitator asks participants to list their job responsibilities, not necessarily in order. This phase could be viewed as a disorganized but much quicker form of the Flowchart exercise.

Once this list is complete, the team is asked to brainstorm and to begin suggesting ways they think any system on any level of the organization can be improved. For example, many teams talk about the need to improve the message system in their office, while others present the current organization-wide shift system as a possible project.

Teams are encouraged to define issues relating to products, production processes, management systems, and the work environment. Nothing is sacred. The facilitator's main responsibilities during this phase are to ask clarifying questions, not let participants get immediately involved in solving the individual problems identified, and to make sure that the definition of each problem as listed is clear.

Once no more issues are forthcoming, the facilitator goes back to the list of trends in the community which affect the employees' ability to do their jobs the way they want to do them and to the list of employee responsibilities. The facilitator leads team members slowly through these lists to make sure nothing has been missed.

Once the list of potential improvements is completed, at least for the moment, the facilitator asks the participants to divide the usually 30 or 40 items into three categories:

1. In-house issues which can be addressed without involving anyone outside the function—this might include bad lighting or improving the filing system.
2. Border issues on which participants must work in conjunction with another function—a common one is bad parts or information coming down the line.
3. Organization-wide issues that affect policy or involve expenditure of a large amount of money and, therefore, must involve upper-level management—this could include the need for a new process control system or more staff.

Once the issues are properly categorized, the facilitator encourages (but does not force) participants to pick the easiest in-house issues to work on first, in order to produce quick results. This allows the team to experience success early in the process, so that team members can prove to themselves that they are capable of creating change and so that teams can prove to upper-level managers who are watching that they can move rapidly and effectively.

This technique was used as part of an effort to improve the operations of a middle-sized city government. The lists presented in Table 3.4* were generated by the secretarial team.

---

* The ** indicates additional items not shown for sake of brevity.

Table 3.4 Breaking the Ice Technique Example

Environmental Trends That Affect My Ability to Do My Job the Way I Want to Do It	Function Job Responsibilities
1. Loss of jobs due to old companies moving out 2. Crime on the rise 3. Influx of unskilled labor 4. Loss of pride in city 5. Deteriorating neighborhoods 6. Increase in drug-related activity 7. Rising taxes 8. New industries require new skills but training unavailable 9. City lacks plan/direction 10. Homes being turned into apartments 11. **	1. Help integrate activities of department 2. Word processing 3. Filing 4. Answering queries 5. Coordinating with other departments 6. Keeping master schedules 7. Photocopying 8. **
Organization Trends That Affect My Ability to Do My Job the Way I Want to Do It	**Projects to Improve Operation (Categorized as Level 1, 2, 3)**
1. Policies change without my knowing or being asked for input 2. Threat of layoffs 3. Unwillingness to invest in needed technology 4. Managers frequently do not communicate well 5. Often hard to get needed information 6. Frequently get calls that have nothing to do with our department 7. Lack of necessary training or cross-training 8. Departments do not know what other departments do 9. Do not know where files are when someone is using them 10. Phone directory often confusing 11. **	1. Develop system for users to write names on a tab when removing files from cabinet (1) 2. Improve intercom system (3) 3. Central library for records (3) 4. Link all computers (2) 5. Cross-train within office (1) 6. Bring someone in from information systems function to answer questions (2) 7. Set up employee education program so we can learn what other departments do (3) 8. Rearrange offices to make work flow easier (1) 9. Revise in-house phone directory (2) 10. **

Holistic Techniques Used to Discover Solutions

The techniques discussed in this section are Force Field Analysis, Idealized Design, Modified Idealized Design, Search Conference, Process Function Deployment, and Service Blueprinting. As with the previous section, these

Table 3.5 Listing Example of Force Field Analysis

Current Situation:	Work force moral deteriorating
Ideal Situation:	All employees 100% committed to doing their best
Worst Possible Situation:	Employees strike
Restraining Forces	**Driving Forces**
Recent downsizing	Stable work force
Added responsibilities	Cross-training
Managers who don't listen	New quality process
Lack of opportunity for employee advancement	Management's promise of no more layoffs
Poor downward communication	New computerized technology
Recent pay increases for highest levels	Beginnings of teach approach production

techniques are more whole-organization centered. The difference is that they don't stop at identifying the problem, but are more focused on discovering the solution.

Force Field Analysis

Force Field Analysis, developed by Kurt Lewin (Lewin, Lippit, and White 1939), begins by identifying two diametrically opposed sets of social forces which exert pressure on any sociotechnical system. Lewin contends that "restraining forces" are those forces that continually are pushing the current situation toward the worst possible outcome. "Driving forces" are those forces that are continually pushing it toward the best possible outcome. The objective of a Force Field Analysis exercise is to identify the members of both sets in a specific situation and their relationships (Table 3.5). Once this is done, participants must find ways to reduce the number and power of the relevant restraining forces while at the same time increasing the number and power of the relevant driving forces.

In order to complete this exercise, the following six questions must be addressed:

1. What is the current situation, what would the ideal situation be, and what could the worst possible situation be?
2. What are the restraining forces which are pushing the current situation toward the worst possible alternative?
3. What are the driving forces which are pushing the current situation toward the ideal state?
4. What relationship exists between these two sets of forces?
5. Over which restraining and driving forces do we believe we have influence, and which of these are important now?
6. For each of the restraining and driving forces subject to our influence, what are specific action steps the group can take to eliminate or strengthen them?

In generating the answers to Questions 2 and 3, the following previously defined techniques might be used: Expert Consultant applied by the group as a whole, Brainstorming, Storyboard, Nominal Group, and Modified Delphi. In generating answers to the three parts of Question 1, TKJ can be added to this list. Definition of the ideal situation can also be achieved through the use of the What/Why/How exercise described next. One could also use Idealized Design, which is described in the next section. Inclusion of these latter two techniques in a Force Field Analysis exercise, however, would cause it to be extremely time consuming.

Once identified, the forces should be listed on a flipchart, with arrows indicating whether they are restraining or driving forces. Question 5 is addressed by circling those forces which can be influenced. Participants might also rank the forces, prioritizing them in terms of the relative ease with which they can be influenced beneficially.

Finally, as a means of identifying the "specific action steps" cited in Question 6, Lewin introduces a checklist of further questions to be addressed:

1. Who will do what?
2. What exactly will be done?
3. Where will it be carried out?
4. When will it be done?
5. How will it be augmented?

This is the old "newspaper reporter" checklist adapted to the workplace, also known as the 4W1H checklist. In terms of workplace problem solving, however, the "what" question should probably be addressed first. This change will allow the participants to address the other questions in a more effective manner.

Idealized Design

Idealized Design was developed by Russell Ackoff as part of the interactive planning paradigm. It is used primarily in comprehensive efforts to plan the future of entire organizations. It can, however, also be used in simpler problem solving exercises, as it was in the Bell Labs project where Ackoff first encountered it. Idealized design twists conventional logic around. When faced with a problem, we traditionally define where we are, or what the weaknesses of our current approach or system are. We then prioritize these weaknesses and work on improving them individually.

Idealized Design turns the traditional approach around. Instead of starting where we are and trying to move forward in an often piecemeal fashion, Idealized Design begins by addressing the question of where we would *like to be* ideally, where we should be, and works backward from that point. In other words, instead of defining existing constraints to change and striving to identify the best way to manipulate or overcome these constraints in terms of current conditions and environmental trends, groups utilizing idealization begin by defining what they would consider to be the ideal state. Once consensus is reached on this ideal state, the groups develop plans for bridging the gaps between their current reality and the ideal state, prioritize the involved activities, and then generate action plans.

The major strength of the Idealized Design technique is its holistic nature. It starts by identifying a comprehensive whole which is desired and then molds the pieces of the system in terms of that whole, rather than shaping individual pieces and then trying to fit them together in a way that builds a meaningful whole.

Idealized Design, as noted, is most frequently used when addressing larger, more systemic problems. Moving a filing cabinet would hardly necessitate this technique, unless process participants begin to suspect that the misplaced filing cabinet is part of a larger, office design issue.

Problem solving exercises begin with the total destruction of the system addressed. Once it is destroyed, participants are told to redesign the system in any way they wish. Roth utilized this method in his book, *Comprehensive Healthcare for the US: An Idealized Model* (Roth 2010), which was held up by

President Obama as one of the influencers for what is now known colloquially as Obamacare (known officially as the Affordable Care Act).

The first step in this process is to decide what the solution case ought to produce or do ideally, ignoring factors, such as corporate policy, which might inhibit change. Next, participants identify characteristics that would be necessary if the solution were to achieve the ideal state. The third step is to actually design the new system, getting down to shaping the nuts and bolts which would allow the desired characteristics to materialize. Next, participants define action steps necessary for implementation of the design elements. Finally, participants decide which of the action steps are possible in terms of their current reality and, then, which steps should be priorities.

The key to the success of this approach is for those involved to develop a clear target to aim for and one to which everyone agrees. Once the target is spelled out in terms of characteristics and design elements, efforts are planned that will move the group, sometimes slowly, toward the target. Another strength of the approach is that once the current reality has been adequately "destroyed," imaginative thinking is encouraged. The technique can be presented as a cooperative group game or a fantasy exercise, the results of which threaten no one. Usually, participants begin to understand the full value and power of the technique only when they start working on the actual system design elements and realize that the gap between their reality and the ideal is not as wide as first imagined.

Results of an Idealized Design exercise must meet the following criteria:

1. They must be technologically feasible. The design cannot incorporate nonexistent technology or technology that is not cost effective. For example, a steel-producing facility powered entirely by solar energy is not technologically feasible at this time.
2. The solution designed must be capable of surviving in the current internal/external economy.
3. The solution designed must include or be linked to an apparatus that allows constant revision based on the continual learning of employees.

As an example of a successful Idealized Design exercise, consider the following scenario of a luxury resort situated on the west coast of Mexico. The surrounding region was extremely poor. Two problems were presented: (1) the company wanted to attract foreign vacationers, especially from the United States, and (2) the company wanted to control the local population.

Natives were mugging tourists and destroying resort property. Townspeople who had been given jobs by the company were not delivering services with the appropriate attitude. They were often sullen and uncontrollable, even when threatened with dismissal.

The company had reacted to this hostile environment by donating a new jail as well as funds to increase the local police force. It had built a wall around the resort compound. Caddies on the golf course had been trained to double as bodyguards.

The first step taken by the consultants hired by the company was to survey people from the United States who had previously vacationed abroad. They were asked to describe the atmosphere they sought. The number one priority they defined was to have contact with the local culture. The number two priority was a safe environment.

With these two requirements in mind, the consultants then spent time at the resort. What they found was a closed environment—guests ate at the resort, used the private beach, and were entertained by the staff. The town adjacent to the resort was relatively uninteresting. The few small restaurants in the town catered to local residents, and there was little for tourists to buy in the way of crafts, indigenous clothing, or other goods. Streets were dirty, and buildings were run down and unattractive. The landscape was mainly dry brush with a few trees. The two major sources of income were subsistence farming and fishing. The resort bought none of its food locally.

The townspeople interviewed by the consultants resented the resort and its constant display of wealth. It rapidly became obvious that if the resort owners wanted to improve the attitude of local inhabitants and at the same time encourage customer contact with the local culture, they needed to change their approach.

The next step was to redefine the problem(s). A team was formed, made up of the people involved. They framed their ideal state as a question: "How could the company develop a resort operation that would attract U.S. tourists and prove profitable not only to the company, but also to the local community and to the region as a whole?"

Design characteristics needed to achieve this ideal state included:

1. Clean up the town and make it more attractive.
2. Develop a marketplace in the town that would cater to tourists.
3. Develop a crafts manufacturing complex that would take advantage of the region's reputation for wood carving, pottery, and weaving. Invite

tourists into the complex to watch the craftspeople at work and perhaps to take lessons.
4. Encourage local farmers to raise materials used by the craftspeople, such as gourds, reeds/grasses, wood, and leather. Support and coordinate their efforts.
5. Mount or support a government project to reforest the surrounding hills with hybrid trees that could survive in the local climate.
6. Mount or support an effort to plant shrubbery and grasses for livestock to feed on and to prevent erosion.
7. Use the skills of local fishermen to help make game fishing a major attraction for resort guests.

Design elements defined as necessary to turn the desired design characteristics into reality included:

1. The company should establish a department for regional development. Its purpose would be to provide an interface between company operations and regional inhabitants. It would:
   – Conduct necessary surveys and research.
   – Define what the region might be capable of supplying.
   – Match the cost of developing these capabilities against long-term benefits.
   – Seek government and private funding for projects that seem cost effective.
2. A series of town meetings would be held, where ideas generated by the idealization team would be presented and input would be sought from local residents.
3. A joint committee of town leaders and resort managers would be formed to oversee the activities of the department for regional development.

Modified Idealized Design

The concept of Idealized Design can also be used in smaller projects. As mentioned, the only requirement is that the project deal with a system. For example, suppose members of a factory maintenance department are having trouble keeping their tools safe from theft or loss. The smaller ones tend to disappear, and the bigger ones cannot be found when needed. Tools are left lying all over the plant. The company buys and supplies tools to maintenance workers but is unhappy about the expense involved.

The workers expressed the problem as follows: "We don't want to have to spend half the day running around looking for tools or standing in line at the supply cage to get new ones." When asked to define the ideal arrangement, they eventually came up with: "Tools available immediately when we need them." When asked what characteristics such a system would have, they identified the following:

1. The company would issue each worker one set of small tools that could be carried on a belt or in a toolbox.
2. The company would provide a safe place for employees to leave tools when not using them.
3. The large tools would be kept together in one place when not being used and would be returned to that place after use.

Design elements eventually included the following:

1. Maintenance workers would buy the small tools themselves. The company would pay for the first set. The company would replace them only if broken. Otherwise, the employees would replace them.
2. The company would provide each worker with a locker in which to store tools.
3. The company would fence the locker area in and lock it up at night to prevent theft.
4. The large tools would be kept in a large chest that can be moved to big jobs. Workers who take tools from the chest are responsible for replacing them.
5. If a large tool is missing, work orders would be checked to determine who used the tool last.

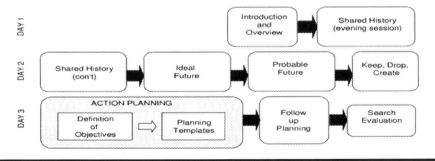

Figure 3.3   Search Conference Stages.

6. The chest would be left in the fenced-in area at night and would also be locked.

A company following this process to discover and implement the solution would find that not nearly as many tools are lost or stolen.

Search Conference

The Search Conference technique, developed by Fred Emery (Emery 1995), is the most global. Rather than addressing the problematic system directly, it starts by exploring the containing environment of the system, thus encouraging a broader perspective. The objective of the technique is to help participants: (1) develop a shared perception, (2) define a mutually desired future, and (3) identify ways of achieving that future.

The process can be shaped in several different ways, largely depending upon the nature and size of the organization and group involved. A stock set of stages exists, as seen in Figure 3.3, and stages can be chosen based on the situation* (Amudavia and Mango 2003). The stages can also be modified.

As an example, a Search Conference was conducted for a coin-operated equipment service company attempting to reorganize and improve the effectiveness and profitability of its operation. Representatives from all major functions and all different levels were included.

The process began with participants identifying general trends in the United States that they considered important. Next, they identified trends in the United States that they considered to be important to their specific industry. The third stage included an oral history of the coin-operated service industry. The fourth stage included a history of the company outlined by the president. The fifth stage was a reference scenario in which participants described a probable future for the organization in both financial and nonfinancial terms if current trends did not change.

The sixth stage focused on the generation of a "desirable future." Here participants defined and listed the ideal characteristics they would like to see their organization develop. These characteristics were then grouped according to three common themes: growth, customer relations, and organization design.

---

* Adapted in 2003 by David M. Amudavia and Nelson Mango. Original source was from A. W. Martin & R. F. Rich (1998). Program for Employment and Workplace Systems, School of Industrial and Labor Relations, Cornell University, unpublished report.

Finally, in the seventh stage, design elements which gave the organization the desired characteristics were generated for each theme sector. The sixth and seventh stages obviously incorporated aspects of idealization. The next step was for participants to begin planning implementation of the design elements.

Process Function Deployment

Another effective approach is the Process Function Deployment method developed by Myron Tribus (Tribus 1975). It has been used extensively to diagram many different types of processes and workflows. Basically start with the previous tools such as Flowchart and Search Conference, but then go one step further in identifying the methods to be used to define the solution. Tribus suggests the following set of questions which can be used by management to check for consistency of application and use:

Why have you selected these as your key processes to diagram? The response to this question demonstrates whether or not a team is, in fact, involved in strategic continuous improvement. It also determines whether the team and the leader share consistent views as to priorities. If this is not the case, either the leader's priorities were not clearly stated or the team members know something the leader should know about.

What will constitute excellence when you undertake to improve this process? How did you arrive at your definition? First, determine if the team is clear about what improvement means. In addition, because asking the customer is the only way to learn about excellence, the leader can determine whether the team is attuned to the customer's needs. Finally, according to Tribus, it will be clear whether the team is merely doing what will suffice or is striving for the best possible performance.

What will you measure as the work of improvement progresses? How will you know, before you get to the end of this effort, whether or not you are really making progress? The purposes of these questions are: (1) to discern the quantitative measures the team will use, (2) to encourage the team to use quantitative measurement if they are not so inclined already, and (3) to allow the leader to help the team use the abilities of others who can demonstrate the use of the quantitative tools.

How will you keep the leader informed of team progress? Will you send emails? Update a portal or website? Broadcast a voicemail? Have meetings? How often should these be expected?

76 ■ *Strategic Decision Making for Successful Planning*

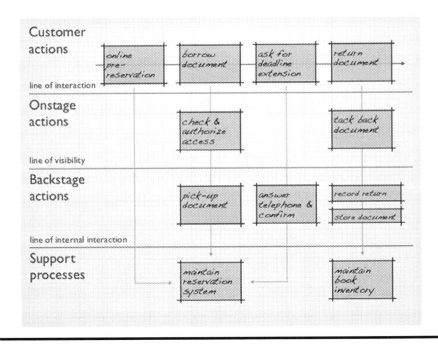

Figure 3.4 Service Blueprinting Example.

Service Blueprinting

Another approach used extensively for service organizations is the Service Blueprinting method developed by G. Lynn Shostack (Shostack 1984), chairman of Joyce International and editorial advisory board of the International Journal of Bank Marketing and the Service Industries Journal. You can see a sample in Figure 3.4*.

A service blueprint is a diagram that illustrates the relationships between different services areas such as people, devices or paths, and processes—that are directly tied to the view of the customer. Service blueprints are helpful in complex scenarios spanning many service-related offerings. They are especially ideal in customer experiences that are omnichannel, involve multiple touchpoints, or require coordination of multiple departments.

For the same service, you may have multiple blueprints if there are several different scenarios that it can accommodate. For example, with a restaurant business, you may have separate service blueprints for the tasks of ordering food for takeout versus dining in the restaurant.

---

* Image by Yves Pigneur. Creative Commons Attribution-Share Alike 4.0 International license. Uploaded July 3, 2017 to commons.wikimedia.org/w/index.php?title=File: Service_Blueprint.jpg&oldid=507869797.

Service blueprints can give an organization a more comprehensive and holistic understanding of all of its service along with the underlying resources and the processes that make it possible—even those that are invisible to the user. This holistic understanding provides strategic benefits for the business.

Evaluation of Holistic Techniques

These techniques are not designed for use in individual problem solving efforts or focused group problem solving efforts. They are based on the belief that no problem stands alone, that each belongs to a network or "mess," and that because of this, no matter how effectively the original problem is addressed, the desired results will probably not be realized due to constraints that exist elsewhere in the network.

The holistic techniques are broken down into two classifications. The first includes the Flowchart, Two Words, and Breaking the Ice techniques, which are used to help identify the problems in the network as well as their interdependencies. The second classification includes Force Field Analysis, Idealized Design, Modified Idealized Design, Search Conference, Process Function Deployment, and Service Blueprinting, which are used mainly to dissolve problem networks and discover (and possibly deploy) solutions.

With the possible exception of the Flowchart, all these techniques encourage boldness and originality, utilizing the intelligence and imagination of the participants. They also encourage all stakeholders affected by a problem network to play an active role in its definition and dissolution. The techniques in this category are by far the most flexible and provide continuous feedback, although decisions might take longer to materialize due to the increased number of stakeholders providing input.

In summary, the strengths of the holistic techniques, with the exception of the Flowchart, are that they:

1. Encourage boldness and originality
2. Utilize the intelligence and imagination of the participants
3. Encourage all stakeholders to play an active role
4. Take into account and actually depend upon group dynamics
5. Encourage flexibility in terms of the problem network addressed
6. Maintain interest over the course of the exercise

7. Encourage development of an appropriate vehicle for the implementation of solutions as a critical part of the exercise

The one possible weakness of these tools and techniques is that:

- Solutions will take longer to achieve due to the increased number of stakeholders involved and, therefore, might not be considered timely, although they are usually more comprehensive and richer in features and designs.

Tools for Measuring Productivity

The techniques described up to this point fit problems and problem networks in a social system, a technical system, or a joint sociotechnical system. It is left to the user to define the dimensions of the problem. This next set of tools, however, is used solely to address problems of production. It does so by measuring key variables in the processes involved. There are hundreds of tools that can be used to measure, but discussed here are some of the most common: Check Sheet, Statistical Control Chart, Histogram, Pareto Diagram, and Scatter Diagram.

Check Sheet

The Check Sheet is simply a written record of how frequently something happens, whether it is the number of fenders that come off the line dented

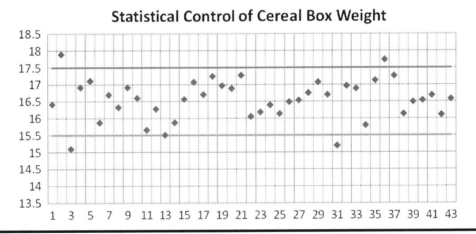

Figure 3.5   Statistical Control Chart Example.

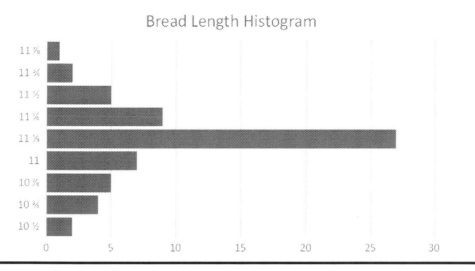

Figure 3.6   Histogram Example.

or the number of potential customers who hang up before a salesperson can get to them. The rest of the tools described in this section can feed off the information collected with a check sheet.

Statistical Control Chart

The Statistical Control Chart, also known as the Shewhart Chart, was developed by Walter Shewhart (Poots and Woodcock 2012) while working for AT&T. It is used to measure variations in a process. It takes samples and plots them against the average.

For example, suppose a cereal box is supposed to contain 16 ounces of cereal. Boxes coming off the line are picked randomly and weighed. The Statistical Control Chart includes a horizontal line across the middle to represent 16 ounces as the desired average. A vertical scale at the left or right edge shows variations, for example, 15.7, 15.8, 15.9, 16, 16.1, 16.2, 16.3. Numbers along the upper or lower edge of the paper denote the sample (1, 2, 3, 4, 5, etc.).

A dot representing each individual sample is placed on the grid at the juncture of the sample number and the defined weight. Two other horizontal lines, one above and one below the horizontal desired average line, show upper and lower control limits. An example can be seen in Figure 3.5.

Employees using a Statistical Control Chart would watch where the dots fall so that they can adjust the machine accordingly, trying to cause the majority of the dots to land on the desired average line. Clusters of dots

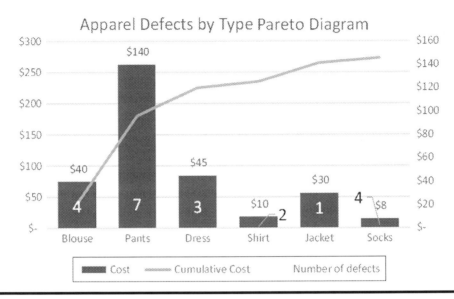

Figure 3.7   Pareto Diagram Example.

above or below the upper or lower control line, or even within the control lines but above or below the desired average line, are easiest to deal with. Randomly distributed dots are more challenging.

Histogram

The Histogram, also known as a Frequency Chart, is a simple tool that is used to show dispersion. It shows a series of bars on a chart to represent categories with, say, ¼ inch representing each of the items in each category being measured.

For example, to discover the dispersion of lengths in a process that produces loaves of bread, count the number of loaves coming off the line that measure 10 ⁶/₈, 10 ⅞, 11, 11 ⅛, and 11 ²/₈ inches. Then, represent each category of bread length with a bar made up of ¼-inch units. If the bar representing 11 ⅛-inch-long loaves is three times as long as any other, there is relatively little dispersion. An example can be seen in Figure 3.6.

Pareto Diagram

A Pareto Diagram provides a visual representation of the relative size of problems. First, a constant unit of measurement is defined (for example, ¼ inch of a bar may be used to represent $10 in cost). Then, using a bar chart,

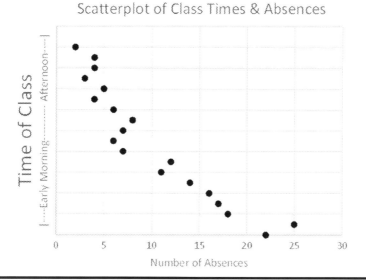

Figure 3.8 Scatter Diagram Example.

the number of one type or various types of defects is plotted against that measurement. The chart may also have a related measure illustrated with a second column which may or may not need a secondary axis. For example, in addition to the cost of the defects, the chart may also show the number of defects. Pareto Diagrams generally also show, again on a separate axis, a line showing the cumulative effect of the different measurements.

An example would be an apparel manufacturing operation where every blouse that has to be rejected at the end of the line is estimated to cost the company $10 in terms of waste. Every pair of pants rejected costs $20. If a manager has to decide whether to deal first with the loss resulting from the blouse operation or from the pants operation, a Pareto Diagram comparing the total daily cost of rejected blouses to the total daily cost of rejected shirts should help make the choice more obvious. An example can be seen in Figure 3.7.

Scatter Diagram

The Scatter Diagram or Scatter Plot is used to show the relationship between two variables. One use of the Scatter Diagram is to verify the relationship between two variables, which may or may not indicate a cause and effect. Scatter Plots can be done to verify relationships between the items on a

Fishbone Diagram. The objective is to discover whether or not a correlation exists. If the points are clustered along an obvious trend line, a correlation probably exists. If they are scattered equally over the diagram, however, chances are that no correlation exists.

For example, to find out if college students are absent most frequently from early morning classes, you could develop a diagram with a horizontal and vertical axis. Place the hours classes begin (8:00, 9:00, 10:00, 11:00, etc.) along one axis. Place the number of absences (1, 2, 3, 4, etc.) along the other. Pick an equal number of classes which begin at each hour, controlling for other variables if possible, and then enter a point on the chart for each day that each class meets to show how many students were absent. You can see in the simple Figure 3.8 that early morning classes are much more likely to have high numbers of absentees than afternoon classes. This sort of tool is a very simple example of the more analytical regression analysis discussed in the next chapter. Basically, when you "eyeball it" to determine if there is a relationship, it is a simple Scatterplot. When you apply mathematical tools to mathematically identify *exactly* how much of a relationship there is, you are doing a regression analysis.

Measuring Productivity Summary

Due to the straightforward and totally focused nature of these tools for measuring productivity, it is not necessary to evaluate them. Generally, the type of data determines which type of tool would be used, and it is generally self-evident which one works best.

Putting It All Together

At this point, we have identified those characteristics an organizational culture should have in order to make it conducive to effective problem solving. We have identified team vehicles that will adequately facilitate the efforts involved. Finally, we have identified the tools and techniques that can be used in the problem solving process itself and have discussed their strengths and weaknesses as well as their relative effectiveness in a wide range of situations.

Now it is time to put it all together, to show how these pieces can and have been combined in a real-life situation. This will be the challenge addressed in the next chapter.

Summary Chapter 3 Questions

- What are the three categories of decision making techniques, and what are the categories based on?
- What are the main subcategories of techniques for individuals?
- What are the specific techniques under each of the subcategories?
- What is the difference between Lateral Thinking and Forced Connections?
- Why are the last two techniques in the Attribute Manipulation subcategory called Morphological? How do they differ from the other four techniques?
- What do all the checklist techniques have in common? How do they differ?
- Why should we Ask Why At Least Five Times?
- What inference can be drawn from analogies?
- What are the four approaches to Synectics?
- What are the three different categories of group techniques?
- Why did William Gordon develop an alternative to Brainstorming?
- What makes the Modified Delphi technique different from either TKJ or the Fishbone Diagram?
- Why would an organization want to introduce competitive group methods?
- What are the three strengths of the Swapping technique?
- What are the strengths of the general group techniques?
- What are the strengths of the holistic techniques?
- Under what circumstances would you use a Flowchart?
- What six questions are addressed in the Force Field Analysis technique?
- For which type of planning is Idealized Design best suited?
- What are the stages of the Search Conference technique?
- Name five tools that can be used to measure productivity. Which are the simplest?

Chapter 4

Choosing the Optimum Analytics

Recently the term "analytics" has been popping up everywhere. Colleges and Universities are offering degrees and certificates in it. Employers, especially, are looking for anyone who has experience in analytics. Courses and workshops are abundant in analytics. But what exactly is analytics?

What Is Analytics?

We'll tell you what analytics is not. It is not new. Analytics has been around for centuries. Two of Aristotle's works on deductive reasoning written about 300 BCE is purported to have been called *Prior Analytics* and *Posterior Analytics**. The term was also used in 1590 and defined as a *method of logical analysis* (2021e). Other definitions include:

- A process in which a computer examines information using mathematical methods in order to find useful patterns
- A system for performing analytics on received data (2021d)
- The science of logical analysis
- The analysis of data, typically large sets of business data, by the use of mathematics, statistics, and computer software
- The patterns and other meaningful information gathered from the analysis of data (2021c)

---

* In case you didn't know, Aristotle lived around 350 BCE (Before the Common Era) and wrote over 200 books and treatises, though not a single one survives to this day.

DOI: 10.4324/9781003198062-4

- The scientific process of discovering and communicating the meaningful patterns which can be found in data
- Concerned with turning raw data into insight for making better decisions
- Relies on the application of statistics, computer programming, and operations research in order to quantify and gain insight to the meanings of data (2021b)
- Information resulting from the systematic analysis of data or statistics
- The systematic computational analysis of data or statistics (2021a)

You will note that the term can apply to three aspects:

1. The domain (i.e., the science of ...)
2. The process (i.e., the method of ...)
3. The results (i.e., the information resulting from ...)

The sentence *In the science of analytics, analytics produces analytics* is a perfectly valid and grammatically correct sentence*.

WHY THE TERM ANALYTICS?

I personally suspect that the term analytics is used in such a widespread way because people were turned off from the term statistics, which is really the synonym of the word analytics (and is equally applied to the three different aspects of the term: domain, process, and results). When people think of statistics, they tend to think of an extremely difficult college course they were forced to take, of which they remember little except that they never thought they would ever actually need to USE that knowledge. For generations statistics/analytics was the domain of isolated academics in their ivory towers who were good in math because of the extensive mathematical equations necessary in order to get a decent answer from a set of data. Often, when I talk to people who have been doing analytics for years, when I mention that they are doing statistics, they have no idea (or actually deny it) because they never realized that they could do statistics without complex formulas and terminology. Statistics is actually the science of seeing patterns in data and estimating the chances that the reality represented by the data is true or false. So is analytics.

---

* Similar to another of my favorite grammatically correct sentences: *Programmers program programs*.

In any case, one of the reasons analytics is talked about so much in this day and age is because data* is so much more accessible. In years gone by, the only way to get data was to laboriously set up surveys and polls and experiments. Generally, the data was painstakingly and manually entered into a computer system. Then once you had the data, you conducted (or hired someone to conduct) the appropriate statistics. This analysis would answer whether your hypothesis was likely to be true or false. The results also provided you with an appropriately couched answer to the statistical question you originally asked.

Few people knew the ins and outs of normalizing and categorizing the data so that it could reveal real information. College-level statistics classes notwithstanding, few understand what is meant by all the statistical terms such as Type I or Type II error, variance, standard deviation, correlations, significance, etc. Outside of statisticians and pollsters, people don't usually understand the underlying meaning of research conclusions. The news media would often report conclusions in a misleading way (and social media even more so).

SOCIAL MEDIA, NEWS MEDIA, VENDORS, EVEN RESEARCHERS OFTEN LIE

I've seen misleading conclusions reported, time and time again, even in academic research when the researcher didn't really understand the underlying statistics. I have read "the result wasn't statistically significant, but it was positive." That's a lie. No, it wasn't positive. If it wasn't statistically significant, it means that *no conclusions* about positive or negative can be stated. It means we still don't know the answer because the sample wasn't big enough to make a conclusion based upon the results received.

Even more often, I've seen vendors present statistics in a misleading way, causing me to write an article on the topic, *Lies, Damn Lies, and Statistics* (Rhoads 2005). Suffice to say, we all need to be very careful about reported conclusions unless we have read and understood the original research. Then we can judge both the experimental design and the conclusions for ourselves.

---

* For years I have argued with editors about whether terms like data and analytics and social media are singular or plural. The style guides will call them plural, forcing odd-sounding phrases like *the data are*, or *social media say* …. Throughout this book these terms are treated as singular *because they ARE singular*. Data is one thing, just as a ream of paper is one thing despite there being 500 pieces of paper in a ream. Analytics is one thing, and it produces one thing (analytics). Social media is one thing, despite the billions of records or hundreds of different sites which are components of it.

Why Do We Need Business Analytics?

Business analytics is essential to improvement processes. Business analytics helps businesses optimize their performances. Implementing analytics into the key performance measures of a business can help reduce costs by identifying more efficient ways of doing business.

A company can also use data analytics to make better business decisions and help analyze customer trends and satisfaction, which can lead to new and improved products and services.

Big Data

These days, data abounds. Tons of it. The term "big data" has been applied to the huge amounts of data in a variety of structures that are available to those who know how to dive in and get it. While computers have been around for more than 50 years at this point, it took human beings that long to figure out how to more easily store and "code" data so that it could be accessible to those who wished to conduct statistics on it.

Big data can be large or huge, structured or unstructured, discrete or continuous. Some people characterize it by the 3 V's: Volume, Variety, and Velocity. These three vectors refer to the amount of data (volume), the different types of data (variety), and the speed at which the data can be processed (velocity). Also remember that big data can have multiple sources; the real power of big data is being able to combine information from multiple sources.

Benefits and Pitfalls of Big Data

As noted, one of the benefits of big data is that there is a much larger variety of types of data available in a timely manner. Often insights and patterns can be discerned simply by sampling and looking at big data sets. For academics, utilizing big data enables them to "find significance" much more easily. Since there is a bias against publishing research unless if finds significance, that can make it easier to publish and share findings.

Regardless of whether data is big data or not, the old GIGO adage about garbage-in, garbage-out applies. Unfortunately, much of the data that is available is dirty—i.e., it has been entered or gathered in inconsistent ways which make the underlying data suspect.

For example, many people review the so-called "analytics" on their website and believe that the "hits" to their website are equivalent to the number of people who have seen their site. Nothing could be further from the truth. A "hit" might be a human being looking at the site, but it might just as easily be another computer looking at the site. (Programs roaming on the world wide web called "bots" go to the websites for a variety of reasons, and they count as "hits.") While the analytics attempts to differentiate between human and bot, they rarely do so accurately. Furthermore, each time a single human being clicks on something or scrolls somewhere on the site, it is counted as another hit. Most web hosting systems do not bother to explain this (because everyone would like to believe the myth that hundreds or thousands of people are coming to their website every day).

Another example is inventory systems that use inconsistent descriptions or different levels of granularity. Any operational manager responsible for inventory control can describe the myriad of difficulties in keeping track of inventory. There are many common problems, mostly surrounding the difficulty of granularity.

Granularity refers to the level at which a unique item exists. Imagine that we own a mom-and-pop knickknack store. We sell decorative candles. We can order a skid of candles from any one of three different vendors. We take the skid and break it apart into three levels of inventory: cases, boxes, and individual candles. The candles come in either small or large, and either red, blue, green, or white. For a small knickknack store none of this is any problem. When we sell the items, we know that the individual small candles are $2 (regardless of color) and the individual large candles are $4. A box of 12 small candles is $20, and a box of large candles is $40, a case of small is $240, and so on. When we want to reorder, we just take a look at the inventory that is left. If all the red candles are gone, we break open another box of candles and convert the one box into 12 individual candles and/or put them on the sheet to reorder.

This process is easy for a human, but for a blind and dumb computer system it is very difficult. It is very difficult to properly figure out what items are in stock, how much to sell each candle for, which vendor to purchase from, and which items need to be reordered. Most inventory systems in use today don't work at that level of granularity, choosing to ignore color, for example, when identifying the SKU (stock keeping unit), resulting in only 18 unique identifying numbers instead of 72. These systems rely upon a human being who can easily recognize which color needs to be ordered. Unfortunately, that wouldn't work in an online system because (oddly enough) people don't want to be surprised by what color candle they ordered. Some online systems get around this by adding an "attribute" field and expecting the buyer to type in the color, or choose the color from the list. This, then, gets into a huge programming issue because each product would need a different attribute list. This is just one example of the complexity involved when trying to provide an online purchasing experience and clean up an inventory. And inventory that is not clean leads to sales records that are not accurate or reliable for many purposes.

> **BIG DATA AND CONSPIRACY THEORIES**
>
> The ease with which researchers can find significance is also one of the downfalls of big data. Often patterns are perceived *which are not real*. In the television show *Star Trek Voyager* in the late '90s, there was a character named Seven of Nine who was a former Borg with a lot of technology installed in her brain. In one episode, she had downloaded too much data, and it made her thinking process go haywire. She started making connections and concocting conspiracy theories, one right after another. She started to think, and act on, crazy ideas. Similarly, big data can lead us down the rabbit hole into seeing patterns that aren't there and making conclusions that are patently false. The computer cannot detect the difference between coincidence and real connection; it is up to thinking human beings to disqualify items that are not likely given our understanding of human dynamics.

Where Does Big Data Come From?

There are numerous sources of big data. Among them are:

- OLTP (On Line Transaction Processing)
- ERP (Enterprise Resource Planning)
- SCM (Supply Chain Management)
- CRM (Customer Relationship Management)
- Social Media (sites such as Twitter, Facebook, Instagram, Snapchat, Pinterest, YouTube, Yelp, etc.)
- Search Engines (sites such a Google, Yahoo, Bing, Baidu)

The growth of these categories of systems means that what formerly were off-line human-to-human transactions (such as going down to the corner grocery store and buying candles) has now become one or more records of data in a computer system somewhere. The drastic drop in the price of storage and the increased speed of data access have both contributed to the ability for businesses to represent all of the different aspects of the supply chain: idea, design, source, manufacture, inventory, order, sell, pay for, delivery, and after-sale follow-up activities.

SPEED OF TECHNOLOGY

Back in 1999, I worked for a large credit card firm just as big data was becoming, well, big. I was responsible for the project management of the VLDB (Very Large Data Base) which was to store all of the credit card transactions for all of our customers so that the data could be deep-mined in huge data warehouses and resold to other companies who could then market new products and services to people based upon what they'd already purchased. Back then, this idea was very new, and the senior leaders of the firm thought that this was just the thing to take the company into the next phase of growth. Back then, however, storing and analyzing all that data was also relatively new, and it was expensive. We had hired a high-priced expert who had implemented two other VLDBS projects of 10 terabytes of data. We also purchased special technology large enough to handle up to 30 terabytes of data. The project had a budget of about 30 million dollars.

Alas, the project was never finished. Due, in part, to the firm missing its financial targets and its subsequent announcement of the plan to sell people's data, the bottom fell out of the entire banking industry and most banks lost 30% of their stock price in one day. A year later the government swooped in with privacy concerns and the senior leaders of the company were demoted or fired. (By that time, I had already gotten laid off with a nice package, so it wasn't a big deal to me personally.)

Fast forward 20 years. A few months ago, I purchased, for myself and my own tiny company, a 10-terabyte hard drive. It cost less than $200, quite a bit less than 30 million dollars. It was added to the slew of other multi-terabyte hard drives that I own, so that altogether I have about 75 terabytes of data sitting in my home office (though most of it is redundant backups).

Knowledge Management

The science of knowledge management is the study of how pieces of data relate to each other, and how information can be stored and retrieved efficiently and effectively. Knowledge representation is the result of information that has been engineered so that it can be visually or electronically reviewed. Thirty years ago, knowledge engineers attempted to represent knowledge by spending intensive, prolonged, and frequent sessions with experts. The idea was to take the implicit knowledge in the brains of the experts and put it into data format so that it could be shared and reproduced. These systems were known as expert systems, and it was a branch of artificial intelligence. (The other branches were natural language processing, visual recognition, neural networks, and machine learning.)

PERSONAL EXPERIENCE WITH KNOWLEDGE REPRESENTATION

In order to write my dissertation at Lehigh University, I built an expert system to enable schools to become more effective. The title of my dissertation was "Knowledge Representation of Effective Schools." My doctorate was delayed by a year because two of the members of my dissertation committee would not agree on the method I should use in order to build the expert system. One professor wanted me to review the literature and determine the rules of the system from that. The other professor wanted me to seek out a noted expert on effective schools and interview that person, producing a representation of what that person thought were the rules for effective schools. In the end, I did both. I can't say, however, that the system actually helped any schools become more effective. The expert system I designed had the same flaw as all other expert systems which caused their downfall; the scope was too narrow. The problem was that to build an expert system, one had to start with a specific question-problem-solution. The initial question, however, is often the crux of the matter. If people knew what the question was, they really don't need a system to determine the problem and solution. The real role of an expert is not to determine the solution, but to ask the right question. And only a human can do that. The expert system can't figure out what question to ask. This is why the medical field is still ruled by human doctors despite the billions of dollars poured into medical diagnostic systems during the '80s and '90s.

Difficulties with Human Knowledge

For over 50 years, scientists have been trying to get computers to be as intelligent at humans. Television and movies often portray computers as thinking and talking, providing analysis and the "right answer." This was a common scene in science fiction even as early as the original *Star Trek* where James T. Kirk would ask the computer for its analysis of complex sets of data, which it dutifully reported verbally in a few seconds of blinking lights and beeps and boops. There are several problems with this scenario, making it most unlikely ever to be real (at least not in our lifetime).

Computers can follow simple step-by-step logical instructions. But they cannot handle directions that are incomplete or ambiguous in any way. Computer don't "get" humans. Take something as simple as happy or sad. Despite millions of dollars spent on studying what seemed to be a very simple problem, computers still cannot recognize human emotions from subtle body language. Humans, even children, do this all the time without even thinking about it.

INSTRUCTIONAL PROCESS MODEL

Before being convinced by my dissertation committee that I wanted to build an expert system (because at the time, that was where the government money was), I had worked for nearly two years on a different topic; identifying the characteristics of a good teacher so that those characteristics could be reproduced in a computer aided learning system. After all that time, hundreds of articles and thousands of hours thinking about it, I finally came to the conclusion (which, in truth, hit me like a ton of bricks in 1988 as I was walking down my stairwell one day) that no matter how much information I got or how hard I tried, a computer couldn't come close to mimicking a good teacher. The reason was that good teachers utilized the *look on the face* of the student to determine what topic to teach next. If the student looked confused, the good teacher would step back and teach a component topic of the current topic. If the student clearly understood the lesson, the good teacher would move forward to the next lesson, perhaps even skipping a few if it was obvious the students already understood it (again, simply from the look on the face of the student and the speed of understanding of previous lessons).

If a computer can't discern the emotions or state of mind of the student by the look on their face, there was no way that a computer-aided lesson would properly match the level of understanding of the student. That's why computer tutorials are usually useless; they either go way too slow for the student who already understands most of the topic, or way too fast for the student who doesn't. In the final analysis, good teachers use a *characteristic model* of the student while the computer-aided instruction could only use a *buggy model* (i.e., wait for the student to make a mistake and then re-present the missing concept again even though repeating the same lesson over and over does not enable the lesson to be learned). I came to this conclusion over 30 years ago, and I'm still waiting for a computer that can interpret the emotions behind the facial expression. It still doesn't exist.

Natural Language Processing

Computers still can't quite handle natural language, though Siri and Alexa and all the natural language processors that Siri spawned make a really good effort. But the truth is that a four-year-old has better language capability in a larger variety of contexts than the most sophisticated computer in the world—still, today, in 2021 (Faller 2020). Why? Well, the easiest way for me to explain is to share the sentence provided by my artificial intelligence professor at Lehigh University when I was working on my doctorate. Dr. Hill asked us to consider the following sentence:

> *The boy hit the other boy with the girl with the blond hair with the hammer.*

Picture it. What vision does this sentence conjure in your mind?

Now try to diagram this sentence grammatically. How do you know the hammer is in the hand of the first boy and was the instrument used to hit the other boy? How do you know why the boy hit the boy? How do you know the blond hair is on the girl and not the boy?

Logically this sentence makes absolutely no sense. It says that one boy picked up the girl and hit the other boy with her. We know that's not what happened and we know why. The boy was jealous of the other boy because he was with the girl with blond hair. We know this because we read the sentence in the context of the human condition where girls with blond hair and boys, as shown in Figure 4.1 might mix with jealousy and end up with

Figure 4.1 The Boy Hit the Boy with the Girl with the Hammer.

violence perpetrated by hammers. There is no computer in the world that could figure out the meaning of the sentence without the human context.

Identifying the Context of Business Data

Business data has the same problem without context. Take the following inventory list:

4 tires
2 windshield wiper blades
5 quarts of oil
1 oil filter
4 petunias
6 spark plugs
2 headlight lamps

Anyone reading will immediately recognize six of the items as normal automobile maintenance supplies. A ten-year-old child could probably tell you the fifth item doesn't belong. But how would a computer know? It wouldn't. There is no way to program a computer so that it would immediately recognize that flowers don't belong with automobile accessories without explicitly telling it so.

No computer, no matter how powerful, can identify the *relationship* between two items meaningfully without being explicitly told. Computers can store billions of facts and figures—but not in context. Computers can sort and organize information, but they cannot turn that information into knowledge. Computers cannot analyze. Computers cannot make judgment calls. If you cannot clearly and unambiguously describe the rules that are accurate 100% of the time, the computer cannot follow the rules. That means they cannot follow common rules of thumb. There still are no computers that can predict the weather as well as a human being can (though they have gotten a lot better in recent years and can now confirm that it is raining this minute if it is indeed raining this minute. Weather predicting supercomputers are independently accurate for about a six-hour window. Beyond that, they need humans to clarify the models).

The volume and quality of relationships surrounding nouns and verbs that can be stored by the human brain is exorbitant. The brain is much more capable in this regard than a computer. A human brain has over 100 billion neurons. If you include the glial cells that support and nurture each neuron, you have millions of times that. In comparison, there are only a little more than 50 billion computers on the public Internet. Even if you factor in each integrated circuit chip, there is still more processing power in the brain of a six-month-old baby than there is in all the computers of the world combined.

Dirty Data and GIGO

One of the tasks that computers simply cannot do is clean up dirty data. This task has got to be one of the most difficult, laborious, and thankless jobs in all the world. (Well, okay, maybe cleaning up latrines beats it, but not by much.) One would think that given its importance, all data stored by computers by now would be clean and pristine—but it is not. Most of the information stored is contaminated in some way: duplicate records, inaccurate entries, incomplete information, and so on. Dirty data is the scourge of every computer system. Garbage-in, garbage-out.

Though still a problem, we have gotten better at cleaning up dirty data. Plus, the volume of data tends to overcome the difficulty of dirty data. If you have 1000 records to analyze, having 200 of them be duplicates or incorrect would nullify any conclusions you might draw. But if you have 100,000,000,000 records, the fact that 20% of them is wrong means that you still have 80,000,000,000 valid records upon which to base your conclusions. Going back to the dirty inventory; one can still predict purchase trends even if the granularity is not consistent.

Or not. Which is one of the mucky little secrets of analytics; despite the volume, it is still possible to come up with the exact wrong answer. If your goal was to see whether the red candles or the blue candles were going to sell better next year (based on existing sales), and the red candles might be under the names magenta, scarlet, and maroon while the blue candles are all called blue, you might come to the conclusion that blue will sell better because it has a higher number but that's only because the red candles were split among different colors. That's why it is up to human beings to develop the *art* (and yes, it is an art, not a science), of interpreting the meaning and context behind the myriad of data in order to discern real patterns and form generalizable conclusions.

Tools of the Trade

Just because we need human beings to cognitively and creatively conduct the analysis, doesn't mean we don't need computers. We do. New technology, both hardware and software, has recently transmuted the world of analytics from the ivory towers of mathematicians and statisticians to the real world, dealing with real data, for any typically intelligent manager. The ability to review thousands, millions, or billions of records graphically and pictorially has changed the game. Now we can easily see patterns without math.

There are several software tools that help us do that. I am hesitant to list exactly what software is in the category of analytics because they change so rapidly that by the time you read this, many will be different. To demonstrate, Table 4.1 is a list of business intelligence software published by Gartner Group, a consulting firm that rates various types of business software in what they call a "Magic Quadrant" (2021f). The list in Table 4.1 shows and the replace the phrase list in Table 4.1 at the end of the sentence with the phrase and if the software was on one or both.

As you can see, only about half of the names on 2021 list were contenders in 2011, just ten years earlier. Half the list dropped off and more than half were new. So, while you might want to recognize the names of software in the field of analytics, it is more important for you to recognize the category of software so that should you need business analytics, you have somewhere to start. Data Analytics software is sometimes called Business Intelligence or Competitive Analysis software. Regardless of what it is called, it makes sense to choose the software that is already associated with the transaction system where the bulk of the data is located. That's why you will

Table 4.1 Magic Quadrant of Business Intelligence/Analytics Software

Name/Publisher of Software	From Which List
IBM Cognos Insight	On both 2011 and 2021
Information Builders	On both 2011 and 2021
MicroStrategy Visual Insight	On both 2011 and 2021
Qlik	On both 2011 and 2021
SAP Visual Intelligence	On both 2011 and 2021
SAS Visual Analytics	On both 2011 and 2021
Tableau	On both 2011 and 2021
TIBCO Spotfire	On both 2011 and 2021
Oracle Endeca	On both 2011 and 2021
Microsoft PowerPivot with PowerView	On both 2011 and 2021
Amazon Web services	On 2021 list
Board	On 2021 list
Domo	On 2021 list
Google Looker	On 2021 list
Info	On 2021 list
Pyramid Analytics	On 2021 list
Sisense	On 2021 list
ThoughtSpot	On 2021 list
Yellowfin	On 2021 list
Alibaba Cloud	On 2021 list
Actuate	No longer on list
Arcplan	No longer on list
Bitam	No longer on list
Board International	No longer on list
Corda Technologies	No longer on list
Jaspersoft	No longer on list
LogiXML	No longer on list
Panorama Software	No longer on list
Salient Management Company	No longer on list
Targit	No longer on list

see the top publishers of ERP, CRM, SCM, and other OLTP systems on the list (and showing up more often than not in both Magic Quadrants). Since it really isn't the tool (despite what these software vendors might have you believe) but the talent of the analyst that can provide the business intelligence, which one you choose doesn't really matter. And they all basically do the same foundational tasks.

How to Tell If It's Good Data

Data that comes from a variety of sources can be categorized on many different levels. These levels include:

- Data source reliability
- Data content accuracy
- Data accessibility
- Data security and data privacy
- Data richness
- Data consistency
- Data currency/data timeliness
- Data granularity
- Data validity and data relevancy

The reliability of the data source is important. An ERP system, for example, would be considered a more reliable source than social media. A source is reliable if the information can be tracked back to the original source, and the person or persons responsible for that source are known.

Related to reliability is content accuracy. How sure are we that the data accurately reflects the underlying reality? Sales data is more accurate than order data because someone paid money for the item, and that won't generally happen unless it is a real sale. Of course, social media is not known for its accuracy, and neither is customer relationship management systems where people might provide fake information in an attempt to avoid being pressured into buying something they don't want.

> **WHEN IS A SALE NOT A SALE?**
>
> Even sales data can be unreliable, however. I personally know more than one author who, instead of buying books directly from their publisher, went onto Amazon and purchased a lot of copies of their own book in one day. This puts Amazon's heuristics into a tizzy and raises the level of the book to the best seller's list—at least for a short time. Once the expected recurrence of the sales doesn't happen, the book will slowly sink lower on the list until it is no longer a best seller, but by that time the author has already been noted as a best seller.
>
> I discovered how Amazon's heuristics work when one of my books suddenly found its way to the best seller list. (And no, I didn't purchase any copies of my own book.) But because it was a textbook, when a lot of students would purchase the book at the beginning of September, it bumped up the status to best seller because the heuristic isn't smart enough to figure out that it's a textbook. It figures it's going to see the same level of sales every week for the whole year and accounts for it accordingly. This is an example of when big data can give the exact wrong impression. By the end of the year the book has sunk back to its low status as a poor seller—until the next September when it shoots up to the top again for a few months.

Accessibility does not just mean that we have access to the data, but also whether the *format* that data is in is accessible. For example, a Word document or PDF with names and addresses is just about useless because the information is not provided in a format that is accessible to the computer. The information needs to be parsed into first name, last name, street, city, etc. A CSV (Comma Separated Variable) file is a more accessible standard for transferring data from one system to another, but the data must be available in short discrete fields that don't contain control codes or special characters like quotes. If the data contains pictures, URLs or websites, emoticons, paragraphs of data, or formatting codes such as line breaks, italics, boldface, etc.—it is not necessarily going to be accessible to the system.

One of the bugaboos with data is keeping it safe and private. Information such as people's social security numbers, account numbers, credit card info, etc., are well known targets for data thieves. Lesser known, however, is that people's names, emails, phone numbers, birthdates, and relatives' names can also be very risky because data thieves can also use this information to steal someone's identity. People are constantly worried about keeping their data private, and yet also want to have the convenience of credit card information already stored and putting their birthday in social media so that others can wish them well. It's a tough balance.

Richness refers to how much detail is included in the data. Having someone's username and phone number is one thing, but to also have their name, address, what they purchased, how much they spent—well, that's a much richer data set. Getting pictures and locations is even richer. Social media information is generally much more "rich" than financial or sales data in ERP and SCM systems.

Data consistency is important and difficult to get. We previously described some examples regarding consistency of inventory data. Sometimes a company will hire a new person who enters the data in a completely different way than the previous person. Neither is right or wrong, but it would be inconsistent. Inconsistent data is dirty data, and often it must be manipulated to make it consistent. Going back to the candle example, an additional field called "color category" could be added so that magenta, maroon, and scarlet could be grouped under the color category of "red" so that "red" and "blue" can be compared.

Timeliness is another important aspect of data. Old data is often useless data. Imagine a company trying to sell a data set of people who looked up phone numbers in a phone book. Would this information be helpful or relevant today? Very few people use phone books anymore, so if the data is no longer current, it is no longer useful.

Granularity is one of the most difficult aspects of data. As described earlier, granularity is the level of detail which the data contains. More data with more fields and additional information is more granular than summary data with fewer fields of additional information. How granular the data should be is entirely dependent upon the questions that you want answered. Again—part of the art of analytics is knowing how much granularity you need for a given situation.

The final two are validity and relevancy. Different from accuracy, validity is whether or not the types of information are appropriate for the types of questions being asked. And relevancy is whether the data matters. For example, if we were trying to ascertain if people were willing to purchase a new kind of fitness watch, whether or not they have already purchased a fitness watch would be relevant. Whether they liked ice cream would probably not be relevant (though how much ice cream they eat might actually be relevant).

Preparing Data

There are many different ways to prepare data to be utilized in analytics. There are few rules to this step other than to clean the data without changing it beyond validity. The possibilities are:

- Data preprocessing
- Data consolidation
- Data cleaning
- Data transformation
- Data reduction

Data preprocessing is whatever needs to be done to get the data into a format that can be viewed and assessed. Once it can be viewed and assessed, it may need consolidation (such as combining individual sales records into weekly or monthly sales totals records). It also may need cleaning: eliminating duplicates, clarifying categories, resolving inconsistencies, evaluating and dealing with incomplete records, etc. For example, incomplete records can be eliminated entirely, or the incomplete portions of the information can be replaced with the average from the other records. (Which one depends upon how many records are incomplete, why they are incomplete, and how important the missing information is to the analysis.) Generally, the data will then need to be transformed into analytical fields.

Analytical fields can represent the underlying data which is often in a format that cannot be analyzed as is. For example, if the addresses have country in them, they can be transformed into country codes so that if someone wrote "United States" and another wrote "United States of America" and a third wrote "America," they would all convert to USA. Categorical information is just text data, like country. Additionally, categorical information can be transformed into a series of yes/no variables. A yes/no variable is also known as an *dummy* or *binary* variable, or an *indicator*. A yes/no variable is usually assigned a value of 1 for yes and 0 for no. If our analysis needed to know whether a record was foreign or domestic, we could assign a 1 to the domestic records (i.e., where country is equal to USA) and a 0 to the foreign records (i.e., where country is not equal to USA). Another transformation might be to group age (which is a continuous variable) into a categorical group (0–20, 21–40, 41–60, 61–90, 91>) so that an analysis can be done by age group.

Finally, the data may then be reduced to just the analytical fields, stripping out the rich details so that analytics can be completed. Just the relevant fields would be left after the variables are selected. Finally, instead of testing the entire dataset, a sampling of the dataset may be taken. For some analysis, such as logistical regression analysis, the data may be split into three datasets: one dataset to develop the model, one dataset to test the model, and the final dataset to conduct the experiment using the model. For other analysis, a stratified sample is taken. A stratified sample is when a certain number of records with a certain value are selected for analysis, such as wanting a certain number of representative records from each country in the world.

In any case, the goal is to have the final analytical fields properly represent the underlying rich data. As already mentioned, the process is more akin to a work of art than a scientific process.

Foundational Tasks of Analytics

What are the basic analytical tasks needed for strategic decision making? Well, let's start by identifying the common tasks for any strategic planning process:

- Conduct a current situation analysis
- Determine the planning horizon
- Conduct an environment scan
- Identify critical success factors
- Complete a gap analysis
- Create a strategic vision
- Develop a business strategy
- Identify strategic objectives and goals

A couple of these steps require analytics, most notably a current situation analysis and conducting an environment scan. These might require any one of the four differ types of analytics.

Four Type of Analytics

The four types of analytics are descriptive, diagnostic, predictive, and prescriptive.

Descriptive analytics is just that; visually presenting the information available without any specific question in mind. It is what *is*. Describing the count (number of), the average (mean, median, and/or mode), the sum, the variance and/or standard deviation of various groups within the data; these would be considered descriptive. Also visually representing the numbers by size of bubble or box or color or some other visual representation. How many were sold in each region? How many phone calls were received on that topic? How many patients utilize integrative healthcare practices?

Diagnostic analytics focuses more on *why* something happened. This is where hypothesizing comes in. Often, we have to look around and figure out which types of data would be able to answer the hypothesis. Did the weather affect bathing suit sales? Did the television advertising sell more than the social media advertising? Did people who utilized integrative healthcare practices see a decrease in symptoms?

Predictive analytics moves to what is *likely going to happen* in the near term. If the weather impacted bathing suit sales, what happens if we have a cold summer? How many weather models predict a cold summer this year, and how many say it will be hot? What would happen if we decrease television advertising and increase social media advertising? What would happen if medical doctors included integrative healthcare practices in their scope of treatment?

Prescriptive analytics *suggests a course of action*. If the likelihood of a cool summer (as measured as an average of five different weather models) is above 65%, we should decrease our bathing suit inventory by 15%. If 95% of the patients with chronic health issues who utilize integrative healthcare practices see a decrease in symptoms, medical doctors should include integrative healthcare practices in their scope of treatment for patients with chronic health issues.

Steps of Analytics

There are several steps to conducting analytics.

1. Determine which type of analytics is needed. (Often all four types are needed.)
2. Determine the data requirements in order to fulfill the needs of the type of analytics needed.

3. Identify the types of data available (pictorial, categorical, ordinal, interval, continuous [numerical], and binary [dummy or indicator variables]).
4. Determine how the data should be grouped.
5. Collect the data.
6. Prepare the data as described in the Preparing Data section.
7. Determine the appropriate analysis for the type of data collected and transformed.

Which Analytical Tools to Use

It is beyond the scope of this chapter to provide a course on statistical analysis, but people doing analytics should at least have some idea of which types of analysis can best answer which types of questions. The goal is to provide conclusions based upon the known data. And while there are hundreds of statistical and analytical tests that can be used, they generally fall under one of these general categories: descriptive statistics, data visualization, regression analysis, group differences, and multivariate analysis*.

Descriptive statistics and data visualization are both examples of analytics that do not include inference. Descriptive statistics and data visualization are the most common analytics both because they must be done prior to doing any inferential analysis (i.e., any analytics requiring a conclusion) as well as being relatively easy for people to understand. Inference, also known as predictive or prescriptive, is when you can make generalities beyond the data. With data visualization and descriptive statistics, all you can do is look at the data and say what it is.

Regression is odd because it can be used in a descriptive way, but it can also be used in an inferential or prescriptive way. Regression cannot establish causality, but it can say how strong a relationship between two or more variables is.

Grouping to determine group differences, however, always involves inference. That's why you group—so you can make inference beyond the data about the population at large. Instead of just saying "the average number of bathing suits sold last year was 259,856," by doing grouping you could say

---

* An excellent place to go in order to figure out which statistical test to use on which type of data using any of the four most common analytical tools is https://stats.idre.ucla.edu/other/mult-pkg/whatstat/, published by the UCLA Institute for Digital Research & Education. Last accessed on March 30, 2021. This website had how-to links to each of the four statistical analysis tools: SAS, STATA, SPSS, and R.

"next year we expect to sell 376,987" and aren't just guessing at the answer, but have actual data to support the statement.

Descriptive Statistics

While data visualization shows colors, pictures, shapes, and sizes, descriptive statistics are usually just numbers, as shown in Figure 4.2. Descriptive statistics include average (which is the same as the mean), or the median (the middle number in a range of numbers), or mode (the most frequent number in a range of numbers). It could also be a sum, a ratio, or percent.

Data Visualization

For example, the percent of Gross Domestic Product (GDP) that each country spends on healthcare is represented in this Tableau example in Figure 4.3 showing the number as a reflection of the gray shading. South Sudan at .108% is the lightest shading of all the countries in the world while the United States of America is 2.095%, which is the darkest shading of all the countries in the world. This is still a simple, descriptive statistic, and doesn't provide any inferences at all about why there is such a difference, what is likely to happen in the future, or what we should do about it.

The data visualization in Figure 4.4 shows sales by category utilizing size of bubble. It is easy to see that the big sellers at this office supply company are paper, labels, copiers, and envelopes with fasteners, accessories, and art coming up behind them. But again, we can't go beyond that simple information. We can't say there is a relationship between them, or if we make changes to our process the number would change either one way or another.

Regression Analysis

If you want to know if two different data points have a correlation, you would do a regression analysis. Basically, the data points are plotted to see if they form a line or an ephemeral blob. The line means they have a relationship (and the proximity of the points to the line determines how strong the relationship is), and the ephemeral blob means there is no relationship between the two variables. As can be seen in Figure 4.5 there is a strong relationship between Carbon Dioxide Emissions and Energy Usage (which only makes sense) shown on the left. However, on the right there appears to be no relationship between the percentage of GDP spent on healthcare and

Country/Region	Avg.	Health
United States	6,967	16.12%
Norway	6,753	9.71%
Luxembourg	6,331	7.51%
Switzerland	6,136	10.67%
Monaco	5,126	3.86%
Denmark	4,911	10.07%
Netherlands	4,328	10.52%
Iceland	4,180	9.58%
Austria	4,117	10.61%
Sweden	3,920	9.18%
Canada	3,825	10.15%
France	3,825	11.02%
Germany	3,809	10.90%
Ireland	3,636	7.92%
Belgium	3,631	9.71%
Australia	3,581	8.63%
Japan	3,268	8.59%
San Marino	3,264	5.40%
Finland	3,252	8.32%
United Kingdom	3,059	8.48%
Italy	2,650	8.69%
Andorra	2,394	6.32%
New Zealand	2,307	8.85%
Spain	2,254	8.48%
Greece	2,030	9.26%
Portugal	1,843	9.95%
Israel	1,744	7.61%
Slovenia	1,616	8.55%
Cyprus	1,538	6.62%
Bahamas, The	1,460	6.48%
Qatar	1,434	2.60%
Malta	1,354	8.28%
Singapore	1,290	3.64%
United Arab Emirates	1,112	2.68%
South Korea	1,074	6.04%

Figure 4.2   Average Healthcare Cost Per Capita and Percent of GDP.

108 ■ *Strategic Decision Making for Successful Planning*

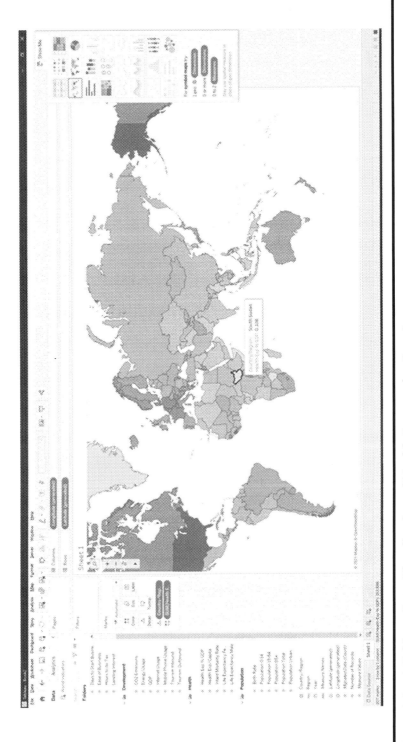

Figure 4.3   A Tableau Data Visualization of Health Expense by Country.

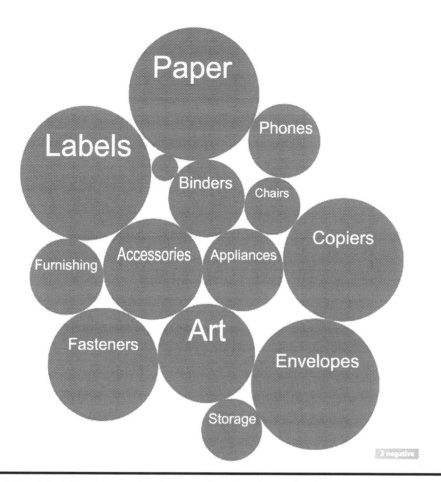

Figure 4.4　A Tableau Example of Data Visualization Sales by Category.

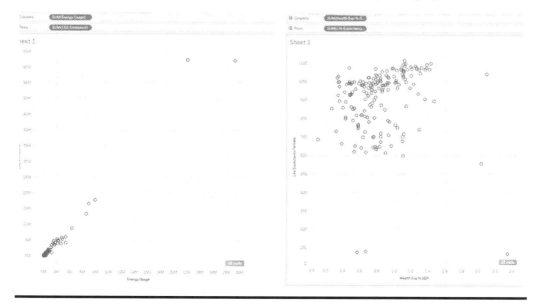

Figure 4.5　Comparison of a Strong Correlation (left) to No Correlation (right).

life expectancy (which actually doesn't make any logical sense, but there it is). This is where we remind everyone that correlation is not causation, so even if the data seems to "make sense," there is no proof here, for example, that higher energy use *causes* higher carbon dioxide emissions. It might be a third factor actually causes both, so lowering the carbon dioxide emissions would not necessarily decrease energy use (or vice versa).

Whether the relationship is really there or just a coincidence, of course, is the function of all those mathematical equations that we learned in our college statistics course, along with the *p* value which tells us whether or not the correlation is significant enough to warrant being called a relationship. That tells us exactly at what point the line becomes a blob. But with easy-to-use analytical tools, the exact point no longer seems important. We can see for ourselves whether there is a relationship or not.

One of the difficulties with regression analysis which determines the extent to which two variables are related is that both variables must be *continuous numerical variables*. Much of data, however, is one of the other types of variable. The other types are *categorical, ordinal* (which is categorical but with a specific *order* to the categories), *interval* (which is the same as ordinal, only the units between the categories are equal), or *binary* (discussed earlier as a yes/no variable, also known as a dummy variable or indicator).

Group Differences

Furthermore, as noted, regression analysis cannot prove causality. For that we need some kind of grouping, which is why analysts often take a continuous variable and put it into groupings like age group, experience levels, salary levels, etc. Once you have groupings you can do experimental designs to determine causality between the variables. A simple regression analysis between weekly sales and average temperature would provide the correlation between those two numbers. But if you wanted to prove that hot summers increase bathing suit sales, you could obtain daily temperatures in a variety of places and categorize them as hot, cool, or control (perhaps a neutral temperature). You could hypothesize that you will sell more bathing suits in the hot places than in the cool places or the control. If you do, then you can state that the hot places caused more bathing suit sales. (Truth be told, however, you might find, if you include deserts in your hot places, that hot temperature does NOT cause more bathing suit sales. Then you might want to test for the presence of pools as the actual cause for bathing suit sales. Hot temperature may be correlated, but would not be a cause, just a mitigating variable.)

But this step toward the *why* and the *what would happen if* and *we should ...* is a large one. We've just tipped over into *inferential analysis*, which means we are now trying to generalize the findings from the sample of the population into other samples from the same population. Descriptive analytics describes what already happened, and is focused backward. Inferential or *predictive* analytics is focused on what will happen in the future. For these we use statistics such as a t-test or an analysis of variance (ANOVA) if the variables are numerical, or a non-parametric test such as a chi-square or Fisher's Exact Test if the variables are categorical.

Multivariate Analysis

Analytics is often most interested in determining which variable is the *most* influential in a certain outcome. For this we need to analyze many different variables at the same time. There are many types of multivariable regression techniques to do this, such as logistical regression analysis, MANOVA analysis, discriminant analysis, factor analysis, etc. Many of these analytics attempt to find the "goodness of fit" to a model which determines which variables are actually influential and which ones are just along for the ride.

BINARY LOGISTICAL REGRESSION ANALYSIS

One of the studies that I did was a binary logistical regression analysis. This type of statistic is most commonly used to calculate things like your credit score. Your credit score is a "probability" that you will pay back whatever money you owe. But it depends upon a mixture of other variables like how long your credit accounts have been open, how often you've paid late, how much overall credit you have, etc. Binary logistical regression analysis is especially suited for categorical factors and specifically designed for predicting membership in dichotomous groups, such as business success or failure, project success or failure, personal financial success or failure. Similar to multivariate regression analysis, logistical regression analysis performs a stepwise analysis, either adding or removing factors one at a time, until it arrives at the optimum predictive (but parsimonious) factors.

Just in case you were wondering, the study I did identified the factors that led to a small business utilizing their technology effectively. Email

Characteristics (76–100% of employees had email), Operating System (Windows), Number of Employees, Web Domain Characteristics (Owned), Source of Technology Information (Top Consulting Firm), were found, in combination and in that order, to be significant predictors of Technology Effectiveness. All the other factors (Company Size, Market Size, Web Use Characteristics, Connection Characteristics, Role of Decision Maker, Perceived Value of Technology, ROI Measurement, and Entrepreneurial Characteristics) did not add enough value to the predictive quality of the formula to remain in the equation. If I were a company trying to improve our use of technology, based on these analytics, it would make more sense for us to make sure we own our own web domain, ensure that everyone in the company used email, everyone had the same easy-to-use operating system, and we should consult the top firms about our technology. How we use the web, whether or not there was a return on investment, and whether or not the people we hire were entrepreneurial would not be factors that would be as important (Rhoads 2008).

Summary Chapter 4 Questions

- What is meant by the term "Analytics"?
- What are the three characteristics of big data?
- What is granularity? Why is it important when analyzing big data?
- What are some of the sources of big data?
- What makes human knowledge so difficult to represent to a computer?
- Why is so much of the available data "dirty"?
- What are some of the programs considered "analytical"? Has the list changed much in the last ten years?
- What are the categorizations that we can make of data sources?
- What are the steps to preparing data for analysis?
- What are the four types of analytics?
- What are the steps to conduct an analytical analysis?
- What is the difference between descriptive statistics/data visualization and inferential (or predictive) statistics?
- What is different about regression analysis?
- What analytical tool would we use to establish causality?

Chapter 5

Mapping the Optimum Approach

The optimum approach means making sure training and implementation are done properly, and at the right time.

On the Optimum Track with Just a Few Adjustments

A growing number of organizations have been developing an interactive attitude as well as the holistic perspective from which it arises. Many have been putting optimum teams into place for quality improvement programs. Some are even developing reward systems that encourage teamwork and continuous improvement instead of backstabbing and the status quo. These organizations truly empower their employees and involve them in designing any changes which will affect them. These companies effectively utilize the expertise of their employees. Unfortunately, however, most of them, while on the optimum track, still need to fine-tune their approach.

A major weakness in the approach some of these companies take lies in their attitude toward training in general, and training in decision making skills in particular (Roth 1989a).

There are two types of training in any normal work situation. The first is the training one must receive in order to meet job responsibilities. This might include training in what information to give customers, what buttons to push to make the machine run, what cabinet to put a specific file in, how to run a maintenance check, or what form to fill out in a specific situation.

DOI: 10.4324/9781003198062-5

Employees are supposed to receive this kind of training immediately after being hired. They also are supposed to receive it when any change occurs—when a new type of account is brought in, a new technology is introduced, when a promotion is received, or when the employee is shifted to another function.

The second type of training concerns what to do when an aspect of the organization or segment of a system with which the employee interacts stops working, or is not working as well as it should. The second type of training considers the possibility that the aspect of the organization or segment of the system might work better if redesigned. While the first type of training focuses on getting employees ready to do what is necessary, the second type focuses on preparing them to help improve products, production processes, management systems, the work environment, and so on.

It is this second type of training that involves the decision making techniques and tools discussed in Chapter 3. However, this second type of training sometimes delivers the wrong skills, can be overdone, and frequently suffers from inappropriate timing.

This is not to say that training is not important to decision making and strategic improvement efforts. Not only is it important, it is critical. Yet it is not the *only* critical part that has to be done right, and it should not be the initial concern of organizers. The traditional focus on training as a necessary first step, in fact, is one of the major reasons so many strategic improvement efforts that start out with promise and enthusiasm end up producing very little of the desired positive change.

In order to explore the validity of the above statement, we must first ask why it has been assumed until now by a vast majority of those given responsibility for orchestrating decision making and improvement activities in organizations that the formal training of participants must precede all else. Why are the early months of so many large-scale improvement efforts almost invariably spent in classrooms training great numbers of team leaders, facilitators, and/or middle managers? It would be assumed that these leaders would then, in turn, teach the techniques they learn to the workforce. But is this the best way?

Several definable reasons exist for this wrong-headed training-up-front approach. First, as noted, training is obviously a critical ingredient of the cultural change necessary if the quality of the product or service offered, as well as that of manufacturing processes, management systems, and the work environment, is going to improve. The problem, however, is that we have confused the two types of training. One type of training allows us to meet job responsibilities. But the training that focuses on making decisions and strategic improvements is the second kind. This second kind of training is better performed as *Just In Time training*. Just In Time training is analogous to Just In Time inventory; the concept that instead of providing all of the inventory at one time in one place, the inventory is produced just as it becomes necessary to ship. With Just In Time training, we wait until the training is needed, and then produce it just in time to be used.

Operational training for daily responsibilities must necessarily be formalized. Everyone needs it. Specific things must be included. Such training offers a well-defined set of skills which everyone must learn. A lot of it, therefore, can be presented in the classroom.

The catch is that while the skills needed during this first type of training can be spelled out with a high degree of exactitude, those required for the second cannot. Therefore, when the second type of training is being offered in the classroom, the "teacher" might actually be teaching the wrong thing.

The best approach to solving a problem or making a strategic improvement cannot usually be defined ahead of time. It cannot be spelled out until the decision or improvement itself and the unique characteristics involved have actually been identified. This usually happens in the trenches, where the perspective and atmosphere are very different.

Some trainers react to this realization with overkill. They pile on technique after technique during classes or seminars and hope that employees will leave with the necessary arsenal*. To the contrary, however, the most frequent result of this tactic is that employees leave the class and do not remember much of anything that has been taught.

Other consultants react by ignoring the reality of the situation and attempting to pound into the heads of the employees the one technique which they claim fits all situations That one technique, of course, does not fit all situations, and once employees get back out into the workplace, they waste a lot of time and grow rapidly frustrated trying to create a marriage between a problem and a technique that enjoy little synergy.

A second reason up-front classroom training has been used more frequently has to do with time constraints. In-house trainers usually have a very busy schedule. They have one or two days to deliver their package at each facility. Hanging around for an extended period of time is not part of their responsibility. Their job is to spread the word as widely as possible. They are judged at least partially by the number of bases covered and/or the

---

* Sort of like the voluminous number of techniques included in Chapter 3. Hopefully the sentence about forgetting them all does not apply to you as well.

number of employees "educated." They are not judged by the effectiveness of the results of what they teach in terms of the bottom line.

Finally, consultants brought in to train have an additional constraint—cost effectiveness. Consultants can ask for more money when training or presenting to a large group in a seminar setting than when spending an extended period of time helping individual teams work through problems or shape improvements.

The Best Model from a Macro Perspective

When we shift our perspective from individuals and teams to the macro picture, the traditional up-front approach to training does not work well either. Such efforts are usually top-down. As a result, by the time that all the required and desired sessions have been completed with staff on all levels and employees are finally turned loose to solve problems or to make improvements, enthusiasm has waned (if it has been generated at all).

At the same time, because it is top-down, traditional training in decision making techniques tends to get lost among the many other types of training mandated by upper-level management—zero defects program training, safety program training, technical expertise training, training in cost-cutting techniques, preventative maintenance training, etc.

Also, the traditional top-down approach to training in decision making techniques may not always generate the desired commitment to improvement. In fact, it can often have the reverse effect. What it can say to some employees is:

> Because management thinks you can't figure out how to identify problems and make improvements in the systems you've been working with for the last 20 years, we've brought in experts to teach you the necessary skills. The results of this training are going to be amazing. With the new skills we're going to teach you, we believe that you will suddenly be able to identify all those problems that have been lying around for all these years without your noticing them.

SHORTSIGHTED MANAGEMENT

As an example of such managerial shortsightedness, consider the true story of a paper mill where the sheet of pulp/paper being run along the webbing of one of the large paper-making machines kept tearing. This cost the company a lot of money because the machine had to be shut down for 20 minutes to an hour while the sheet was patched.

No one could figure out why the sheet kept tearing. Experts were brought in from corporate. Consultants were hired. Every inch of the webbing was examined. The pulp mixture was tested and experimented with. But the tears continued.

One day, while the mill manager was standing by the machine watching it run, an old-time employee happened to walk by. The manager said, "Jess, I don't get it. We've tried everything, but this sheet just keeps tearing."

Jess hesitated a long while, then with a shake of the head said quietly, "You haven't been looking at the right thing."

The manager glanced sharply toward Jess and said, "What are you talking about, Jess?"

Jess pointed and replied, "See that window up there on the wall above the machine? When it gets really hot in here, people open it to help cool things down a bit. When the breeze is coming from the southwest, it blows directly through that window and tears the sheet."

The manager's response was, "Jess, we've been working on this for six months. Why didn't you say something?"

And Jess replied, "I didn't want to get into trouble. I'm not supposed to think about things like that. I was told to stick with my own job."

The key is that most workplace problems could be solved more rapidly and comprehensively if managers simply asked the employees dealing with the system involved for their input, listened carefully and sincerely to the response, and then asked the employees to help make the necessary correction.

Employees know what the problems are in their areas of expertise better than anyone else. They also frequently know the solutions to the problems. What organizations need is the culture, the attitude, the perspective, the vehicle, and the type of training which will allow management to take advantage of the employees' knowledge and their ability to make improvements.

With this objective in mind, an alternative to making formal process-related training the initial and primary focus of decision making and improvement efforts is to make it part of more results-oriented activities. The most important objective of organizers, if this alternative is adopted, is to very quickly get employees directly involved in improvement efforts. It is to quickly begin generating highly visible results based on employee expertise in both the production process and the work environment.

Training, in this scenario, is delivered on an as-needed just-in-time basis. Team facilitators are trained on the job as consultants bring the first teams up. Further process-related training needs are identified and frequently designed/met by the team members themselves.

Into the Trenches

The case study in the final chapter of this book is presented in order to further explore the strengths of action-oriented training in decision making. The organization, Jan's Technology Services, is hypothetical, but based on a real company started in 1993. No training was given to the top-level managers. They were simply told what was going to happen so that when it did happen, it would be less threatening.

The next step was for the manager to identify a head facilitator. That person would work closely with the consultants. The consultants would be responsible for teaching the head facilitator everything they could about team building and decision making. The objective was for the head facilitator to take over the process as quickly as possible.

The new head facilitator then identified a group of team facilitators. Neither the head facilitator nor the team facilitators, once identified, were given up-front, formal, classroom-based training.

The manager, together with the direct reports, was then asked to break the organization chart down according to function so that a network of decision making teams could be created. This was relatively easy to do. The work in this company has definite, well-defined stages. At least one team was formed to represent each of these stages.

Within three weeks of the initial discussions with the manager, the action part of the approach, coupled with on-the-job training, commenced. The consultants started bringing up hourly teams using the Breaking The Ice technique. Team members were not formally taught the technique, but were simply led through it.

The on-the-job action-oriented training for the head facilitator began with that person watching a consultant working with the first decision making team. The head facilitator then assisted in working with the second team and eventually took the lead in working with the third or fourth teams, with the consultant observing, supporting, and critiquing afterward.

This same approach was used to teach the facilitators how to run team meetings. The consultant or head facilitator would run the first few meetings and then turn the team over to the facilitator and observe.

Eventually, the facilitators in the network took over the entire team building and team management process. The consultants, at this point, began to function mainly as troubleshooters and resources.

In this way, teams were defining projects and producing positive results within three to four weeks of their start. Also, at least some of the required training was being completed, but in a more positive manner in that it was "real life" rather than classroom oriented. The facilitators were learning their trade by participating in an actual exercise that produced actual results, actual problematic challenges, and actual commitment, rather than by sitting in a classroom having the steps explained to them and going through mock drills.

The only training that team members had received thus far was again on the job and consisted of being guided through a simple, common-sense approach to decision making. This approach included the steps of problem identification and exploration, alternative solution development and analysis, cost-benefit analysis of the preferred solution when relevant, and action step definition. Formal training of any type, in fact, was offered only when the team members defined a need for it themselves. Such requests came relatively quickly, but almost without exception they were for training in skills necessary to meet their normal job responsibilities rather than for process-related skills.

The only people who did eventually request additional training in process-related skills were the facilitators. As the in-house people took increasing control of the team network, they began to realize that in order to keep it productive, they needed ways to stimulate more ideas. At this point, additional techniques were introduced, depending upon the situation. For example, a lot of decision making exercises started with Brainstorming in one form or another. Again, if a management system problem had a large political dimension, Force Field Analysis might be used.

The facilitators had their own monthly meetings at which they discussed process issues and the projects teams were working on. If a facilitator's team was bogging down in a project, or was losing interest, or had come up with a problem it did not know how to address, various techniques were offered by the consultants to see which would best "fit" the situation. The facilitators then carried these back to their team meetings and introduced them.

Once the teams had enjoyed a number of successes on smaller projects and had developed a sense of ownership, facilitators were also offered the tools for measuring productivity. These tools were introduced to the teams on an as-needed basis. A team might come up with a project where one of the tools, say a Check Sheet, a Statistical Control Chart, or a Scatter Diagram, might be of use. At this point, the facilitator would introduce the tool as an alternative or as an aid to achieving a solution. The team would then decide whether or not to use it.

Corporate-Wide versus Individual Facility

One might argue that more formal process-related training is necessary when starting a strategic decision making effort at the top of a corporation, rather than somewhere down among its units. In this instance, the CEO is not the only one who has the power to block or support the necessary changes; a line of vice presidents, division managers, and so on, can also affect this process. It is necessary, therefore, to develop the same level of understanding and acceptance in all of these people that was developed up front in the CEO.

More than likely, however, such an approach to training would again not work. The weaknesses of traditional top-down efforts have previously been discussed. These weaknesses include excessive time commitment, lack of understanding, and lack of ownership.

A more acceptable alternative when an entire corporation is involved would be to familiarize the CEO and maybe a few key reports, gain their tentative support, and then immediately drop down several layers, pick a facility, and get the approach at least partially in place. Consultants would begin building the team network at, say, a production facility or in the human resources department several months before beginning full-scale corporate executive-level familiarization.

This staggered approach would prove beneficial in many ways. For one, executive-level familiarizers would be able to say: "Don't just listen. See for yourselves. This is what we are talking about. This is how it works." By this time, a good number of improvement teams at the facility or department would be involved in projects, and several would have produced results. The facility or department, therefore, would provide a "living laboratory" to complement the information consultants were delivering to upper-level managers at the corporate level.

Another benefit would be that once the necessary top-level managers had developed the necessary degree of understanding and commitment, the pilot site could function as a showplace. Staff from other facilities and departments could visit and learn from the pilot site during their familiarization phase.

Finally, one last obvious benefit would be that facilitators from the pilot site would be able to function as consultants at new sites across the corporation, helping to train their counterparts at these sites on the job.

Succeeding at Decision Making

Decision making is a major part of our everyday lives. We make decisions continually as individuals, both at home and at work. Common sense and experience are our two best allies. On occasion, however, a variety of techniques can help us to broaden our perspective in order to come up with new alternatives and better solutions.

Group decision making situations are more complicated because more than one perspective is involved. The best solution for one participant in such an effort might not be the best for all. Techniques are needed, therefore, which help us to understand what others are thinking and saying and which encourage the integration of individual perspectives into a far richer group perspective. Finally, techniques are needed to help generate the necessary degree of group-wide commitment to the final solution.

When we reach the organizational level, *in decision making* between the *level*, we must deal not only with individual and group perspectives, but also with those of organizational segments and the organization as a whole. Effective decision making at the organizational level becomes a very complex matter. A lot of time, energy, and money can be wasted by setting up decision making efforts and carrying them out in the wrong way.

In order to succeed at the organizational level, we ultimately need a culture (especially a reward system) that encourages participation in and commitment to the processes involved. We need the optimum attitude and perspective. We need a vehicle which allows the most effective utilization of employee expertise. We need an accurate understanding of the value of the various techniques and tools at our disposal. Finally, we need to know how best to fit all these pieces together into a systemic whole which will allow us to achieve the desired results.

This last need requires an organization-wide process model. One such model, which has been used successfully, will be presented in Chapter 6.

Summary Chapter 5 Questions

- What is one of the major weaknesses of the approach some companies take toward developing an interactive attitude?
- What are the two types of training?
- Why is Just In Time training the best way to handle training?
- What does the traditional top-down training approach often say to participants that causes the opposite of the desired effect?
- Who are the best people to ask to solve operational problems that are encountered?
- Who were the only people in the example from the case study to request additional training?
- What is meant by the staggered approach to training?

Chapter 6

Overview of the Ideal Decision Making Model

Introduction

The Ideal Decision Making Model (IDMM) is a ten-step model that can be used to diagram and make any type of business strategy decision that requires more than a superficial analysis and documentation to effectively reach the optimum solution. It is typically applied to autonomous work teams, but may also be applied by an individual decision maker. The steps in this process are sequential in nature, although some steps may be omitted or replaced as needed. The suggested ten steps are as follows:

1. Document the decision to be made in a charter
2. Identify the scope of the decision
3. Collect initial data and survey the customers and stakeholders
4. Define and diagram the process in order to understand current circumstances
5. Establish the process performance measures and targets
6. Diagram the causes and effects
7. Collect data on causes
8. Analyze data
9. Develop and consider possible options
10. Measure success or failure

DOI: 10.4324/9781003198062-6

These ten steps can be grouped into six macro categories as follows:

- The decision to be made
- The process
- The causes
- The numbers
- The solution
- The future

Understanding the Decision to Be Made

In many cases, people often start improvement activities without first understanding why the decision must be made. Decisions almost always start with a problem to be solved. Often, people become uncomfortable and wonder whether or not the real or correct problem is being addressed or whether there will be a more important issue to work on right around the corner. Problem areas become much clearer when the actual circumstances are compared to the business objective, the process requirements, or the customer expectations. The bottom line is that problem areas must be "discovered."

Three steps are included in this category: (1) document the decision to be made in a charter, (2) identify the scope of the decision, and (3) review data on customers and stakeholders. It is important to set priorities among decisions to be made, choosing the ones that appear to be most significant in terms of the following categories: quality, volume, delivery, and cost. Problems are often hidden despite the fact that they usually exist all around us, like low-hanging fruit waiting to be picked. Decision making activities begin with understanding the facts, organizing the data, and exposing them through data analysis.

Step 1: Document the Decision to Be Made in the Charter

The selection of the decision in the strategic improvement process provides the team with its "Balance Scorecard" to measure how closely actual performance matches the performance promise. The data that the team uses to evaluate and select the issue to work on must come from the team's processes. This is called the "voice of the organization."

According to the Union of Japanese Scientists and Engineers (JUSE), selecting the strategic improvement issue for decision making can be enhanced by the following requirements:

- The issue is directly tied to the workers' personal areas of authority
- The problem or issue urgently requires resolution
- The organization's managers and leaders are interested in the issue
- The workers are able to employ their own opinions in the problem solving and are able to collectively make decisions
- An evaluation of the project can be made in terms of financial effects, the expected benefits are positive, and it appears that the employees will be able to take pride in the results
- The proposed strategic improvement is in line with the long-term strategic plan or the yearly plan
- Dramatic results are expected from the improvement activity
- The time period potentially required by the project is appropriate

Of course, not all decisions can meet all of these requirements, but the more they do, the likelier success will ensue.

The decisions to be made and the problems to be solved should be written in paragraph format and should include a description of why the particular issue was selected and included in the group *charter*.

A *charter* is a written grant or document conferring certain rights and privileges to a local branch, chapter, or group and which outlines the principles, organization, and function of the group making the decision. Most decisions are not made by a single person in a vacuum. For the solution to any problem to be effective, other people need to be involved in the decision.

The identification and documentation of the team charter is the critical first step in the decision making process. Ironically, it is also the least understood and most frequently omitted or short-circuited. The nucleus of the charter revolves around the establishment of a performance promise that the team can consistently deliver in order to ensure success. According to Bob Lynch of QualTeam (Lynch, Werner, and Lynch), flawless delivery on the performance promise to customers and stakeholders depends upon seamless execution internally. Seamless execution is the result of strong links between internal customers and suppliers. The charter enables every team to consider its role in helping to accomplish the greater purpose of the organization by considering these relationships.

The charter can be viewed as a chain of objectives, which begins with a statement of the mission of the team, followed by the supporting purposes. The length of the mission statement should be between 25 and 50 words. The mission statement describes the decision which must be made, which is the core purpose of the team. The next section covers team organization and the reporting structure, followed by team member responsibilities. This is followed by the procedures of the team's activities. The following are the key items typically covered within the framework of the charter:

1. Team mission and objectives
2. Products, services, and/or information provided
3. Synopsis of team processes, customers, and their valid requirements
4. Competitive benchmarks, if known
5. Supplier requirements, if available

Step 2: Identify the Scope of the Decision

One of the most important steps that either must be done as the charter is being written or immediately afterward is to document the *scope*. The *scope* is a description of the boundaries of the team decision making; what they will *and will not* consider under their purview. If the scope is too narrow, then the team will not be able to accomplish their goals because their decision making cannot change the underlying issue since it is not under their control. But if the scope is too broad, the team will get bogged down in trying to do too much, and will not be able to make any progress on any one of the specific goals. So it is extremely important that the scope match the issue at hand.

Step 3: Collect Initial Data and Survey the Customers and Stakeholders

As noted before, years ago the only way to obtain any data was to develop a survey and gather the results. But in this world of big data, often we don't have to wait until we've designed and deployed a survey to get data. Often, the data we need already exists within the systems. It makes sense to review this easily available data before going to the trouble of designing and deploying a survey. If we don't find the answers we need, then we can deploy surveys out to the customers and/or stakeholders.

   A key point in this step is for the members to put themselves (as a team) in the shoes of the customer and identify areas to focus the team on. Some of the areas to cover are:

- Quality
- Speed/timeliness

- Cost and functionality
- Availability and flexibility
- Responsiveness
- Durability
- Reliability

This level of initial data gathering is not the same as the more detailed, more in-depth data gathering that we will do later in the process when we are considering different options for the strategic improvement program. This initial data gathering is considered the "voice of the customer" which helps us to determine and/or confirm the decision to be made and the scope, both of which are documented in the charter. The data may cause the team to refine their scope or change their focus to a different, higher priority, decision.

Understanding the Process

Once the decision to be made is fully understood, the process to make the decision needs to be fully explored. This category includes two steps: defining and diagraming the process, and establishing the measurements to be used.

Step 4: Define and Diagram the Process in Order to Understand Current Circumstances

This step involves creating a support or working group (if one is not already in place) in order to get started, followed by creating the activity plan and completing the diagram and Flowchart of the initial documentation package. The working group is usually in the form of a team or an employee-involvement group interested in a certain problem area. If the scope of the activity is very broad, the project can be broken down into smaller components and spinoff teams can be created at this time. A "communication" team or even a "quality assurance" team may be part of the decision making activities.

Once the theme is selected and the working group has been formed, the next activity involves building a project rollout plan of activities and key milestones. The plan should be constructed around the management cycle, starting with the vision.

> Management cycle = vision, strategy, planning, organizing, implementing, and controlling.

Once the plan has been developed, the following activities should be performed as part of the diagramming and flowcharting activity:

1. Develop a statement that explains the overall purpose of the business process:
   - Prepare a one sentence draft that describes why the process exists.
   - Verify that the statement incorporates language that covers cost, schedule, and performance, such as reliability, timeliness, etc.
   - Check to see that the statement is one that the business leaders would endorse.
2. Define the valid process scope:
   - Identify where the process starts or begins (the first activity in the process).
   - Identify where the process ends (the last activity in the process).
   - Identify all major activities within the process.
   - Identify the key inputs that are required from outside the process and the suppliers that provide them.
   - Identify the key outputs from the process and the business partners/customers who receive them.
   - Identify those major activities and processes that depend upon this process or upon which this process depends for support or input.
   - Check the process scope to ensure that it takes into account known significant problems/opportunities for improvement.
   - Identify related processes that are specifically excluded from the process scope.
3. Identify the key activities that occur in the process and the position or person who performs them and their related inputs and outputs:
   - List all the positions or players in the process and the activities by name.
   - Identify the various inputs that are needed for each activity and the suppliers that provide each input. Group activities where possible.
   - Identify each output from the activity groupings and the customer/business partner who normally receives the output.
   - Identify those activities where there is a need to verify/check/inspect the output in order to effectively complete the next activity without delay or modification.

- When the output does not meet requirements, identify the activities that need to be performed instead of, or in addition to, the normal next activity. Identify the position/person who performs these activities when the output does not meet requirements.
- Identify all additional inputs required for these additional activities, as well as the suppliers that provide the inputs.
- Estimate the frequency of occurrence of these nonconforming situations.
4. Create a process map or Flowchart, based upon the information outlined above:
   - Number the activities identified in Step 1 according to the sequence in which they normally occur.
   - Using a block, square, circle, or other symbol on the Flowchart, enter the name of each activity identified and the position/person who performs it.
   - Map out the process, generally starting at the left and proceeding downward and/or to the right.
   - For those activities identified as needing a check or inspection, create a decision block following the activity block that indicates whether or not the next normal activity can be performed without delay or modification.
   - Enter the name of each additional activity identified above in a series of blocks, thus creating a secondary process path. Connect the last block and resume the normal flow.
   - Estimate both the elapsed time and the applied time that it takes to complete each activity. Post the numbers above or next to the corresponding block or symbol.
   - Use off-page connectors to continue the flow where necessary.
5. If the Flowchart becomes too detailed, modify the scope of the process defined in Step 2 and create a summary, higher level macro flow.
6. Additional usefulness can be derived from the Flowchart by labeling and grouping activities into "value-added" and "nonvalue-added."

Step 5: Establish the Process Performance Measures and Targets

In order to develop process measures, it is necessary to identify (1) categories of measure, (2) units of measure, and (3) levels of measurement, as outlined in the following five items:

1. *Categories of measure* identify "what to measure" in a process. Cost, schedule, and performance quality are three such categories. Other relevant categories include quantity, timely use of resources, and leadership.

These basic categories of measure should be broken down into more specific levels of customer requirements, using a scorecard matrix as a tool. David Garvin, in his *Harvard Business Review* article entitled "Competing on the Eight Dimensions of Quality (Garvin 1987)" suggests the following customer requirements as part of the quality categories of measure:
- Performance—The primary operating characteristics of the product
- Features—The "bells and whistles" that supplement the basic function
- Reliability—The probability of a product malfunctioning
- Conformance—The degree to which a product's design meets standards
- Durability—The life of the product in terms of economic and technical dimensions
- Serviceability—The speed, courtesy, competence, and ease of repair
- Aesthetics—How a product looks, feels, sounds, tastes, or smells
- Perceived quality—Inferences about quality reputation based on images, models, advertising, or brand

2. *Units of measure* identify the "how to" measure. The units of measure are ratios, ratings, and absolute numbers.
   - *Ratios*—Indicate the percent or rate. Examples of ratios include percent of on-time performance, percent of desired applicants hired, percent turnover, percent system availability (or unavailability), percent rework, percent of process goals met, percent above or below budget, percent overtime, etc.
   - *Ratings*—Indicate satisfaction or perception. Customer ratings are usually along a numerical scale. Dimensions of quality can be listed and the customer is asked to rate the service, products, and persons involved in a process. Each dimension can also be further ranked both on a scale of 1 to 5 and in terms of priority of importance.
   - *Absolute numbers*—Indicate occurrences over time. Examples include number of customer complaints, number of new customers, number of training courses completed, number of programs tested and completed, downtime due to equipment failure, turnaround time, dollars' worth of cost savings and value added, etc.

3. *Levels of measurement*—This is the "why" of measurement. There are three levels of process measurement: mission measures, process output measures, and process variable measures.

- *Mission measures*—The business results that the process directly impacts on a macro level. Mission measures are the indicators of the fundamental accomplishment of the process in relation to the satisfaction of business objectives. If the process team has stated its charter, then mission measures are the quantitative indicators of its success against it. Mission measures include indicators of quality, speed, cost, customer satisfaction, employee satisfaction, revenue, and profitability. Generally speaking, there should be at least one mission measure for each process.
- *Process output measures*—The indicators of the success or worth of the process outputs. They are used to track the products or services of an operation and they drive mission measures. Examples include number of reports generated, number of programs finished, number of projects meeting deadlines, etc.
- *Process variable measures*—The measures that indicate the performance of the process itself, before outputs are produced. They are used to maintain and improve quality by tracking the process. Examples include number of calls answered before the third ring, time taken to produce a program design, effort needed to correct errors, etc.

4. Define the measurements that will determine whether and to what extent the requirements defined previously have been satisfied, beginning with those for the process mission, followed by external process outputs.
   - Identify any existing measures that relate to the requirements. Evaluate the existing measures to determine whether or not they meet all the criteria for valid measures. If they do not, modify them or drop them.
   - For all critical requirements for which there is no existing output measure, determine the appropriate type needed: ratio, rating, or absolute numbers.
   - Ensure that the characteristics of valid measures are satisfied in describing these new measures.
5. For internal process measures, ensure that practical measurements for both effectiveness and efficiency are developed as indicators of process performance.
   - Identify measures for those activities that must be performed in order to identify process fail points, which are those activities for which there is a need to check/inspect during the process flow.
   - Repeat the steps above to identify measures for all other critical requirements for the outputs/inputs within the process flow.

The next activity involves setting targets. Targets are numeric values that show what level of improvement the activities must achieve. Their focus is on how things ought to be. However, if targets are set too high, there is danger that the plan will fall apart. It is important to carefully judge the current level of progress and the ability to improve in order to set targets at attainable levels that provide sufficient stretch.

Understanding the Causes

In order to make a good decision, it is important to understand the causes, which means diagramming them and collecting data on them.

Step 6: Diagram the Causes and Effects

Either a Flowchart or Fishbone Diagram (or both) can help with diagramming the causes and effects which can be used for this purpose. Additionally, Process Function Deployment and Service Blueprinting can be especially helpful with this task.

Step 7: Collect Data on Causes

Understanding the current situation does not mean just understanding the state of the process at the present time. It also means being aware of the history and variations over time, as well as the state of control. Accomplishing all this requires looking at data and compiling Pareto Diagrams, Histograms, Statistical Control Charts, and other quality tools. It also requires the use of stratification when collecting, organizing, and compiling data. The purpose is to gain an understanding of how bad the problem situation actually is. It is also important to understand changes that have taken place over time and to understand problem areas in detail.

This step differs from the earlier initial data gathering in purpose and level of detail. The initial data gathering was helping to define and scope the problem to determine the decision to be made. Now we need data to define and evaluate the potential solutions. We may also need data in order to establish baselines for scorecards or a performance matrix.

The following items should be performed when collecting data as part of Step 7:

1. Identify the purpose of collecting data, including which specific data is required, how the data will be used, and how the data will be displayed.
2. Identify which data is to be collected and used for analysis.
3. Identify who will collect the data (usually the people closest to the work the data represents). It is important to communicate why the data is being collected.
4. Determine when the data will be collected. If sampling is to be used, specify the time of day, week, month, and shift. All data must be collected in a timely manner. Monthly is usually the longest interval and daily is usually the shortest. If the data is coming from existing systems, make sure it has been prepared properly as explained in Chapter 4.
5. If not already available, decide how the data will be collected. The use of carefully designed forms or spreadsheets can be helpful. Be sure that they are simple, easy to complete, self-explanatory, and take a minimum amount of time to complete.
6. Decide how much data will be collected and determine the appropriate sample size. The use of a technical resource or statistician may be needed at this point.
7. Collect the data, tabulate, and display using the quality tools discussed in Chapter 3 and Chapter 4.

Understanding the Numbers, Solutions, and the Future

The remaining three categories each has only one step related to it. In order to understand the numbers, we must analyze the data. In order to understand the solutions, we must develop the different options. In order to understand the future, we must measure whether or not we met the goals we set out to meet with the decision.

Step 8: Analyze Data

According to a Japanese saying, if the analysis of data is done properly, then the problem is already half-solved and the decision is just about made. When people cannot discover appropriate ways to solve a problem, it is almost always because they lack a sufficient understanding of the problem and because the analysis of causes was done poorly. The true multiple causes of the problem must be uncovered and efficient corresponding corrective action must be taken.

When a shotgun approach is used (corrective action taken based on a whim), the effort rarely yields an effective resolution. The starting point for strategic decision making is the level of variability, which is documented through the process of understanding current circumstances. Using variability as a base, it is important to define the relationships between the characteristics and the results and to seek out the true causes of the variability.

As noted in the chapter on Analytics, it is beyond the scope of this book to teach the hundreds of tools available to do the analysis, but it is essential that the tool chosen matches the goals outlined in Step 1.

Step 9: Develop and Consider Possible Options

This step consists of three separate activities within the decision making model:

1. *Researching the improvement plan or hypothesis*—Once the real causes of the problem are known, the next step is to establish a corrective action plan to eliminate those causes.
   - It is important that the corrective action plan be specific. Abstractions will not be useful.
   - Use a 4W1H (who, what, where, when, why, and how) checklist to clearly specify who will do what.
   - Use a TKJ diagram to research the many corrective action plans by breaking down traditional ways of thinking and drawing out new ideas.
   - Use a corrective action diagram of some kind.
2. *Planning and executing the improvement plan*—The corrective action plan that was researched and established is now ready for implementation in this activity. Since there is usually more than one item in the corrective action plan, it is necessary to schedule the various items so that the effects of each can be verified. Execution of the plan is often broken out into a separate project plan or perhaps even a different team.

Step 10: Measure Success or Failure

This last step involves evaluating the corrective action to determine whether the strategy influenced the measurements chosen to evaluate the decision.

The idea is to determine how much the key performance metric improved, how much the average was changed, or to what extent the variability was reduced.

Once the strategic improvement plan has been implemented and found to be successful, two additional activites are needed. The two activities are: standardization and establishing full control. To ensure that the effects of improvement activities are not just temporary, standardization through documentation is necessary. Standardization is defined as the tasks necessary to prevent circumstances from returning to their previous state once improvement activity has been implemented and the results verified. A key part of this step is recurrence prevention, which is implemented to maintain the results and effects of improvement activities that eliminate the true causes of the problem. Examples of standards include technical engineering standards, operational standards, and standards relating to systems and work methods (Schon 1971).

Once standardization is in place, a system of full maintenance control is needed to sustain the benefits of improvement over the long haul. Setting up a control system generally requires defining control characteristics, discovering control items, establishing control limits, and defining responses to out-of-control situations. To fully establish control, it is important to establish a system to execute the PDCA (Plan-Do-Check-Act) cycle effectively and in a timely manner.

Verifying and reviewing the results of improvement activities is probably the most important step of all ten. It is also the one that is skipped even more often than the charter development. Many times, organizations go through all the continuous improvement programs, identify the problem, find the solution, make the decision, implement the program—and then stop. They often don't circle around back to see if the improvement they planned actually came to fruition. Often they are just happy to finish the project and would rather not know if they somehow missed the mark and no improvements were seen for all their work.

Chapter 7 will now offer a case study of an organization effort in which the Ideal Decision Making Model was successfully used, incorporating many of the techniques and tools discussed in Chapter 3 and dealing with many of the issues discussed in other chapters.

Summary Chapter 6 Questions

- What are the ten steps of the Ideal Decision Making Model?
- What are the six macro-categories those steps can be grouped into?
- How can selecting the strategic improvement issue for decision making be enhanced?
- What is a charter and why is it important?
- What key items are included in a charter?
- What is a scope, and why is it important?
- What are some of the areas to focus on when gathering data from the customers and stakeholders?
- What two steps are involved in understanding the process?
- The project rollout plan should be constructed around what cycle? What does that entail?
- What three aspects of the measures need to be identified?
- What are the eight quality categories of customer requirement measures?
- What kinds of tools can help identify the cause of an issue?
- What three activities are involved in the last step (Step 10) of the Ideal Decision Making Model?
- Which step of the Ideal Decision Making Model is the most important (but the one most often skipped)?
- Once the plan has been implemented successfully, what two activities are necessary to maintain the success?

Chapter 7

Integrated Case Study: Jan's Technology Services

This case study will demonstrate some of the tools and concepts discussed in the previous six chapters of the book. The company is hypothetical, but the examples are based on real-life experiences.

The Company

Jan's Technology Services, better known as JTS, was founded in 1998 by Jan "technology is my middle name" Billings. Within ten years, JTS had development offices just outside of 14 cities throughout the United States, from Miami to San Jose. JTS developed full stack technology systems that interfaced with legacy systems. Jan owned 80% of JTS, and Kim Peters, a long-term partner, owned 20%. JTS was able to finance expansion through company profits and a long-term loan agreement with First Customer Federal Bank.

JTS' marketing strategy was to create displays at technology expos and trade organizations, providing demo systems fortified by a well-trained and knowledgeable sales staff and a strong service department. Jan thought that support services were so important to JTS' customers that each of the 14 cities had its own in-house support department. Ongoing support and training for customers and partners were coordinated through the central office.

By the end of 2020, annual sales averaged $60 million and net profits $3.5 million. The service department averaged an annual loss of $500,000, which

DOI: 10.4324/9781003198062-7

Jan considered an acceptable expense because it allowed JTS to maintain at least a 10% gross margin pricing advantage over its competitors.

Changing Conditions

JTS' marketing strategy had worked well for many years in the beginning—especially during the Y2K scare when many companies needed work done on their legacy systems. But after the dot-com bust in 2001, conditions began to change significantly. JTS was still profitable ($1 million on sales of $35 million), but it was obvious at the time that some adjustments were needed. So, they underwent a major move from an individual sales channel targeting decision makers to working much more closely with network, hardware, and software vendors, and consultants bundling the technology development and programming work with the larger infrastructure projects, sold by the vendors.

That also worked well for many years. The business expanded its footprint beyond the 14 cities in which it had offices, and established relationships in just about every major corporation in the United States. But now the strategy was running into some major problems and needed to change again.

Among the changing conditions was a string of new competitors, especially from overseas, which resulted in frequent price wars. Some competitors even mimicked JTS' in-house support service departments and provided superior 24-hour support and just-in-time training. Another issue was the fact that because the majority of jobs were through other channel companies (network, hardware, and software retailers as well as consulting companies), JTS no longer had a direct connection with the buying company. That made it difficult to upsell or cross sell.

Furthermore, while JTS was a "full stack" developer (meaning that they did networking, back-end database work, programming and middleware, as well as front-end website or mobile client work), it was getting more and more difficult to find full stack developers. Most developers were specializing in only one of the levels.

Finally, the number of legacy systems had dropped significantly over the past 20 years, so the "specialty" that differentiated JTS services was not needed quite as much as in prior years.

As a temporary measure, JTS began increasing its advertising budget and hiring more salespeople who joined local trade organizations like chambers of commerce, which resulted in increased sales but at lower profit margins.

Jan and Kim knew that it was only a matter of time before this temporary strategy was doomed to fail, because increased sales were accompanied by increases in other expenses, advertising, office, storage, and more sales staff.

Jan was constantly monitoring the company's numbers, including measure such as sales, daily sales calls, and closing rates of salespeople. Jan used to joke, "Making money is easy. You just increase sales and reduce expenses!" Which, of course, wasn't so easy. Reducing expenses too much would break the very spine of JTS. Increased sales would also cost money. For every dollar of added expense, sales had to increase by seven dollars. And then came the pandemic, which impacted businesses everywhere. While certain technology services such as networking infrastructure and work-at-home systems had an uptick, overall business was down by 60%. By year-end 2020, Jan was no longer joking. If expenses remained the same and the sales forecasts were on target for next year, JTS would barely break even. Jan wasn't sure how to explain this to First Customer Federal Bank, which could pull the plug on JTS overnight if it felt "insecure," as the loan agreement was worded.

Quality Comes to JTS

Kim Peters, Jan's long-time partner, approached Jan about some recent articles describing how other companies had improved customer satisfaction while increasing productivity. Kim said the concept was fairly simple—find out what is most important to customers and give it to them. Kim was still a little vague on the subject, but told Jan that JTS needed to create some structures, develop a long-range "game plan" designed to meet customers' needs, involve the people at JTS who did the work, and train them in the use of quality tools.

Jan was a little skeptical about Kim's ideas. Hadn't JTS always been oriented toward its customers? Didn't JTS have an annual strategic plan, with defined objectives for each store? Weren't employees free to volunteer ideas through the suggestion program? As for structure, it was clear who was in charge, wasn't it? Besides, Kim's ideas (which included a lot of training) would cost plenty, at a time when JTS was watching every cent!

Discussions about Kim's ideas continued for several months without resolution. Kim finally engaged a consulting company to create a proposal for the training and to do a preliminary survey and analysis of JTS. Their report caused Jan's blood pressure to rise several points, because it suggested that over 15% of JTS' customers were no longer satisfied in general and over 45% were dissatisfied with the support service department in particular. The report also noted that there were pockets of discontent among JTS employees regarding compensation, reduced opportunity to make sales, and having to deal with unhappy customers.

Matters became worse at the July 20th meeting when JTS' accountant reported that first-half earnings were a negative $175,000! It was probably coincidence, but on the same day, Jan received four extremely critical letters from customers who wanted to cancel their contracts and pull the development projects they had ordered, citing poor service as the reason.

The next morning, Kim was surprised when Jan asked about the project previously talked about, specifically, how much would it cost to put it into place and how long would it take. Kim suggested they meet with the KWB Group, which had conducted the survey and whose specialty was improving customer satisfaction and performance.

During the meeting, the KWB consultants explained their improvement process and tried to learn the level of Jan's commitment. Persuaded that Jan was committed and would devote sufficient resources, the KWB Group agreed to work with JTS.

Establishing a Strategy

To begin the implementation program, Alex Martini of the KWB Group conducted a three-day high-level executive workshop, which was attended by Jan and Kim Peters and the other members of the executive committee (Baker Rubio, vice president of sales; Jamie O'Leary, vice president of finance and treasurer; Norma Vogel, vice president of administration; and Drew Emerson, vice president of service).

Alex spent most of the first day reviewing the benefits of improving customer satisfaction, involving employees and identifying key measurements and the need for an overall strategy. None of the executives were able to describe JTS' mission, or reason for being in business, other than it related to "making a lot of money."

There were many questions and much skepticism about the need for a formal mission statement, but Alex was able to persuade most of the group that accomplishing financial objectives could not occur in a vacuum. Those who were not so convinced agreed to keep an open mind. Alex shared the mission statements of various successful companies and suggested that it was time JTS developed one. However, it would only be meaningful if the people of JTS defined the company's mission. Alex couldn't do it for them.

The next morning's session focused on drafting the mission statement. Suggestions ranged from "being the largest company in the country" to "being the dominant developer of systems in the 14 states in which they had offices." In facilitating the workshop, Alex thought the ideas offered were a good start, but they needed to be more specific, more customer oriented, and should include a time frame. On the other hand, a mission statement must be flexible enough to accommodate changes in technology and the marketplace.

Jamie O'Leary commented that all of this was very interesting, but as vice president-finance and treasurer, there was some question as to whether some high-sounding mission was going to pay the bills. "Are we drafting our epitaph?" Jamie asked facetiously.

Alex thanked Jamie for raising the issue and promised to connect it later with something to which they could all relate. Alex couldn't help but quote one of Dr. W. Edwards Deming's remarks to the effect that a company without a mission is "... like taking a trip in an automobile by looking out the rear-view mirror. You need to know where you want to go and point in that direction!"

It was an agonizing day, but by dinner time, the executives had developed their first draft of a mission statement, one they all could live with. It read:

> The mission of JTS is to become, within five years, our customers' preferred provider of development and programming services for their businesses in our market areas, providing continually improving value while exceeding their needs and expectations through the active participation of all JTS employees.

Alex commented that they might want to fine-tune the draft later, but it was an excellent beginning.

To start the third day of the workshop, Alex said that the fun was just beginning. Now that they knew where they wanted to go—the mission—they had to decide what was necessary to get there—the strategic objectives—by land or by sea. Later on, they would need to establish ways to measure their progress toward meeting their objectives.

Alex divided the executives into two groups and asked them to brainstorm lists of what they thought had to be accomplished, on a broad level, to achieve the mission. Later, they would combine the lists and use the TKJ process to come up with several key categories. For example, one way to support the mission might be to increase sales levels by providing free training or support (rather than charging extra for these services, as was JTS' policy), but these ideas could be grouped under "incentives" or even the broader category of "improve customer satisfaction."

The workshop was extended to four days. The group finally agreed on six strategic objectives which had to occur in order for JTS to achieve its mission:

- Achieve and maintain at least 95% customer satisfaction with all development and programming services.
- Achieve and maintain at least 95% customer satisfaction with all support agreements.
- Become and continue to be market share leader in all service categories.
- Achieve and maintain at least 95% employee satisfaction and involvement.
- Achieve and maintain reputation in each community served for high quality and as being responsible corporate citizens.
- Achieve and maintain stable financial condition, maximizing shareholder value.

One learning experience for everyone was having to function and communicate as a team. For Jan, it meant "leaving the stripes at the door." Through Alex's encouragement, everyone felt free to criticize anyone else's ideas, which was a rather unique concept at JTS.

Alex said that the next step would be the development of priority or key activities necessary to achieve the strategic objectives. For example, what specific activities were required to achieve 95% customer satisfaction? One such key activity might be to create an outstanding management system by developing processes to assure that constant excellence and quality every day were not left to chance. Identifying these key activities would be the subject of the next week's workshop. Alex suggested that the participants might want to discuss these ideas and possible supporting activities with the people in their departments.

Jan issued a memo the next day to all employees, stating the mission statement and the strategic objectives and explaining their significance. Plans were already in the works for Jan and Kim to visit all the offices to communicate the reasons for the changes and to answer questions and concerns. It was critical that employees be kept informed and their fears addressed. While employees may have been fearful of current conditions continuing (flat sales and profits, competitor inroads), they would be just as fearful about the impending changes, even if they knew that the changes were absolutely necessary.

The next week's workshop was very trying for all concerned, but by Friday all the key activities necessary to accomplish the strategic objectives had been identified. The first objective would require successfully accomplishing several key activities, such as improving customer satisfaction with value and pricing and improving effective/caring communications with customers.

For the second objective, the group decided that a few of the same key activities applied, such as improving effective/caring communications with customers. They also added some activities, including reducing the number of missed commitments and providing high-quality support service.

Next, for each key activity, the group identified one or more indicators to determine how they would measure their performance. For example, to measure progress towards increasing the number of support calls solved on the first call, the number of customer support requests solved on the first call were tracked. All of the key activities, their indicators, and their related strategic objectives are shown in Table 7.1.

To determine the indicators for the key activities, lower level measurements would also have to be established, usually on an office-by-office basis. At the end of each measurement period, the lower level indicators would be summarized in a company-wide indicator. This process would require each business unit to track its data accurately and consistently.

Once all the indicators had been established, the next step was to gather the actual data, not an easy task. JTS already had some of the information in its files, such as sales revenues and expenses, but much of the data did not exist, such as the number of times a customer had to call to resolve a support issue. It had been three years since the last employee survey, and customers had not been formally surveyed in years. The files were full of various customer comments, most of which were complaints about support service.

Table 7.1 Strategic Objective Table

Strategic Objectives	Priority Activities	Indicators
Achieve and maintain at least 95% satisfaction for all development and programming services	• Develop outstanding quality and delivery system • Improve customer satisfaction with value & pricing • Improve effective/caring communications with customers	• Customer Satisfaction Index (CSI) Summary • Process Indicatory Summary • CSI Pricing component • CSI Communications component
Achieve and maintain at least 95% satisfaction on all support services	• Developing outstanding quality and delivery system • Improve effective/caring communications with customers • Provide high-quality support service • Increase the number of support requests resolved on the first call	• CSI Communications component • Process Indicators—Support Requests • CSI Communications component • CSI Repair component • Total number of support requests resolved on the first call
Market share leader	• Improve development and introduction of innovative development and programming services • Improve competitiveness	• Percent of sales on new development and programming services • Customer survey results
Achieve and maintain at least 95% employee satisfaction and involvement	• Improve employee satisfaction by providing knowledge and experience • Improve communication with employees	• Learning hours per employee • Percent participation on teams • Employee survey results
Achieve and maintain reputation for quality and corporate citizenship	• Develop outstanding quality and delivery system • Encourage employees to participate in community affairs • Reduce number of complaints to Better Business Bureau	• CSI Summary • Percent of employees involved • Total complaints to Better Business Bureau
Achieve and maintain financial objectives, maximizing shareholder value	• Increase revenues • Reduce operating expenses • Increase return on investment	• Total revenues • Total expenses • Net profits + shareholders equity after tax

At Alex's urging, Jan and Kim continued to explain to all employees what the new measurement system was attempting to accomplish. Employees might naturally have assumed that with performance being more closely monitored, some heads might roll if the indicators moved in the wrong direction. The partners tried to emphasize the positive; that no one at JTS could improve without keeping track of results, like weighing in when on a diet. Despite such encouraging statements, many employees remained unconvinced. Alex hoped that the integrity of the data would not suffer.

Jan was not as worried about the integrity of the data as much as the sheer volume. "Do you realize that to know what's going on in my company, I've got to go through zillions of reports and indicators? I guess the days are gone when I could just look at the sales figures and know what was happening!"

Jamie O'Leary continued to harp on a favorite theme: even though all these measurements tied to performance and customer satisfaction might be nice to have, nothing was more important than the bottom line. "Try paying the rent with customers' compliments!" was Jamie's standard operating phrase.

Alex continued to plead for Jamie and the others to be patient. Alex tried to remind everyone that JTS was actually remodeling its 20-year-old management structure, which had not changed radically from the days when JTS had one outlet. "You didn't create your existing management structure overnight and you're not going to put a new one in place overnight either. We've got to take things one step at a time, and you've got to have faith that JTS not only will take care of its customers better, but will achieve or surpass its financial objectives."

Alex asked all the executives to read copies of two reports which had been distributed, both of which related to a well-developed concept: the Balanced Scorecard. Though the Balanced Scorecard has been around for nearly 20 years, it is as relevant and useful today as it was when first introduced—even more so since it has withstood the test of time.

The Balanced Scorecard

What Alex asked everyone to read was "The Balanced Scorecard—Measures that Drive Performance," written by Robert S. Kaplan and David P. Norton and published in the *Harvard Business Review* (Kaplan 1992), and "Improving and Measuring Corporate Performance with the Balanced Scorecard," a summary and analysis of many companies' experiences with the scorecard, written and edited by James A. Ryder (Ryder), Jr.

In the next executive workshop, Alex asked for someone to summarize the essence of the Balanced Scorecard and why it might be useful at JTS. To Alex's surprise, Jamie O'Leary offered to describe the meaning of the process. Everyone sitting at the horseshoe-shaped table glanced at each other and sat forward in their seats. Jamie didn't usually volunteer for presentations.

"I think I see what you've been getting at, Alex," Jamie sheepishly admitted. "It appears that the Balanced Scorecard answers some of our concerns about the measurement system we've been implementing."

"My reading of the process is that we'll be identifying several key categories which are really critical to our success, measuring how well we're doing in each category and balancing them against each other. It means that at the end of the month, we'll look at just a few numbers or indicators within each category to tell us how we're doing. That seems to handle Jan's problem about being inundated with numbers. While the rest of the organization may need to measure performance in some detail, we'll be taking a broader view and having a better handle on where we're going and how well our strategic plans are succeeding, if at all."

"I'm sure all of you remember from the *HBR* article that Kaplan and Norton recommend four key categories, each from a different perspective: customer perspective (how do customers perceive us?), internal business perspective (how are our internal processes performing?), innovation and learning (are we continuing to improve and able to add value to our customers?), and financial perspective (are we satisfying the needs of our stakeholders?)."

"As you may recall," Jamie chuckled, "I've been a little more than concerned about the last category, the financial perspective. Well, I have to admit that maybe focusing completely on the bottom line could be a mistake. The authors of the two reports make a good case for paying attention to the other categories as well, because they have a heavy impact on the financial category. It'll just be hard living with some lackluster financials and reconciling myself with new records for customer satisfaction."

"Excuse me, Jamie," interjected Kim. "I don't think the Balanced Scorecard concept says that the financial category is last. All the categories are on an equal footing, to be balanced. We shouldn't accept declining customer satisfaction even if accompanied by record earnings either. It just means we look at all four categories and try to manage the business by not improving one category at the expense of the others. Hopefully, we'll find that improving customer satisfaction goes hand in hand with improvements in the other categories. Isn't that how the rest of you view this?" Heads around the table nodded in agreement.

"Well, I guess I went a little too far," admitted Jamie. "That's absolutely right. You want to manage your business by reviewing and balancing all the categories. I think what brought me around to believing in the concept was the authors' distinguishing between outputs and output drivers, the items which drive or impact financial success. As a matter of fact, they are saying that financial measures, such as sales, profits, cash flow, return on investment, etc., are important, but by the time you put together your financial reports, those numbers are history. On the other hand, by following the progress of the drivers, such as customer satisfaction, we can act before it's too late."

"The authors have also found that companies which did well in the nonfinancial categories also met their financial objectives, over the long run. Perhaps I have been too focused on the immediate cash flow and the bottom line only because I'm the first person our suppliers call when the bills aren't paid on time."

"Assuming we want to use these four categories, and I think they are an excellent starting point, we need to establish goals within each category and determine the means of measuring progress toward those goals."

"Alex, didn't we just go through this last week when we developed measurements for how well we are meeting our strategic objectives?" an exasperated Jan queried. Everybody looked over to Alex, who was sitting at the side of the room up against the wall.

"Good question," Alex responded automatically. "Yes, we did develop many measurement points, but for different reasons. What we did last week was to figure out how to measure our performance in many of the key activities which must be accomplished well in order to achieve the strategic objectives. That resulted in many, many data collection points. You may recall, Jan, your anxiety about being overwhelmed with numbers. There is no way you could manage JTS by reviewing those various indicators on a regular basis, from the number of bugs reported to how many times our support reps were called by customers, office by office. Indeed, it was never in the equation that you would be studying that data regularly, unless you were focusing on one specific problem."

"Remember, the whole concept of the Balanced Scorecard is like the gauges on your car's dashboard, to give you a broad picture of the whole situation. Is the oil pressure where it should be? Is the cooling system working? You don't need to know the temperature of the oil or how many gallons are in the radiator, unless you have a problem. As a matter of fact, business intelligence software usually calls the Balanced Scorecard the *dashboard*."

"Fortunately, much of the data we collect for measuring key activities will also be useful for the Balanced Scorecard assessment. What you'll see each month, however, will be limited to a relatively few numbers in each category, telling you how JTS is doing. Is customer satisfaction getting better or worse? Are our internal or core processes functioning as they are supposed to? If you need to dig deeper, the data will be there. If that answers your question, Jan, perhaps Jamie can wrap up the presentation and we can break for lunch."

"Thanks, Alex," Jamie said, strolling to the front of the room. "Just so we don't think the Balanced Scorecard is exclusively for executives, let's not forget that the authors emphasize the importance of cascading the scorecard down through the organization. In so many words, this means that individual departments or offices will have their variations of the scorecard, tailored to their units, to the extent they impact the corporate scorecard. In effect, an office general manager's scorecard might balance his or her financial performance with the satisfaction of the office's own customers and the performance of the store's critical internal processes. The store may not measure innovation at all, since our research and marketing department has direct responsibility for developing new products and services. Of course, innovation will definitely be part of the corporate scorecard."

"I'm sure you noted some of the lessons learned by the various authors, including keeping the scorecard simple and making sure we consider the human elements in its rollout throughout the company. You know how nervous people are now about the new measurement system. Well, I can see the scorecard as throwing everyone for a further loop, saying in effect that JTS is putting customer satisfaction ratings on the same footing as the profit and loss. Some of our old-timers will have trouble stomaching this, particularly when their compensation plans are affected by their overall performance. Any more questions?"

Drew asked, "What was that about compensation?"

Before Jamie could answer, Jan took the floor. "You heard right, Drew. Our thinking is that if we're going to improve in these critical categories, we can't give lip service, saying we want to improve customer satisfaction but your bonus will depend on your meeting your sales or budget objective. Effective next quarter, all incentives and future evaluations will be tied to the scorecard."

Drew grinned and, referring to the sometimes temperamental Dade service manager, said, "Wait until Harper Bull hears about this!"

The group broke for lunch, where Alex sat with Jan and Kim. Alex admitted that the executives were looking a little overwhelmed, what with developing one set of measurements last week and then having to develop what appeared to be a parallel system, the Balanced Scorecard. There was no going back now, but perhaps they should have started with the Balanced Scorecard, developed appropriate measures, and then gradually added measurement points which were not part of the scorecard.

Following the lunch break, Alex thanked Jamie for the presentation and summarized the highlights. The group agreed to adopt the four key categories referred to by Kaplan and Norton. Certainly, success in each of these areas was absolutely essential to JTS' overall success. There was no question that financial results were driven by performance in the other categories. The four categories were:

1. Customer perspective
2. Internal business perspective
3. Innovation and learning perspective
4. Financial perspective

The next step in implementing the scorecard would be to set goals within each category and to establish measurements for each goal. For example, under the customer perspective category, JTS might establish goals relating to development and programming service quality, delivery or service time, and cost/value of percent of customers' business done with JTS. If the goal were at least 95% on-time delivery, then that would be measured from the customer's perspective (and not when the system was developed in a JTS office).

It took two weeks, but the executives finally developed their first Balanced Scorecard. The managers solicited input from their departmental colleagues, trying to involve them in the process as much as possible. The final scorecard, with the goals and measurements, is displayed in Table 7.2. Jan quickly distributed a memo to all employees, sharing the scorecard and the methodology behind it.

Table 7.2 Items in JTS Balanced Scorecard

Customer Perspective		Internal Business Perspective	
Goals	Measures	Goals	Measures
Be preferred provider Retain existing customers Meet commitments for development service Meet customer expectations for support service 95% customer satisfaction with value/pricing	Market share Sales trends Survey CSI: retention component Total bugs reported Total complaints Total support requests solved on first call CSI: pricing component	Increase productivity Develop and maintain outstanding quality and delivery of systems Involve employees in improving productivity in satisfying customers	Revenue vs number of employees CSI Summary Key process and quality indicators Percent of employees on teams Hours of training Employee survey
Innovation and Learning Perspective		Financial Perspective	
Goals	Measures	Goals	Measures
Introduce new development services to market Continue to improve customer satisfaction	Percent of sales from new development services Total development and programming services CSI Summary	Survive Succeed Prosper	Cash flow Monthly financial statements of revenue and expenses by office and department Return on investment

Once the data was collected and formatted into the Balanced Scorecard, it did not take long to ascertain where the scorecard was out of balance, or tilted. The executive council knew that the financial situation was headed in the wrong direction. While information about two categories (internal performance and innovation and learning) was still scarce, the customer perspective numbers were available, and they were alarming. If customer satisfaction were a key driver of financial results, Jan and Kim Peters were not going to sleep well any time soon.

The most difficult part of improving customer satisfaction was deciding where to start. Customers seemed unhappy about everything: pricing policies, credit plans, expertise and courtesy of the sales staff, support response,

response policies, development and programming quality, installation charges, etc. Jan began to wish for an earlier time when a Chicago service organization offered to buy out the company.

Setting Priorities

In their next meeting, Alex suggested to Jan and Kim that JTS could not undo all its bad practices with the snap of a finger. For long-lasting improvement, things had to be thought out and solved once and for all, but that would take time. The only way to proceed while maintaining sanity was to set priorities and attack the biggest problems first, throwing all the company's resources into the fray. Alex was reminded of a Japanese counselor's observation that trying to solve everything at once was like "… chasing too many rabbits. You don't catch any!"

From their surveys and discussions with JTS' customers and employees, it was clear to Alex and associates at KWB that the biggest customer satisfaction issue at JTS was not its pricing policy, but its support service department. It was agreed that all efforts should be focused there first. In addition to affecting the customer perspective category on the Balanced Scorecard, improving customer satisfaction to 95% percent was one of JTS' priority objectives. Without an effective and efficient support service department, that objective was unachievable.

Jan was relieved that the initial efforts would involve only the support service department since that would confine much of the initial training expenses to a relatively small portion of the company. While committed, Jan was still watching expenses pretty closely.

Implementation

Because JTS' support service departments were located throughout the country, KWB's strategy was to do all the training for the 14 service managers in Chicago, located centrally between the coasts. They would be introduced to the general concepts of customer satisfaction and, through improvement, shown how productivity could actually be improved. Training for second-level developers would focus on decision making and team participation. The service reps, who answered the initial phone call and recorded customers' problems, would be trained a few months later.

KWB continued to emphasize that Jan and Kim had to demonstrate their total support for the new way of doing things, a focus on customers and employee involvement, and that a successful culture change was as critical as using the new quality improvement methods and tools.

Initial Training

Seven support reps from the Miami service department were combined with eight from San Jose and six from Chicago for a week of training in September.

The five-day course included quality tools and techniques (Pareto Diagram, Fishbone Diagram, Brainstorming, etc.) and an introduction to the ten-step decision making methodology, the Ideal Decision Making Model (IDMM). The Ideal Decision Making Model employed a four-by-six-foot Storyboard on which each step was represented by a rectangle large enough to display appropriate documentation.

The principal advantages of the Storyboard were to provide a structure for teams while solving problems and to serve as a common communication vehicle. The Storyboard would be placed in a hallway or other common area for others in the department to view. The Ideal Decision Making Model ten-step process is shown in Figure 7.1.

Some training participants were skeptical; they wondered if their paychecks, or even their jobs, would be affected if productivity actually increased. A few remarked that this was not the first "great new program" they had heard about. Many were impressed but did not think management would really support their efforts. Ironically, in the training for service managers, the managers were skeptical that the support reps cared enough to get involved in making improvements. One very skeptical manager was Harper Bull, the Dade service manager.

When they returned to their service benches, the support reps found that their backlogs had doubled in their absence during their week of training; therefore, they did very little during the next ten days in the way of applying their new skills.

When the Dade support reps met for the first time as a team, they agreed to meet once a week (on Wednesdays) for an hour. The team members were Taylor Atkins, Robbie Suarez, Cameron Jacobson, Tommy Perkins, Irwin Katz, Janka Hawkins, and Chris Ingram. The team decided to call themselves the Electrons. Janka Hawkins was elected team leader. They unanimously agreed to follow the "Rules of the Road," suggested in the training class. The rules required that each person's ideas be respected, that everyone listen with an open mind, and that everyone was expected

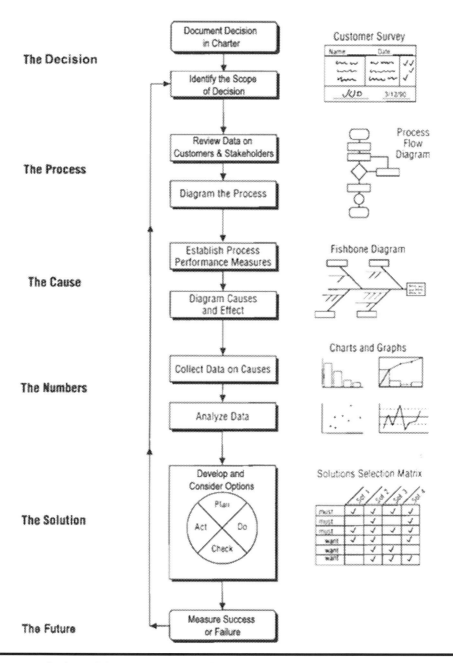

Figure 7.1 Ideal Decision Making Model.

to participate. A copy of the "Rules of the Road" poster is displayed in Figure 7.2.

Alex Martini of the KWB consulting firm was designated as the team's facilitator. Teams were formed at the other 13 JTS locations, but Alex was the only experienced facilitator. The other facilitators were trained in a three-day KWB workshop.

```
1. Attend all meetings on time
2. Keep an open mind to the ideas of others
3. Avoid interrupting
4. Participate
5. Speak with facts, avoid subjective opinions
6. Respect others
7. Give attention to whoever is speaking
8. Let everyone have his/her turn to speak
9. Suspend certainties
10. Share responsibility
```

Figure 7.2   Rules of the Road.

The Ten-Step Ideal Decision Making Model (IDMM) Begins

The teams each went through the model. Here we will detail the process for the Dade Service team.

Step 1: Document the Decision to Be Made in a Charter

Because top management had determined that improving the service department was the number one priority required to achieve 95% customer satisfaction, the Electrons' team charter was impacted. A charter states a team's reason for being, or the mission it is seeking to accomplish. During the course of a decision making team's activities, it is important that the team does not lose sight of its purpose.

At Alex's suggestion, Janka divided the team into two groups, A and B. Each team was responsible for drafting a charter statement. Group A focused on the technical issues ("improve support reps' skills so that support would be done more productively"). The other group had a broader scope ("improve service to all customers, whatever is required").

When the team met as one unit again, everyone acknowledged that a good statement lay somewhere between the two drafts, but they reached an impasse. Some members frequently changed their minds.

Finally, Alex suggested that they identify the attributes of an ideal support service department and try to determine the team's potential role in arriving at that ideal state. For each attribute, the team would brainstorm possible alternatives (if answering the phone promptly were a desirable attribute, alternatives might include adding more people to answer phones, a voice mail system to handle overflow calls, etc.). Using this Morphological

Forced Connection process, the team would then select various words from the alternative lists and "connect" them in novel ways, perhaps arriving at a good charter statement.

This unique exercise created a multitude of new ideas and finally resulted in the following charter statement for the Electrons:

> Our charter is to improve customer satisfaction through identifying key customer concerns about service, specifying the areas where we fail to address such concerns, and taking the responsibility for eliminating such failures systematically, within our service district. We will involve all employees at the company, as appropriate, in order to achieve this objective.

The charter statement was placed in the first rectangle on the four-by-six-foot IDMM Storyboard. Alex commented that the statement correlated well with the broader concept behind the Balanced Scorecard.

Step 2: Identify the Scope of the Decision

The Electrons team felt that the slowness of support (or perceived slowness) was what the team should try to improve. The team selected average support times for all requests as its principal indicator and chose to develop a trend line chart to track the indicator.

Tommy suggested that they should also try to improve reliability and cost, the other two customer concerns. Janka reminded the group that the decision making process, the IDMM, worked best if the team concentrated on fixing only a one problem at a time. Through communications between the Electrons and the management council, management would be informed of the scope. They could create additional teams to address other problem areas if they wished. Or this team could address them after the initial problem was resolved.

With the major area for improvement selected, the next question was to decide whether to stratify, or break down, the problem into more than one issue. Should all slow support times be lumped together? Could they all be solved in the same way? Were some types of support requests more critical to customers? Were long support times associated with only some technicians? Did some types of issues take longer to fix? Was the problem seasonal or based on the day of the week?

The team began to collect information on a Check Sheet, one of the five tools for measuring productivity (see Chapter 3). One of the pages from the team's Check Sheet is displayed in Figure 7.3.

158 ■ *Strategic Decision Making for Successful Planning*

Date	Day of Week	Cust #	Type of Issue	Tech Tier	Solution	Resolved	Time spent	Sessions To Resolved
30-Aug	Monday	685	Finding Menu	1	Showed correct menu	Y	1 hr	1
30-Aug	Monday	875	Broken Monitor	1	Installed new monitor	Y	1 hr	1
30-Aug	Monday	340	Bug in Menu	3		N	2.6 hr	
30-Aug	Monday	476	Finding Menu	2	Showed correct menu	Y	0.5 hr	1
30-Aug	Monday	340	Bug in Mobile	3		N	+15 hr	
30-Aug	Monday	365	Wrong Driver	4	Installed new driver	Y	0.5 hr	1
30-Aug	Monday	685	Finding Menu	1	Showed correct menu	Y	0.7 hr	1
31-Aug	Tuesday	354	Bug in Menu	4		N	67 hr	
31-Aug	Tuesday	235	Bug in Mobile	4		N	23 hr	
31-Aug	Tuesday	567	Bug in Report	4		N	29 hr	
31-Aug	Tuesday	564	Bug in Query	3		N	56 hr	
31-Aug	Tuesday	354	Bug in Menu	1		N	+43 hr	
1-Sep	Wednesday	678	Finding Report	2	Showed correct report	Y	2 hr	1
1-Sep	Wednesday	237	Problem with Query	2	Revised query	Y	4 hr	1
1-Sep	Wednesday	475	Permissions Issue	2	Revised permissions	Y	1.5 hr	1
1-Sep	Wednesday	237	Finding Menu	1	Showed correct menu	Y	1 hr	1
1-Sep	Wednesday	235	Bug in Mobile	3	Fixed bug	Y	+8.7 hr	25
1-Sep	Wednesday	486	Finding Report	1	Showed correct report	Y	0.5 hr	1
1-Sep	Wednesday	567	Bug in Report	3		N	+12 hr	
15-Sep	Wednesday	354	Bug in Menu	2	Fixed bug	N	+34 hr	14
15-Sep	Wednesday	287	Wrong Driver	3	Installed new driver	Y	0.7 hr	1

Highlighted issue is still unresolved
+ means multiple sessions on same issue

Number of resolved issues	345
Number of unresolved issues	205
Number resolved on first call	278
Average calls per issue	3.4
Average sessions per issue	8.34

Compiled by Chris Ingram
Roberto Suarez

Figure 7.3 Check Sheet: Support Calls for Two Weeks.

The training class had stressed that as part of the IDMM, data needed to be collected, analyzed, and stratified from different perspectives to determine if there was a significant pattern. Instead of looking at all long support responses, maybe certain types accounted for the majority (the Pareto principle or 80-20 rule). According to the Pareto principle, a relatively low number of types of causes (20%) may account for a disproportionate number of problems (80%). By looking for such disparities, considerable improvement in an overall situation can be achieved by eliminating just one of the causes.

The first few Pareto Diagrams indicated no pattern. It did not seem to matter which technician performed the support service, what type of service needed support, what type of support was given, or on which day of the week the call for support came in. However, the fifth Pareto Diagram told a different story. The Pareto Diagram is shown in Figure 7.4. It became apparent that while slow support had a number of causes, the top cause of lengthy support times was due to programming bugs. Programming bugs are when the code developed is supposed to do one thing, but either it doesn't do it, or it does something else. It looked like the number of bugs reported was a huge influencer in the number of support requests and that bugs took an inordinate amount of time to fix—many remaining unresolved after dozens of hours of time spent. Furthermore, by reviewing which customers were calling about the bugs, it was obvious that bugs often required multiple calls from the same customer to be addressed. Since bugs were what caused a great deal of the support calls, decreasing the number of bugs would improve on the resolution time and might produce the biggest

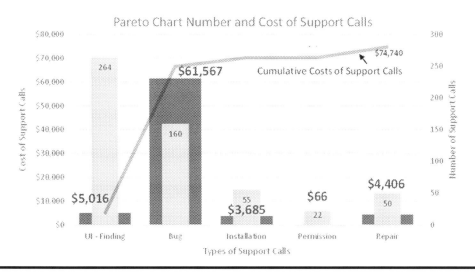

Figure 7.4   Pareto Diagram of Support Calls.

productivity boost. Another chart, a Histogram, was chosen to track the number bugs reported, and those types of calls were stratified for analysis.

Taylor added that nothing could be a worse situation than taking several days, weeks, or months to fix a bug. No wonder customers were unhappy.

Following their decision making methodology, the IDMM, the team developed a problem statement. They tried to be as specific as possible about the nature of the problem. The statement read:

> The top reason for the volume of support calls was the User Interface (UI), where 48% of the calls were from people who could not find what they were looking for in the menus, queries, and reports. But the top reason for *unresolved or long-delay resolution* of support calls was *bugs* because the length of time to fix the bugs. Fixing bugs was far more costly.

A clear definition of the problem would focus the team's efforts to solve the problem. As Alex remarked, "A problem well-described is half solved!"

Since the team was given the goal of increasing the number of support calls that were solved on the first call, it became increasingly apparent that they needed to do something about the number of bugs. Chris wondered if the one-call target was too ambitious. How could they possibly meet that when bugs took an average of over 52 hours to fix?

They considered removing bugs from the list of types, and applying the one-call goal only to support issues that were solvable within one call. "But how would that help the customer?" asked Janka. "Wouldn't they still be waiting weeks or months for a solution—if they ever get one considering the number of still unresolved requests?" The rest of the group had to agree.

Except for Taylor. "All software has bugs. The customers just have to get used to it. We can't do anything about the number of bugs or the time to fix them."

Tommy nodded; "And how do we know that this issue is the top issue? More calls come in because people can't find things. They aren't properly trained, obviously. Maybe that's more important to them." After some further conversation, the team decided to go to the horse's mouth and find out what was, and was not, important to the customers. That would give them a clear indication of priority between the high number of UI-related support calls and the high cost of bug related support calls.

Step 3: Review Data on Customers and Stakeholders

Cameron had gathered some additional data, going back to the beginning of 1998, and found that the average JTS support time ran between one and four days for the first ten years. After that, the number of days slowly ticked up until it reached the current 35.6 days, as shown in Figure 7.5. Obviously, some support requests were taking even longer than that!

Some team members were shocked that the number of days had increased so drastically over the years—and that no one had noticed it. Cameron noted; "Maybe it's like the frog in the hot pot of water; the heat increases so gradually and it takes so long to notice that the water is approaching boiling that the frog never thinks to jump out."

The group brainstormed over 40 potential reasons for the increase. They continued the discussion until they could agree with the following list of top five reasons:

- Increased complexity of technology
- Lower level techs hired for both programming and support calls
- Increased pressure from sales to release software that had not met specifications
- Decrease in the quality testing budget
- Increased sophistication of end user who were more vocal about issues

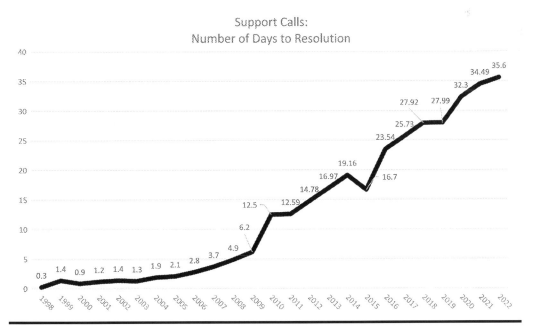

Figure 7.5 Historical Average Days for Support Call Resolution.

Data was available from several sources to determine customers' concerns and needs. JTS had an accumulation of letters and other comments about its support service; most were negative. Many of the service personnel had long-lasting recollections of numerous problems. Most of these data were not organized or compiled, but simply filed in cabinets with support requests.

With Alex's help, the team designed a two-part survey that would be given to each support service customer during the next 30 days, beginning November 1. The first part asked customers to rate their concerns regarding support service on a scale of 1 to 5, where 5 indicated extremely concerned. A total of eight items were listed for rating, including the friendliness, courtesy, and knowledge of the support representative, time to resolution, costs involved if any, etc. The second part of the survey sought customers' opinions about how well JTS was performing in each of the eight categories, based on a scale of 1 to 5, where 1 indicated extremely poorly.

The two parts of the survey would tell the team not only what JTS was doing poorly (and well), but the degree to which such poor (or good) performance mattered to customers. Because they were asking the same questions from two different perspectives (concerns versus how well), the answers would not be influenced by the direction of the questions, so that the underlying experiences were more accurately reflected in the data.

At Irwin's suggestion, the team agreed to call at random 200 customers who had called for support in the past 30 days (during October) and ask them the same questions. The telephone sample would be designated Sample Y and the other survey Sample X.

All the team members participated in the survey. A major problem was the failure of a few support service reps (who were not on the Electrons team) to solicit feedback from every customer. After Janka complained, Harper Bull, the service manager, reluctantly ordered the reps to survey all customers. Harper was still a little more than miffed about the bonus package being tied to customer satisfaction rather than productivity, as it was in the past. More surveys were produced, but this alienated some employees (and a few customers who did not want to take the time to answer questions).

Taylor, Irwin, and Chris were responsible for compiling and analyzing the survey, which produced the following results:

1. A total of 347 customers were surveyed, 187 in Sample X and 160 in Sample Y (the telephone surveys).
2. The responses from both groups surveyed were virtually identical.

3. Using Pareto Diagrams, Taylor, Irwin, and Chris documented the findings. Both samples indicated that the time for bug fixes was the chief customer concern (68.02% and 70.32%, respectively, out of all possible concerns) and that JTS deserved the low grade it got for its consistently slow support times. The combined Pareto Diagram is displayed in Figure 7.6.

In the telephone surveys (Sample Y), Irwin said that once it was clear that the time to fix bugs was a problem, they began asking customers what they thought was an acceptable time. While 15% of those surveyed said that a week was acceptable, 65% thought that two working days was the absolute maximum, and 17% indicated one day. Some customers said that the answer depended on the type of bug.

Other team members stated that the "explosion point" for most customers seemed to be about three days, even if they were told in advance that the bug fix would take longer.

Additionally, Tommy and some team members were curious as to why the number of support calls they get for the User Interface was so voluminous, but few of the customers cited that as a concern. So, they asked a few of the customers about it. The consensus seemed to be that, while additional training and better documentation might help, getting a live person to

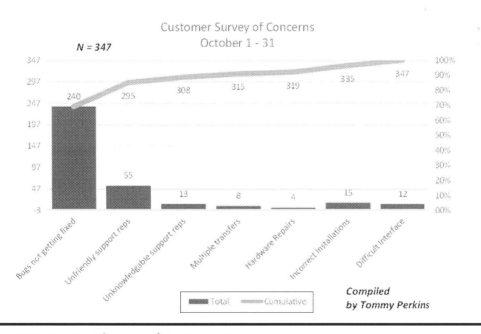

Figure 7.6 Pareto Diagram of Customer Concerns.

simply tell the customer where to find what they were looking for appeared to be a "bonus," a positive, rather than a negative. Indeed, the most positive reviews came from people who had called to get help finding something or learning how to do something they didn't know how to do. Some people went on and on about how helpful the support staff was, and how much they appreciated their patient guidance. Unfriendly support reps did garner 15% of the concerns, but the interface received less than 4% of the concerns despite the fact that those calls constituted 48% of the support calls.

The team discussed all of this at the following meeting. Janka wasn't sure of the next step. "Where do we go from here, Alex?"

Alex answered "Well, we have definitely uncovered that the customers are happy when they call for help with the interface, and unhappy when they call for help with bugs. And the internal cost of answering those two types of support calls are clear. But what do your senior leaders think? Have you asked them?"

So Janka set up a 15-minute meeting the following week with Jan, Kim, Baker, Jamie, Norma, and Drew, the executive team. After explaining the findings of the group, the executive team was asked to provide their opinion. After much discussion, the upshot was that the executive team ...

- Was highly concerned about the volume of calls on the interface and the cost of those calls
- Even more concerned about the even higher cost of the calls on bugs

"There's no excuse for those bugs!" railed Jan. "The programmers who release buggy code should be fired! Heads will roll!"

Drew, apparently familiar with outbursts from Jan, tried to calm things down. "Jan, be realistic here. It's not usually the programmer's fault that they are forced to release buggy code. Sales is often adamant that the code be released on time, even when the scope for the development has changed. And the testing department has lost three quality control testers and they haven't been replaced for the past 10 months."

"We can't help it if the customer still wants the completed system implemented even if they change the scope," Baker chimed in.

"And we can't afford to hire more people. Quality control seemed to be the best place to cut costs so that we can stay afloat," remarked Jamie.

Norma added, "We also had to cut the training staff and offer less documentation and training than we had in years past. Often, our documentation reflects the previous version of the software instead of the current version. That might be why so many people have to call in to find things."

While it became very obvious that there were many issues to consider, Janka tried to bring the discussion back to the specific decision at hand. "While we understand that both of these are concerns, the team needs to focus on one of them, at least at first. We can either figure out the root causes of the high volume of UI calls, or figure out the root causes of the number of bugs in order to decrease those types of calls. What we are looking for is input from you as to which one we should focus on."

Jamie's answer was swift, "We are losing over $67,000 a month because of those calls related to the bugs. There is no question that we need to focus on that." While heads nodded around the room, Janka appeared to get the answer needed to go back to the team.

Step 4: Define and Diagram the Process

After the meeting, completing Step 3 of their IDMM, the documentation was posted on the storyboard, and the Electrons moved onto the next step—documenting the existing process. How was the JTS service department releasing and tracking buggy code now?

Although there were quality control procedures, there was no comprehensive description of the process from code release to post-implementation. Since the team members worked in the service department, they had the best understanding of the current code release and implementation processes, even when those processes did not equate with prescribed procedures.

Following the IDMM process, the team began to develop a process flow diagram, or Flowchart, to show all the activities that occur from the moment a customer calls to report a bug until the time the customer is satisfied that the bug has been fixed satisfactorily.

There are many advantages to using a Flowchart. First, a Flowchart is a visual representation that shows the linkage of all key activities, something verbal descriptions often fail to achieve. With a Flowchart, it is easier to identify critical points, such as when people have to make decisions (which can lead to delays) and when certain activities must be accomplished before other activities, or processes, can begin. Measurement points can be placed on the Flowchart to assess whether the process is operating properly and is in control.

Through the exercise of developing a Flowchart, a team or individual gains insight into its current process. Team members often identify various "what if" scenarios that may not have occurred to other team members.

Working with Post-Its, the Electrons team brainstormed all of the steps and activities they thought occurred between the time a customer first calls JTS through completion of the support service. One Post-It was used for each activity. The reason for using Post-Its is they allow for flexibility if team members change their minds about the sequence of steps.

Janka suggested that for the time being, they identify the process from a macro or global standpoint (i.e., the "big picture"). Once the process was documented, they would take each major activity and develop micro Flowchart steps. For example, in the earlier stages of flowcharting, they would not get into details such as describing what occurs when a customer reports a bug that turns out not to be a bug. Rather, the Flowchart would succinctly state: "start bug fix process." The macro description might also indicate that the "tech contacts customer," rather than several mini-activities, such as "look up customer contact, review system coded, log into system," etc.

Two meetings were required for the Electrons to develop the macro Flowchart and reach consensus that it was a true representation. They identified six key macro activities:

- Customer needs a form, report, query, or some other information from the system that they are not able to get.
- Support Service rep takes customer call, writes up support request, and identifies the area of the system involved.
- Developer is assigned.
- Developer contacts customer.
- Developer fixes bug.
- New code is released, customer satisfied.

Not reflected on the macro chart were everyday occurrences, such as what occurred when no developers were available to be assigned, when the developer could not locate the source of the bug, when the bug fix could not be completed in one session, or when there was a scheduling problem. The macro Flowchart is displayed in Figure 7.7.

The next step was for the team to create a detailed, or micro, Flowchart showing these types of everyday occurrences. One difficulty was determining the degree of detail to include so as not to get bogged down. Within

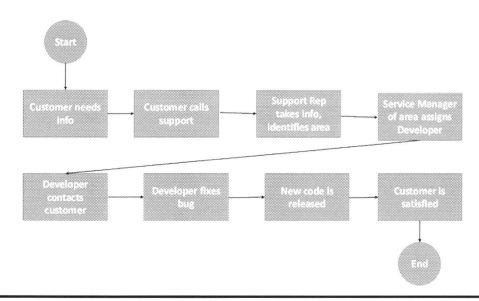

Figure 7.7 Macro-Level Flowchart of Bug Fix Request.

micro activities lay sub-micro activities, and there was a tendency to want to include every possible scenario. The team's micro Flowchart is shown in Figure 7.8.

The micro Flowchart included numerous diamonds, or decision points, that reflected various alternative sequences. As a sanity check, the team had some of the nonteam members review the Flowchart to ensure that it was accurate and easily understandable. Harper Bull, the service manager, said that the process flow diagram "looked OK."

Alex complimented Janka and the team on their high level of cooperation and their progress up to that point. (Sometimes people in the same department can have major disagreements about how they perform their work, which adds to the time taken to develop such a chart.)

Step 5: Establish the Process Performance Measures and Targets

Janka reviewed the IDMM Storyboard and pointed out that the team was almost to the half-way point in its journey. The Storyboard contained all of the documentation for the first four steps. The team then had to decide which points in the process flow diagrams were critical, where measurement points would be established, and those places where data had to be collected and analyzed.

Before proceeding, Alex pointed out that the process of constructing a Flowchart was a good example of why a team benefits from following a

168 ■ *Strategic Decision Making for Successful Planning*

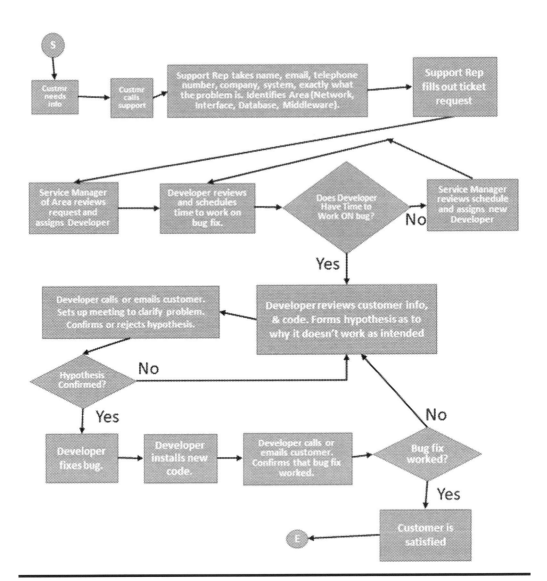

Figure 7.8 Micro-Level Flowchart of Bug Fix Request.

structured decision making process. Without a Flowchart (which shows visually all of the activities involved in making bug fixes), the team would have been only guessing about what to measure. It might have measured the wrong things, which were not necessarily critical to improving fix time. For example, while the number of times the service phone rings before being answered may be important for other reasons, the extra few seconds does not significantly impact the total bug fix time.

As Janka approached the Flowchart (which ran the length of the 17-foot meeting room), Tommy wondered why they needed additional measures.

After all, the team knew that bug fixes were averaging over 50 days. It was up to the team to improve that number down to one day, wasn't it? A few other members looked similarly befuddled. Janka glanced at Alex, a little unsure about what to say next.

Cameron, who had taken several quality improvement courses, asked to respond. Cameron acknowledged that while Tommy was absolutely right, that their goal was to achieve 95% of the target (which was one day, not 50 days), the total bug fix time was an outcome indicator or "Q" indicator (for quality). Unfortunately, outcome indicators are necessarily after the fact; they do not provide any information about what is happening before the end result.

What Step 5 is about, Cameron stated, is developing meaningful measurements, known as process indicators, that tell more about a process, so the process can be modified it if it is not operating properly. For example, the team might want to measure the time between requests for support service and assignment of a developer, or the time necessary to schedule the bug fix, or how many times developers are reassigned because they do not have time in their schedule to look at the code.

Obviously, not every point on the Flowchart needs to be measured. What the team had to do, Cameron summarized, was to select critical points, or milestones. With more data, the team would be on its way to analyzing the causes of late bug fix times. Once the improvements were implemented and proved successful, these key measurement points would be required to monitor the steps in the process.

At Janka's suggestion, the team began establishing measurement points on the process flow diagram. They agreed to put a Post-It with a large "P" at any point suggested by a team member as long as he or she made it clear what would be measured (days, minutes, number of occurrences or failures) and why it might be important. Once all the process or "P" indicators were posted, the team would evaluate the overall importance of each one. Another factor was the relative difficulty of collecting the measurements.

Irwin suggested that, depending upon their analysis, the team might have to establish further measurement points once they had identified key problem areas.

After four meetings, an exhausted team agreed on the following process measures:

- Number of calls regarding bug fixes
- Number of such calls where time was critical

- Number of calls where customer apparently knew which area of the system had the problem
- Number of calls when customer was uncertain about problem ("doesn't work")
- Time to make assignment to developer
- Number of times developer did not have time to be scheduled when needed
- Number of bug fixes per day per developer
- Number of bug fixes for the same customer
- Average time of bug fix
- Number of times developer had the wrong hypothesis
- Number of times developer fixed problem, but customer did not believe the problem was fixed, requiring a second attempt to fix the bug
- Number of bugs fixed on first attempt
- Number of bugs not fixed on first attempt
- Number of bugs fixed but requiring more attempts
- Number of attempts required for bug fixes needing more than one attempt
- List of categories why bugs were not fixed on first attempt (wrong hypothesis, replacement code incorrect, additional problems caused by code, etc.)
- Average days to bug fix
- Number of times customer was mistaken about area for problem
- Number of times developer completed bug fix within one day, compared to total number of bugs fixed

While not all team members agreed with these measurements (some members wanted more points), they agreed that these measurements would provide much more information than they had previously. As the IDMM proceeded, they thought that they could always develop more, particularly as the search for problem areas intensified. The 19 measurements were reviewed against the Flowchart, and exactly when in the process the information could be collected was noted. The points were designated by "Ps," as shown in Figure 7.9. They were:

P1: Number of time-critical calls
P2: Number of calls with area of system (certain or uncertain) and for same customer

Integrated Case Study ■ 171

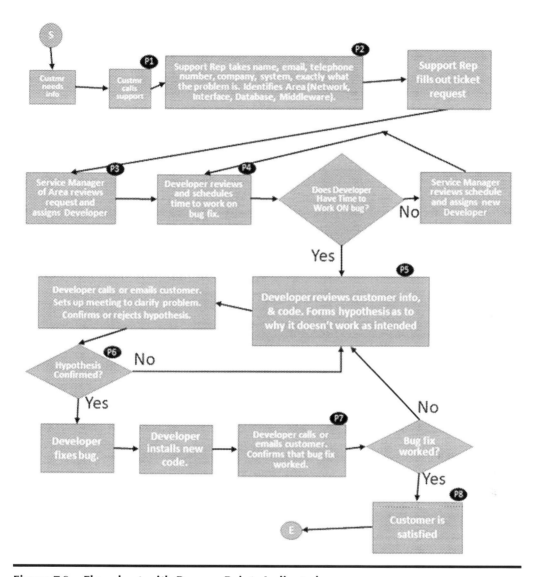

Figure 7.9 Flowchart with Process Points Indicated.

P3: Time to make assignment to developer
P4: Number of times developer did not have time to be scheduled when needed
P5: Number of bug fixes per day per developer
P6: Number of times developer had wrong hypothesis
P7: Number of times customer did not agree problem was solved
P8: Average days to fix bug

The "Q" indicators, reflecting the output (or end result of the process), are listed here:

Q1: Total number of bug fix requests
Q2: Total time to fix bug from call to completion
Q3: Percent of bugs fixed correctly the first time

These indicators measure the success of the bug fix process from the customer's perspective. The customer is much more interested in having the bugs fixed correctly the first time (an outcome) than whether the service manager takes too long to assign a developer.

Collecting the data would be very useful in verifying the team's determination of the root causes and would be the basis for assessing whether improvements were actually made.

Alex signaled to Janka that the measurement points they selected looked good and that the team could consider Step 5 to be completed.

Step 6: Diagram the Causes and Effects

The team was then prepared to analyze the possible causes. Tommy and Taylor said that they already had the answer—that developers often had to work on new customer projects and could not drop everything to fix bugs from previously completed projects—especially if they weren't the developer on the original project. No one should expect them to be able to fix a bug created by another developer. Robbie, who was a developer, disagreed; the service manager assigned developers in accordance with their experience on the project with the bug.

Janka refocused the group on the process and reviewed the cause-and-effect shown in the Fishbone Diagram (Figure 7.10). The problem statement was inserted into the head of the fish (the "effect"). The team agreed there were several generic categories, or bones, any of which could have caused the late bug fixes. The generic bones were people (developers, support reps, service managers), areas (network, interface, database, middleware), the environment (customer systems), and methods (procedures, forms, diagnostic process).

The team decided to group these major generic bones into four major ones: people (developers/support reps/service managers), areas, environment, and methods. Starting with each major bone, the team brainstormed the possible root causes. It was important to ask "why" enough times to assure that

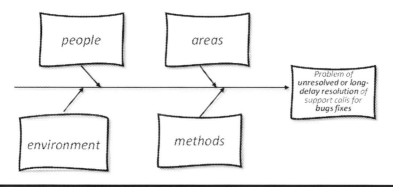

Figure 7.10 Fishbone Diagram: Major Bones.

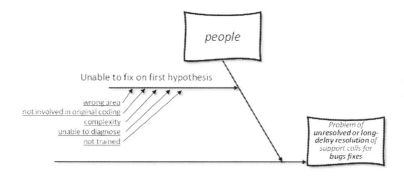

Figure 7.11 Fishbone Diagram: People Bone.

they were not just identifying symptoms. After all, if they fixed only a symptom, the problem would resurface someday. For example, if a developer was identified as the reason the problem occurred, it was important to ask why the developer ("people") failed to fix the bug on time. If the explanation was that the developer made the wrong hypothesis, it was important to determine why he or she made the wrong hypothesis, and so on.

With the first major bone, the team asked "why" several times. There were several bones off the major "people" bone, including "unable to fix on first hypothesis." Following that path, the team identified several smaller bones, including "not trained, wrong area, not involved in original coding, complexity, unable to diagnose" (see Figure 7.11).

Taking one of the minor bones, "wrong areas," the team went further down that bone and brainstormed several "whys," including "customer wrong about area." The next "why" was "customer not knowledgeable," which may have been the result of "customer not asked right questions." Why was that? There might be several reasons, which would include "rep didn't ask right questions," which may have been the result of "inadequate training of reps" or the fact that reps were not always involved in coding. This portion of the people bone is shown in Figure 7.12.

Tommy suggested that the main problem was because the customer did not provide the right information, but Robbie reminded everyone that they were not supposed to ask "why" beyond their area of control. They could control what questions to ask the customer, but they could not control what the customer might volunteer.

Having identified what they believed to be the root causes for the "people" bone, the team highlighted (clouded) the items for emphasis. This is shown in Figure 7.13.

The team then asked "why" regarding the other major bones (procedures, equipment, and methods) and found essentially the same root causes, all of which were related to obtaining incomplete information when the customer first called due to lack of training or questions first asked, or the developers who understood the code were not available, and the documentation was not sufficient. These root causes were highlighted (clouded) as well.

The team observed that often multiple attempts to fix the bug were required because the right developer was not initially available, or the wrong

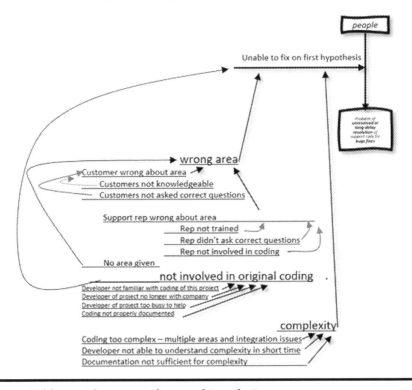

Figure 7.12   Fishbone Diagram: Subpart of People Bone.

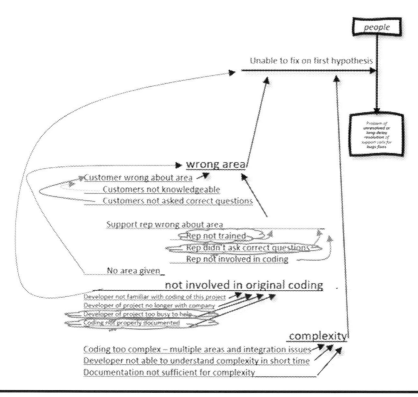

Figure 7.13 Fishbone Subpart of People Bone with Root Causes (Cloud).

area for the bug was initially noted, or the documentation was incomplete. These scenarios were prolonging the average time for a fix because multiple hypotheses meant multiple contacts with the customer. Furthermore, there was no quality control of the bug fixes, so the bug fix for one call often caused bugs in another part of the code. But more often, the problem was that the original area was not properly described so the bug got assigned to the wrong developer.

Robbie, who often fixed bugs, expressed adamant agreement. Most of the time (noted in an exasperated voice), the only instruction on the service order was that the "system didn't work." The form did not require more information and the support service reps did not ask for more details. And, Robbie sighed, customers did not understand, because they felt that they had "explained everything that was wrong to the rep!"

With its preliminary analysis of the root cause completed, the team needed to verify its conclusion with hard data by examining the process performance measurements it had been collecting. This verification would take place in Step 7.

Step 7: Collect Data on Causes

The information gathered through the process performance measurements was invaluable. While team members had ample first-hand knowledge of the situation, evidenced by their cause-and-effect diagram, they could not be certain of their conclusion until they looked at the numbers.

Before agreeing to any changes the team recommended, particularly the expenditure of money, management wanted to see supporting data. Since the beginning of the quality effort at JTS, management was prone to remind everybody to "speak with facts."

Charts were prepared by the team, displaying the number of bugs that were fixed in the 60-day monitoring period, sorted by the length of time it took to fix the bug. Bug fixes were segmented by the possible reasons, which included wrong area identified, incomplete details on form, developer not available, documentation not sufficient, and "other."

Bar charts were also prepared for all bug fixes. The first one compared bug fixes completed within a single call to those that took longer and/or are still incomplete. The latter comprised 91%! As Robbie had suggested, many support service orders merely stated "system doesn't work."

On another chart, relating to incomplete information, the form was further analyzed. In addition to the cryptic "system doesn't work," other omitted information included the screen the customer was on when they encountered the problem, the information they had input, and the information they received as output, as well as how it differed from what they expected to see.

Step 8: Analyze Data

Cameron suggested that the team employ a Scatter Diagram, a quality control tool, to plot the relationship between incomplete information regarding the problem description and the late bug fixes, to see if a correlation existed.

Data was grouped according to the length of time for the fix and the amount of incomplete information as a percentage. If the team's assessment was correct, there would be a high correlation between the two types of data.

The paired data (88%, 30 days; 67%, 40 days; 74%, 30 days; etc.) was plotted on a Scatter Diagram and an almost perfect correlation was displayed, at a 45-degree angle. The higher the percentage of incomplete data (the

X axis), the longer the bug fix took (Y axis). There seemed no doubt that incomplete information resulted in developers frequently having to make multiple hypotheses, which made it virtually impossible to achieve bug fixes within two days. The team's Scatter Diagram is shown in Figure 7.14.

With its root cause analysis verified, the team began the next step: reducing or eliminating that cause.

Step 9: Develop and Consider Possible Options

Having identified and verified the possible root cause, the Electrons team considered various options to solve the problem once and for all.

Janka referred to the IDMM Storyboard which contained the "mini-steps" of each of the major ten steps. In Step 9, the process of developing and selecting a solution is related to the PDCA (Plan-Do-Check-Act) cycle.

The team would "plan" and select which solutions to employ to eliminate the root cause of the problem. They would then implement ("do") the selected solution or solutions. In the "check" mode, the team would assess whether the solution(s) were effective (i.e., did they reduce or eliminate the root cause). Finally, they would "act" to change the solution or, if effective, assure that the solution continued to be used (i.e., standardize it).

Before implementing any solutions, the team would make a presentation to the management council to formally communicate the team's IDMM and to obtain management approval.

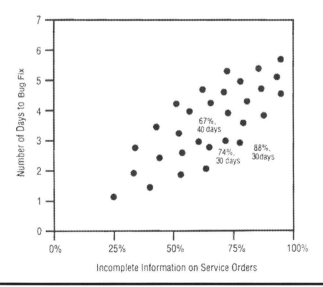

Figure 7.14 Relationships between Incomplete Info and Long Delay.

Plan: Selecting Potential Solutions

In the plan stage, the Electrons looked at several different sources of information. Janka urged the team to keep an open mind about possible solutions. They might consider some ideas that could create a breakthrough, or radical improvement, rather than simply speeding up the bug fix time. One way of thinking, as they gathered information, was based on the concept of "Idealized Design," or identifying the ideal or perfect situation (i.e., immediate bug fix) and working backwards to determine what must be done to arrive at that ideal state.

Robbie and Taylor interviewed several managers who had been with JTS for several years, some of whom used to be in the service department. With no ownership in the current process, these managers might have some valuable input.

Jan was a good friend of the owner of Star Systems, a similar technology development firm in Cleveland, Ohio. With Jan's approval, Irwin and Cameron spent a day with Star Systems' service manager, Karen Roos. They did an abbreviated form of benchmarking to observe and learn how Start Systems' managed to fix bugs on the first call 98% of the time.

Chris researched industry trade journals and various electronic publications to learn if there were any innovative solutions which future technology might offer. Chris readily applied the "Idealized Design" concept. Chris's approach was that the only ideal solution was instantaneous bug fix. In Chris's mind, there had to be a way to accomplish it, although Chris didn't have the foggiest notion how that might happen—yet.

Janka called several programmers' trade organizations (Computer Professionals Organization, TechSpeed, Computer Technology Associates, Information Technology Association) for any input they might provide. The organizations might have statistics on which areas were most likely to have issues, so that JTS could hire more people in those areas.

Tommy spent two hours per day monitoring incoming service calls and interviewing the support service reps. Since they received customers' support requests, they might have some ideas about how to improve the process. Tommy also spoke to the sales department managers to get their feedback and bounce some ideas off of them.

These activities occupied the team for three weeks. During this period, the team did not meet formally.

At the next meeting, each member gave a brief report. Janka suggested that the team list the various ideas on a flipchart. Some ideas might stimulate new ideas. The list would also lead to a structured evaluation of the ideas.

Over 75 ideas were brainstormed, ranging from hiring a special bug-fix group (which could specialize in troubleshooting) to having developers communicate directly with customers (instead of support service reps).

After rehashing these ideas for five hours in an extended meeting, the Electrons multi-voted to reduce the list of 75 ideas to a more manageable number. They agreed on the following seven ideas:

1. Redesign the support service form, with a checklist so that the service reps would be more likely to ask the optimum questions when customers called.
2. Provide special training for the service reps so they would know more about the different areas which might be causing the problems, which would allow them to ask more probing questions.
3. Designate certain people to specialize in bug fixing so that they would always be accessible.
4. Designate certain people in each area to be available for bug fixes.
5. Identify which developer worked on the customer system and directly connect that developer with the customer immediately.
6. Designate one developer to do all bug fixes.
7. Probably the most unique idea, presented by Chris based on the research, was to install remote connection software, which would allow the customer service representative and the developer to see exactly what the customer sees, eliminating the time-consuming task of trying to explain which screen and which item was causing the problem. Chris pointed out that no one else employed this type of system at the initial support contact level, and it would be a great marketing advantage. If this were not an Ideal Design, Chris implored, it was the next best thing.

The exhausted team members agreed that they should wait until the next meeting before evaluating the seven possible solutions.

Plan: Selecting a Solution

During the first 20 minutes of the next meeting, Janka reviewed the IDMM process the team would use to make its selection. The team would not know for certain whether a solution was effective until it was implemented and the results checked, but it was important to use a structured methodology to choose the proposed solutions.

Janka displayed the solutions selection matrix. On the left-hand side of the three-by-five-foot poster, the team was to list the seven proposed

180 ■ *Strategic Decision Making for Successful Planning*

solutions. Each solution would be evaluated and rated by the team according to three criteria: (1) the extent to which the solution was effective and would eliminate the root cause of the problem; (2) whether the solution was practical from the standpoint of cost, the time required to implement it, and how difficult it would be to employ; and (3) the degree to which the solution represented a real value to customers. The poster included a column to represent each of the criteria and a fourth column in which the total of the ratings for each proposed solution could be entered. The fifth column would indicate whether the proposed solution would be analyzed further ("Go"). The team's matrix is displayed in Figure 7.15.

The criteria for each proposed solution were to be rated on a scale of 1 to 10, the latter being the highest (i.e., best or most effective). When all three criteria had been rated for each solution, the ratings would be multiplied. The top score would be 1000 (10 × 10 × 10). Once the ratings were completed, the three or four solutions with the highest scores would be analyzed further. Janka pointed out that it would be a waste of resources to analyze all seven solutions in detail. The matrix would allow the team to narrow the choices down, based on the best combination of effectiveness, practicality, and customer satisfaction, using their collective experience.

Before beginning the rating process, Janka reminded everyone that the scores should reflect the team's consensus, following ample discussion of logic and facts. In particular, Janka said that the team should not vote or average the ratings. If two people disagreed, there had to be a reason for the difference,

Potential Solutions	Effectiveness	Practicality	Customer Value	Total	Comments	Go/No Go
Support Service Form Checklist	6	6	5	180	Difficult to capture issues on a checklist.	
Special Training for Support Service Reps	7	8	6	336	Training would enable better area identification	G
Designate specialized bug fix team	8	3	7	168	Some people good at troubleshooting, others not. Would enable those who are good to specialize in it.	
Designate certain people from each area to	9	8	5	360	Sometimes the area is critical; a database problem can't be diagnosed by a web developer.	G
Directly connect developer with customer	10	5	10	500	Only the original coder can swiftly look at an issue and diagnose it without a lot of research. But developers' job is to work on new projects, and they hate to interrupt what they are doing to fix previously developed code.	G
Designate full time bug fixer	5	2	6	60	Full time bug fixer would be great, until they got overwhelmed by bugs and need more help. Also, this would take away a developer working on paying projects.	
Install Remote Connection software	10	4	9	360	Remote connection software might cut down a lot of the back and forth and increase hypothesis accuracy.	G

Figure 7.15 Solutions Selection Matrix. Scale of 1–10.

which needed to be discussed. Janka pointed to the "Rules of the Road" poster, which called upon everyone to participate and keep an open mind.

Irwin recalled from the training session that it would be less confusing to rate each solution against each of the others, applying one criterion at a time. The seven solutions would be compared to each other from an effectiveness standpoint. The most effective would receive a "10" and the others a lesser rating. Each of the seven would then be rated in terms of practicality and then from a customer value standpoint. The rest of the Electrons agreed that this approach made sense.

Effectiveness

Once the seven potential solutions were entered on the matrix, the team began assessing the effectiveness of each. While Chris's suggestion to install monitoring systems seemed a little atypical, the team agreed that it was probably the most effective solution since the tech would always know what the problem was, assuming that the monitoring system was functioning properly. Accordingly, the team agreed to rate the suggestion a "10." Janka pointed out that the number itself was not as important as the fact that the other ratings would be in relation to it. The practicality (and cost) of the suggestion would be considered later.

The team agreed that the least effective method would be to designate a full-time bug fixer. Not only would it be difficult to find someone who was familiar enough with all the areas AND familiar enough with the previous projects AND was really good at fixing bugs, but it would take one of the developers completely out of action for development, the bread and butter of the company (though that last one was really an issue of practicality, not effectiveness). While Cameron and Tommy thought that this solution rated a "3" for effectiveness, they finally agreed with the others and reached consensus on a rating of "5."

The Electrons finished the "effectiveness" portion of the matrix in one meeting. If they had any difficulty, it was the tendency to consider the cost of the solution, but Irwin's earlier suggestion kept them focused on the one issue—determining which proposed solution was most effective in dealing with the problem.

Practicality

At the next meeting, the team looked at the practicality of the seven suggestions and considered in general terms whether much cost was involved (cash outlay as well as people's time), how long it would take to implement (days versus months), whether it would be difficult to implement (people issues), and the nuisance factor. Janka stressed that the team was not going to do a detailed cost-benefit analysis at that point; that would occur once the list was reduced to a few solutions. Here the team was just using its experience to ask, in the simplest terminology, whether each idea was practical (i.e., did it make sense?).

Much to Chris's consternation, the monitoring suggestion was deemed not very practical in that it involved a heavy outlay of money for installation, training, monitoring software at the service center, and doing specialized training to utilize it effectively. While the cost might eventually be recovered through saved time for developers fixing bugs, sufficient information was not available to assume that the time saved would pay for the service. JTS, as Cameron pointed out, was in no position to gamble on such an investment. Additionally, there was no information on whether or not customers would allow developers to connect remotely to their screens. Customers may consider that a security risk.

Chris was a little upset because of the many hours spent researching the idea. Chris had taken Janka's suggestion about starting with an Idealized Design literally. Chris even hinted about resigning from the team. Taylor whispered loudly to Tommy that worse things could happen. Chris gathered the manual and other materials and prepared to stalk out.

Janka stopped the meeting. "I'm very upset that the team is neglecting the *Rules of the Road* to which you all had agreed in the first meeting. We are a *team*." Janka put heavy emphasis on the final word in that sentence. "We are supposed to give everyone's ideas and comments our full consideration, whether or not it impacts our private agendas."

"Further," Janka exclaimed, "None of the team should be making nasty remarks, as Taylor had just done. Also, Taylor, if you had something to say, you should have addressed the whole group rather than engaging in side conversations." Taylor apologized, and Chris acknowledged probably overreacting to the criticism of the remote connection idea. In the back of the room, Alex remained quiet but signaled to Janka "well done" with a thumbs up.

Chris finally admitted that compared to the other suggestions, the remote connection idea was not the most practical. Robbie suggested that the idea be kept under consideration, but perhaps a bit on the "back burner" if the other ideas were not totally successful. Everyone agreed that the monitoring idea should be rated a "4" in terms of practicality. Chris felt consoled by the fact that the remote connection idea beat out the full-time bug fixer (which everyone quickly agreed rated only a "2" for practicality).

At the other extreme, the Electrons readily agreed that special training for the support reps and designating certain people from each area to fix bugs would not cost very much and could be implemented easily. Both solutions received an "8" for practicality. The other ratings are shown on the matrix in Figure 29.

There was little time left in the meeting, and Janka suggested that the team postpone the rating of customer value until the following week. Janka sensed that emotions were running a little high.

After the meeting was adjourned, Janka and Alex held their usual session to critique the meeting. Alex commented on how well the team had been progressing through the matrix, in particular the "effectiveness" column. They were both pleased they had decided to rank each column separately to maintain focus. Janka was waiting for the other shoe to drop and asked what might have been done differently to handle the episode between Chris and Taylor.

Alex acknowledged the concern but assured Janka that what had occurred was not unusual. Groups go through various stages of development, sometimes being very team oriented, and then revert to more individualistic styles.

In the 1950s, Dr. Bruce Tuckman and Mary Ann Jensen researched team behaviors and identified five distinct stages: form, storm, norm, perform, and adjourn (Tuckman and Jensen 1977). So far, the Electrons had engaged in little storming, but today's meeting was just a sample of what can occur. What helps in this situation, Alex tried to say without preaching, is to maintain the team's focus on the problem and the process without losing sight of the basic principles of quality improvement. For example, rather than reach a "standoff" about how practical Chris's idea was, Janka might have encouraged more discussion to allow Chris and others to share their data and facts. If Cameron thought the idea was not practical, Cameron should tell the group. If Chris disagreed with Cameron, Chris could present data to support the position.

In general, Alex thought that Janka handled the side remarks well. The only question might relate to timing. Janka might have asked Chris to stay through the end of the meeting, refocused attention on the meeting agenda, and saved the little lecture for the five-minute end-of-meeting critique portion just before adjourning. Other members might have critiqued Chris and Taylor instead, saving Janka from having to do so. Alex thought that the more often a team leader is put in the position of "traffic cop," the more difficult it is to maintain a positive leadership role.

Janka and Alex confirmed their regular session to be held just before next week's Electrons meeting. They would review the agenda and plan for appropriate steps should the Chris and Taylor situation recur.

Customer Value

The Electrons assembled again, this time to rate the "customer value" section of the matrix. Tommy reported on the discussions with some of JTS' sales staff, who were very negative of some of the ideas. "The customer wants to hear directly from the developer they worked with during the project—they don't want someone else to work on the bug fix." The sales staff viewed JTS' service department as a competitive advantage. They recognized and understood the difficulty in getting the original developer to work on the bug fix, but to them it was much more important for the original developer to be available.

Robbie acknowledged the point, but expressed concern that what may have been a good selling strategy was backfiring when developers were too busy to fix the bugs. Robbie asked, "Do we lose potential customers by not being able to fix their bugs in a timely manner, or do we aggravate them?" Janka asked if anyone else cared to comment on the issue. No one spoke up, perhaps in reaction to the previous day's little scuffle. Janka suggested they remain focused on the matrix and whether this proposed solution would increase value to customers compared to the other ideas. Alex nodded approval.

The discussion picked up and everyone agreed that whether or not the strategy made any sense, customers would not be very satisfied with different developers working on the code. Although it might be valuable to JTS, customers would perceive absolutely no value. Another consideration, probably relating to practicality, was that the policy could not be implemented immediately, because training for bug fixing would be necessary. This idea was rated a "5."

Chris beamed when the remote connection idea was rated by the team as a "9." Customers would be able to simply show the support service reps what the problem was rather than trying to explain it. The idea that got rated a "10" was the one that customers perceived as most important; the original developer who did the code working on the bug fix.

Some of the other ideas were rated less than "10" because the impact on customer value would not be dramatic. While most of the other ideas might have increased JTS' efficiency, in the customers' minds, JTS would just have been performing as expected; nothing more, nothing less. Of all the other ideas, training the service reps to ask more specific questions was rated slightly higher than simply modifying the check sheet since capturing the info in a check sheet would not have been easy. If the support reps were better trained, customers would be impressed with JTS' thoroughness and professionalism when the support rep answered and relayed the problem to the developer. Customers became very aggravated when they explained a problem in detail to a support service rep over the phone and their comments were summarized as "won't work." When they finally get through to the developer and the developer indicates they don't have a clue what the problem might be (and often goes through the same difficult question/answer explanations that the support rep already went through), the customer has a tendency to get a bit frustrated.

Rankings

With all the ratings completed, Cameron multiplied the team's assessment of each of the seven ideas, as reflected on the matrix. The matrix reflected the four choices with a "G," to go forward to the next level of analysis. The four proposed solutions that received the highest scores were:

- Directly connect developer with customer
- Designate certain people from each area to fix bugs
- Install remote connection software
- Special training for support service reps

Chris and Tommy shook their heads. Janka pointed out that this was not the final team decision, but only the basis for deciding which ideas to scrutinize further. Directly connecting the developer with the customer came in first because of its perceived value to the customer. Designating certain people from each area and implementing the remote connection software came in about even, in second place. The team agreed that since the training the reps idea was a close third and the least costly, it should be considered. The remote connection idea was probably the best long-range solution, whereas the other ideas would result in incremental, less dramatic improvements.

Plan: Analyzing the Four Potential Solutions

Janka reviewed the next sequence of steps. First, the team would conduct an in-depth cost–benefit analysis of each solution, followed by a Force Field

Analysis, and then prepare an action plan to implement the solution which they decide upon. The team would then make a presentation to the store's management council, which would consist of the service manager, the store manager, and others who had an interest in the outcome. Janka and Alex weren't sure whether the Jan and Kim could attend, but Alex knew they would try. Both Jan and Kim were becoming very anxious about the team's progress and authorized the Electrons to meet as often and for as long as possible each week to complete the project.

Cost–Benefit Analysis

The prescribed method in the IDMM was to determine the total cost of a problem, including direct and indirect costs (such as rework and extra hours spent), plus lost revenues which could be attributed to the problem.

The next step was to estimate what the cost would be after implementing the proposed solution(s), which would presumably reflect less time spent by expensive developers, coupled with the added revenues resulting from increased customer satisfaction. In the case of the remote connection software, there might be a case for revenues down the road since it might be possible to charge for support services if the support service reps have access to this important tool.

In effect, the team was to take "before and after" pictures, comparing what the service process was currently costing JTS to what it would be expected to cost in the future. For example, if the current process cost $350,000 per year and the new process might cost $250,000 per year, the company would "gain" $100,000 a year.

The third step was to determine the cost of implementing the solution, which would reduce the gain. Some solutions would be more expensive than others, depending upon the need for training, software purchases, printing, etc. The hypothetical $100,000 gain might quickly disappear if the implementation costs were too high.

As a rule of thumb, Janka said, the cost–benefit analysis should be done over a five-year time frame, considering the benefits for that length of time. Solutions should not be rejected just because they do not pay for themselves overnight. After all, the team was charged with the task of solving problems for the long run rather than coming up with a quick fix. Kim Peters, who attended this meeting, echoed full support.

Members were divided into groups so that each of the proposed solutions would be studied by two team members. There might be some duplication, but the procedure would act as a double-check on each group's data collection and assessment. Each group was to meet with the accounting and sales departments to come up with numbers and estimates.

Tommy wondered why an accountant hadn't been assigned to the team. Alex responded that it was important that the team maintain ownership of the project and that everyone on the team needed to stay involved. Alex's experience was that having "experts" on a team quickly led to members deferring to such experts, which reduced the members' commitment and involvement. Alex reminded the team that the accountants had not been through the training, and while their tracking revenues and expenses may be acceptable for general accounting practices, it was not necessarily suitable for making business decisions, particularly when projections were involved.

The three groups gathered data over the next ten days, interviewing the accountants, office general managers, and sales staff. Compiling the actual expenses involved in making and testing multiple hypotheses (and the related loss of service revenue when a developer was unavailable to work on new customers) was not complicated. It was a little more difficult to estimate what a new process might save, because support service reps and developer utilization would increase. It might turn out that JTS would not need as many developers or support service reps, unless revenues improved considerably—but they couldn't tell until they worked the numbers.

What was particularly mind-boggling was having the office general managers and sales staff estimate the impact on sales of not changing the process at all (i.e., many long delays in bug fixes and customer complaints), nor improving the process in one of the four proposed manners. The sales staff was already concerned about the idea of taking developers from existing revenue-producing projects to fix bugs from older already-paid-for projects. Estimating five years into the future only made matters worse!

Irwin had a novel idea for converting customer dissatisfaction into dollars. In the original Pareto analysis, Irwin noted that there had been few complaints about the interface help requests. By comparison, interface help requests are easier for the support service reps to understand. They almost always understood the problem and could take the customer right to where they wanted to go, requiring virtually no repeat calls.

The team found a high correlation between customer satisfaction with interface help requests and future purchases of JTS products. Unfortunately, there was also a high correlation between bug fixes and future purchases (or lack of them). About eight out of ten customers would continue to purchase from JTS if they had a favorable service experience (such as with interface help requests), compared to only four out of ten who had the opposite experience (such as with bug fixes). The team calculated that for every ten JTS customers with bugs that needed fixing, all of whom would eventually need another system developed, about four would never buy from JTS again. Another two would probably not buy for other reasons (i.e., started buying off-the-shelf software instead of developed software). If the satisfaction with bug fix service equaled the satisfaction with interface help request service, there presumably would be *four additional sales* for every ten current buyers. But they were currently losing those four potential sales. Revenue losses were projected to be even higher because dissatisfied customers with buggy code presumably would not buy other JTS products as well.

Irwin and Taylor reviewed the numbers with the sales staff, who agreed that the figures looked right. Kim, who had become the unofficial head of quality at JTS, hoped the team would not overlook the intangible impact of poor service, which would eventually hurt JTS' reputation in the community and was directly contrary to one of the company's strategic objectives. Kim recited some favorite sayings (e.g., that a dissatisfied customer will tell 40 other people; it's ten times as expensive to get a new customer as to retain an old one).

A cost–benefit analysis was performed on the four proposed solutions. As expected, the least costly proposal to implement was to train the support service reps. There would be some backlogged support calls while they were being trained because for a short time during training, support would get even worse. But Taylor pointed out that by not creating dissatisfied customers (because the bugs took so long to fix), they might be able to sell other products (like support contracts) to such prospects. Tommy and Cameron cringed at this logic, but said they agreed with Taylor's revenue estimates.

Designing the training could be done very economically. Robbie and Chris said they could probably do it, with the support service reps' assistance, in a week. Based on an estimate that perhaps "only" 3.5 out of ten buyers would never buy from JTS again, future revenues would improve slightly.

The direct connection to the developer would be the most expensive. Unlike support service reps who made a decent living but not great money, experienced developers were not easy to find or keep. They were picky about their work environment, and did not like to be interrupted when coding a system for a client. They also didn't like to do documentation, or go back into a system they'd finished in order to fix the bugs. Tommy estimated that if they took away the ability of the developer to either refuse to do the bug fix or reschedule it for a future time, they would lose at least two developers, who would have to be replaced. It would lower the productivity of all the developers to be constantly interrupted.

Janko had an idea: "I wonder if we shouldn't do a cost analysis on this option both WITH and WITHOUT the training of the support reps? Perhaps if the support reps were trained, they could 'feed' the developer the information in a much more comprehensive manner so that the developer didn't need to be interrupted for long. Maybe we could even find some way to reward developers who fixed bugs quickly, and built a 30-minute period into their schedule every day in order to fix any bugs the systems they worked on encountered?"

Tommy had a comment to make about the area-specific developers instead of the one specific developer who worked on coding the system. "The second idea could be thought of as backup to the first one. The developer who worked on the original system isn't always available—sometimes they've left the company. If that developer was not available, rather than just assigning another developer ad-hoc, we should assign the developer based on the area the support service rep identifies. But that only works if we do that training, the fourth idea."

Kim liked this idea and commented that this would enhance the reps' credibility with customers, an intangible but important benefit in the long run. The team acknowledged that with turnover running about one in three per year, the training would have to be repeated annually.

After about 20 minutes of discussion, the team agreed with its earlier assessment that support service reps fielding customers' calls with better questions and a better understanding of the system, coupled with avoiding multiple hypotheses for bug fixes, would increase customer satisfaction more than the other two solutions. Translating this to reduced dissatisfaction and increased future revenues, the team estimated that the "never buy again" number would be "only" three out of ten, compared to the current four out of ten. They acknowledged that some multiple hypotheses bug fixes would still occur, but at least the trend would be in the optimum direction, with relatively little cost. The five-day training was estimated to cost $500 per service rep, including salary and the cost of the service manager's time to do the training. The training would be done on staggered shifts so that the phones would always be covered, though the backlog of support calls would inevitably grow while half the staff was training.

Cameron, who had been quiet for the past few meetings, spoke up. "What if we combined all four? Would that improve revenues and save lost sales enough to cover the cost of all four? Combining these ideas might even result in fewer dissatisfied customers and more additional sales than any one proposal alone. And after all, implementing the new software is going to require training—and if we are already training the support reps, we could save money that way."

The team agreed, and combining all four ideas was designated Proposal #5 on the matrix. Chris was a little shaky about predicting more sales, but agreed with the rest of the group that the "never buy again" category could be reduced to 2 out of 10. Thus, implementing all four proposed solutions would reduce the "never buy again" category by 50%. The cost–benefit analysis is shown in Table 7.3.

Some of the team members seemed uncomfortable with the projections, but Alex assured them that the forecasts were only intended as rough estimates, to be used as a basis for comparing one solution to the others. In fact, lost revenues do not equate directly with profits because of overhead and direct expenses. Also, some expenses may be incurred once while others will be expended each of the five years.

After this exhausting meeting, the team quickly agreed to break until the next meeting, when they would conduct a Force Field Analysis of their selection.

Force Field Analysis

Janka explained that the team needed to identify what might stand in the way of implementing each proposed solution properly (i.e., the restraining forces). Similarly, there might be conditions that would make the solutions workable (driving forces). Some driving forces might offset some restraining forces. The whole purpose was to anticipate difficulties and plan for them.

At Alex's suggestion, Janka split the Electrons into two groups. Chris, Robbie, and Cameron were to brainstorm all the restraining forces on a flipchart, while Taylor, Irwin, and Tommy were to brainstorm the driving forces. Their lists for the combined solution are displayed in Table 7.4.

The biggest restraining force to overcome, which unfortunately did not have a driving force to offset it, was the attitude of the service manager, Harper Bull. It became very apparent that Harper had no great love for customers; they were only necessary evils who were always making unreasonable demands. Harper had previously been service manager at a local stereo store, where customers frequently had to wait three or four weeks to have their amplifiers fixed. In Harper's mind, anybody who wanted any kind

Integrated Case Study ■ 191

Table 7.3 Cost–Benefit Analysis

Category	Current (No Changes) ($)	Proposal 1 (Direct Connect Developer) ($)	Proposal 2 (Developer by Area) ($)	Proposal 3 (Install Remote Connection Software) ($)	Proposal 4 (Special Training for Support Reps) ($)	Proposal 5 (Combine All 4) ($)
Developer Cost	67,000	45,000	35,000	30,000	45,000	38,750
Software Costs	-	-	-	18,000	-	18,000
Support Service Rep Cost (Lost Time)	13,000	1,000	3,000	23,000	23,000	18,400
Lost Revenues	1,20,000	93,000	1,05,000	96,000	1,05,000	60,000
Gross Cost	2,00,000	1,39,000	1,43,000	1,67,000	1,73,000	1,35,150
Gain/Lost From Implementing		+ 61,000	+ 57,000	+ 33,000	+ 27,000	+ 64,850
Five Year Projection		+ 3,05,000	+ 2,85,000	+ 1,65,000	+ 1,35,000	+ 3,24,250
Buggy Software Only						
Average Revenue Per Customer Per Year	30,000	30,000	30,000	30,000	30,000	30,000
Average Number of Customers Per Month Lost	4	3.1	3.5	3.2	3.5	2

192 ■ *Strategic Decision Making for Successful Planning*

Table 7.4 Restraining and Driving Forces

Restraining Forces	Driving Forces
Time for training support service reps	Reduced time to fix bugs
Some reps may not be trainable	More sales, referrals
Some developers may object to fixing bugs	Top management priority
Even after training some reps may identify wrong area	Training of reps and developers—awareness
Customers may object to new remote software	Fewer total bug fixes
Developer productivity may go down a bit	Developers focus more on documentation
Support service reps productivity may go down	Developers focus more on testing/quality
Support service rep quotas	Fewer hypotheses, incorrect fixes
Cost of software	More satisfying job—fewer complaints
Lack of management commitment	

of product or service fixed in two or three days was unreasonable. Even if a bug fix required five hypotheses, implementation, and tests, Harper's response to the cost of development was to raise rates to cover the cost.

It was clear that the ramifications of Harper's attitude would be difficult to counter. Complete cooperation was essential to having the support service reps trained, the need for obtaining more information for customers, scheduling the developers to do bug fixes, and implementing the software. As it was, Harper chided the support service reps if they seemed too "chatty" and asked too many questions of the customers who called in.

Since Harper was monitoring the team's activities closely, questioning their purpose and the time spent in meetings, Janka suggested that the minutes and the Force Field Analysis not refer to Harper directly. They would only indicate that "management commitment" was a restraining force. Harper would probably assume that meant Jan or Kim.

Another restraining force, squeezing time for training into the usual hectic pace at JTS, had no offsetting driving force. However, the problem of developers and support service reps resisting might be offset by their not having to deal with complaining customers, which would improve their overall job satisfaction.

Action Plan

Problems such as finding the time for training were entered on the action plan found in Table 7.5.

Integrated Case Study

Table 7.5 Action Plan

What	Who	When	Indicator of Completion	Completed on Time?	Comments
Design training and plan for Support Service Reps	Robbie and Chris	30 days from date	Harper, Support Service Reps, and Developers Agree		
Schedule the training for support service reps	Janka	40 days from date	Harper sends memo confirming dates		Training should include use of software
Implement the training	Robbie and Chris	60 days from date	Eval sheets from Support Service Reps recevied		
Get specific pricing and choose software	Tommie	15 days from date	Quotes received, 1 chosen		
Get approval from finance to purchase software	Tommie	30 days from date	Signed Purchase Order from Jamie		
Purchase and install software	Janka and Tommie	45 days from date	Memo from Harper		
Work with Area Managers to discuss who would be designated bug fixer	Taylor	30 days from date	Confirmation of scheduled meetings with Area Managers		At least 1 from each area (Use Interface, database, middleware, network) for backup only
Select designated bug fixer	Janka and Tommie	45 days from date	Confirming memo from Norma		

(Continued)

Table 7.5 (Continued)   Action Plan

What	Who	When	Indicator of Completion	Completed on Time?	Comments
Schedule meeting to work with Service Manager and developers to work out process for bug fixing	Janka, Cameron, and Irwin	30 days from date	Confirmation of scheduled meetings with developers and Drew		
Redesign process for developers to fix bugs	Cameron	60 days from date	Confirming memo of new process with Drew		Will include designated time each day for bug fixing and new process using software
Schedule bug fixing training on new process with new software	Irwin	90 days from date	Confirming memo from Norma with dates		
Implement the training for new process with software	Tommie, Robbie, and Chris	120 days from date	Eval sheets from Support Service Reps and Developers received		

Robbie and Chris were assigned the task of negotiating with the support service reps, the developers, and Harper to schedule the training. There were basically two types of training. The first was specific training for the support reps on basic information about the different areas and how to tell which area was the source of the issue (something the developers all already knew). The second was training for all the support reps and the developers on the new process for bug fixes that the developers were also involved in working through. Other items like purchasing and installing the software were assigned as well. It was important that every open item be addressed, with somebody assigned to handle it, and a completion date be assigned. Otherwise, something might fall through the cracks. Because the start date had not yet been established, the due dates were written in relationship to the start date of the project.

At this point, the Electrons had examined the problem of delayed bug fixes and the root causes of the bug fixes and decided upon the combined solutions to counter the root causes. Before going further, it was necessary to prepare a presentation for the management council to formally update the council about the team's activities, review the decision making efforts, and obtain its approval for the solutions.

Plan: Presentation to Management for Approval

Although the Electrons had kept management up to date on their activities through the distribution of minutes and frequent informal discussions, supplemented by Alex's reports to the management council, it was time for the team to make a formal presentation.

In the presentation of the IDMM, the team reviews its data and decision making methodology. During the session, team members present for about 20 minutes, and all questions from the council are deferred until the end. While the official reason for the presentation is to secure approval to implement the proposed solutions, it also serves as a form of recognition for the team's efforts. In reality, management has probably approved the solutions informally as it has been kept informed about the team's progress. An ideal presentation should contain no surprises.

Janka and Alex scheduled their presentation for June 15 in the Dade office training room. Tables were arranged in the shape of a horseshoe, with seating for 15. The team planned to use overheads to illustrate its IDMM Storyboard process. The four-by-six-foot storyboard was mounted on the wall, next to the projection screen. Janka and Irwin were to make the presentation. Chris, who was uncomfortable making presentations, agreed to handle the overheads. Other team members were responsible for reproducing and distributing copies of the IDMM to those in attendance.

The management council included the office general manager (Jordon O'Douls), the two assistant store managers (Sandra Woodall and Pete Swartz), the service manager (Harper Bull), the regional manager (Kennedy Scott), and the vice president of service for JTS (Drew Emerson). Kim Peters also attended. Jordon acted as the chairperson for the presentation. A few salespeople and others from the service staff were invited to observe, along with Alex and some of the associates from the KWB Group.

To begin the meeting, Jordon announced the purpose and format of the presentation and requested that questions be held until the team's presentation was concluded. Cameron distributed copies of the IDMM to everyone.

Janka began. Janka had rehearsed the remarks several times with Alex, but still felt very uneasy. Not only was this their first presentation, but it also was the first presentation of this type at JTS. The team thought Harper Bull would be ready to pounce on any gaps in the team's logic or facts, although might show some restraint in front of Drew, the boss, and Kim.

Once into the presentation, Janka's words flowed smoothly, essentially reciting what was covered on the overheads, gesturing to illustrate key points. Janka reviewed the IDMM through the root cause and verification of the problems (Steps 1 through 8). Irwin then reviewed the seven potential solutions and the team's recommendation. Both Janka and Irwin related the need to improve in this area to the corporate and departmental Balanced Scorecards, emphasizing that they would never be in "balance" unless this major source of customer dissatisfaction was eliminated. Altogether, Janka and Irwin consumed 25 minutes, running a little behind schedule.

Jordon thanked the team for its presentation and invited all the Electrons to join Janka and Irwin at the front of the room to field questions.

At first, no one had any questions. It appeared that most of the management council was overwhelmed by the amount of analysis that the team had undertaken, something that probably was not apparent earlier. Finally, Jordon broke the ice by asking some simple questions, such as how often the team met and for what length of time. Drew wondered if the idea could be applied at other JTS service centers. Others asked what type of difficulties the team may have encountered.

About ten minutes into the questioning, Harper finally raised a point. Janka thought, "Well, here it comes …."

Harper glanced around the room at Jordon, Sandy, Drew, Kennedy, and Kim, not really sure whether it was appropriate to say anything. Finally, Harper spoke up. "I can't believe what I've just seen. I mean this group put a lot of work into this project, spending over six months just to tell us to add a bit of training, all because a few hysterical idiots want us to drop everything to fix their bugs the same day they find them! All software has bugs—and most companies don't even bother to fix them. If you want me to change the damned process and do all this training, I won't get in the way, but I just don't see it!"

Janka and Irwin looked at each other, but before either could say anything, Jordon looked over to Harper and asked if the remark was a question. Harper's shaking head in exasperation while doodling on the handout made the answer clear. Kim looked concerned, but didn't say anything except to thank Janka and the rest of the team members for their efforts.

Jordon and the management group discussed the team's recommendation for about ten minutes and granted their enthusiastic approval. Harper muttered, "Sure, why not?"

With its presentation completed and approval to proceed obtained, the team was ready to implement its action plan.

Following the meeting, Janka and Alex conferred. Alex expressed admiration for how well the presentation went, especially since it was a first. Commenting on Harper's little tirade, Alex said it might have solved the "Harper problem," because now there was no doubt as to Harper's attitude toward quality and customer satisfaction. Perhaps further training would cause a shift in Harper's mindset, but Alex thought it unlikely. At this stage, Alex thought that Kim would probably be in touch regarding Harper.

That evening, the team went out for a little celebration since an important milestone had been reached. Now all they had to do was make their recommendations work!

Do: Proposed Solutions Implemented

In the first meeting following the successful presentation, the team agreed that training the support service reps and implementing the software had priority. Once the initial training was completed, the bug fixing process with the developers could be redesigned and the additional training could be done.

Robbie and Chris had contacted the support service reps and they agreed to help in the training development. This ensured their buy-in and virtually guaranteed that the training would run smoothly.

Tommie was scheduled to work through obtaining the software. Cameron, Taylor, and Irwin were scheduled to meet with the developers in the following weeks for process discussions. Cameron projected that after two or three meetings with the developers, drafting the process could begin. It would then be reviewed by Harper, the reps, and the developers.

They all began planning for the process redesign sessions. The draft was revised six times, the last three times because of changes demanded by Harper. In Harper's mind, the proposed process and questions to ask customers were too detailed. The team eventually compromised by allowing the developers a lot of leeway and freedom on how they actually established the hypothesis and implemented and tested the results. Harper finally agreed. At long last, the completed draft was delivered to the administrative office to print out.

Even though the team had described the proposed training in its presentation and it was approved by the council, Harper wanted to reopen the issue. Harper questioned the need for support service reps to understand how the different areas worked together in the customers systems and balked at committing more than two days of training, compared to the five days recommended by the team and approved by the management council. Taylor learned that Harper was bad-mouthing the Electrons' plan to the support service reps and telling them that they could ask customers all the questions they wanted, but their telephone quotas would stay the same!

At the next team meeting, Janka described Harper's roadblocks. Taylor asked why they didn't just tell the management council about Harper's sabotage, but since they worked for Harper, that could be risky. Alex sat at the back of the room and stared straight ahead, obviously very concerned.

After the meeting, Alex and Janka remained for a short review of the situation. Alex agreed that the team members would be at risk by approaching Jordon, Drew, or Kim. Alex thought the best way to handle the situation was for Alex to tell Kim in their monthly meeting. Kim always wanted to know what was going on and, in particular, why the team might be running behind schedule. Alex could "reluctantly" describe the situation with Harper and let Kim draw conclusions.

Act

Two weeks later the software had been installed, no training had been scheduled because of Harper's foot-dragging. The team was reluctant to start using the software unless they were coupled with the training.

A very demoralized Electrons team sat down at 4:00 p.m. on Friday afternoon to decide where to go from there. Alex arrived a little late, accompanied by Drew Emerson, Harper's boss. Alex asked if Drew could make a statement.

Drew apologized for infringing on the team's time but thought it was important for them to know that the Dade service center would be under the guidance of a new service manager because Harper had just resigned for personal reasons. After about 30 seconds of stunned silence, Robbie asked about Harper's replacement. Drew said that the management council was so impressed with Janka's presentation and knowledge of the service process that Janka was appointed acting service manager, effective immediately. A round of applause filled the room.

After Drew left, Janka reminded the team members that they needed to begin the training as soon as possible. Janka said that with the support service reps' needs in mind, they would support whatever schedule they might agree upon, just as long as it got started! Alex was grinning from ear to ear.

Later, Alex confided to Janka that the project had very little to do with Harper's leaving. Kim had already gotten feedback about Harper's actions and after conferring with Jan had instructed Drew to remove Harper. Drew commented that Kim would get no argument because Harper's attitude problems flowed in all directions.

The initial training was completed in three weeks. The process training for the larger group was completed within the next month. The firm lost another employee—one of the developers—but for the most part, both the support service reps and the developers thought the new process was much better than the old. And the ability to see what was on the screens of the customers saved a lot of time and frustration. Most customers seemed to appreciate the new capabilities when they called in for support. It seemed especially helpful for the interface issues as well! The next step for the team was to assess whether the new training achieved the results intended: did complaints decrease? Was the delay in bug fixing reduced? And because of the comments made about the interface help requests, they decided to add that to the results.

Step 10: Check: Measure Success or Failure

The team agreed to monitor the results of its solutions for three months, beginning July 1, the same length of time as the initial survey period. Also, three months was long enough to assure that the new measures were really beneficial, after the initial enthusiasm wore off.

During the three months, the team agreed that it would meet about every 30 days to review the data and suggest ways to improve the process even more.

After the three months of data gathering ended, the team prepared new charts, corresponding to the Pareto and other graphs which had been prepared last year. It was important that the formats remain the same, to construct "before" and "after" pictures of the data. Only then could the solutions be evaluated properly.

As might be expected, the first few weeks were a learning experience for the support service reps. Previously, their questioning of customers focused on learning which system they were working on and how payment (if not under warranty) was going to be handled. Now, customers were asked to allow the support service reps to watch and take print screens of whatever the problem was. They also asked questions about what the customer was doing just prior to the bug appearing, and what they expected to see differently. It appeared that their increased knowledge of the different areas of the system was very useful. Some customers even thought they were speaking with a developer!

The support service reps' morale increased simultaneously, since they felt that their activities served their customers far more than previously. Janka also eliminated the phone quotas, which reduced a great deal of the pressure to complete phone calls in a hurry.

There was a noticeable decrease in grumbling by the developers about being interrupted since the last half-hour of every day was set aside to work on bugs. And because they were getting such a complete picture of the problem up front, often they could diagnose and fix the problem without even needing to contact the customer. The number of times their first hypothesis was correct increased significantly, and they often now didn't even need all that time to work on bugs. And, because they were more knowledgeable about what kinds of problems arose, they were producing code with fewer bugs—without even hiring additional quality control testing personnel. Janka, now promoted to full-time service manager of the Dade service center, was happy because JTS' reputation for quality service was on the rise.

More significantly, it appeared that customers were calling less frequently about bug fixes (though they seemed now to call even more frequently for interface help). Those who did call to complain apparently were surprised by Janka's demeanor, which suggested that Harper had not always been especially helpful or polite.

Janka and the team couldn't wait for the 90 days to end so they could assess the final numbers. Was it their imagination, or were bug fixes taking less time? Because the data fluctuated from week to week, it was difficult to tell. The summary indicators for the Balanced Scorecard and the key activities were inching in the right direction.

Within a week of the end of the 90-day period, the Electrons compiled the numbers. They can be seen in Figure 7.16.

In Figure 7.17 the original costs for support calls are compared to the costs after implementation. There has been a drastic change—a savings of $32,219. While the costs for User Interface requests appears to have gone up a bit because the volume of those calls was even higher, the cost per call has gone down for both User Interface and bug fixes. The number of days to resolution has also improved from a high of 49.2 (which occurred right after the implementation, when the support service reps were undergoing training) to a low of 31.2, which are numbers the service department hadn't seen in over a year. The number of days to resolution is plotted in Figure 7.18.

Another revelation was that the overall indicator had improved. The total number of support requests solved in one call went from less than 10% to more than 72%. And the number of customer complaints went way down.

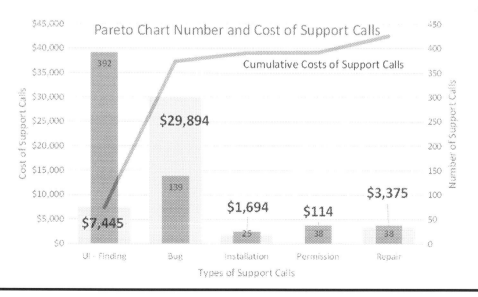

Figure 7.16 **Pareto Diagram of Support Calls.**

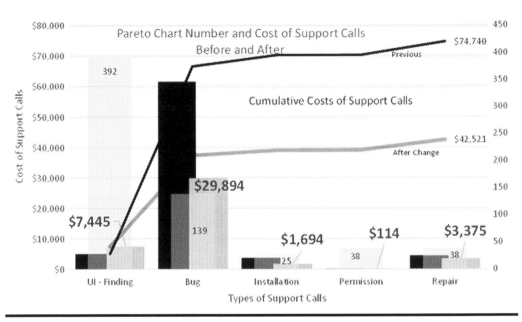

Figure 7.17 Pareto Diagram Comparing Before and After.

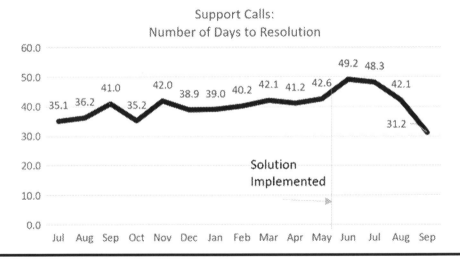

Figure 7.18 Number of Days to Resolution.

Irwin pointed out the obvious—that the numbers were clearly better. The solutions had made a difference. However, the numbers still were not quite good enough. They wondered whether the team should just go ahead and make its presentation to the management council or delve into some other issues that might require different solutions, some of which might require the management council's approval following a presentation.

Robbie thought that more information on the bug fixes might be useful. Robbie knew about a few bug fixes had nothing to do with having the proper area or the information the support service reps could gather. Not every bug could be fixed in one day.

The team agreed to gather more data on the points Robbie had brought up, so they would not be including those instances when a one-day bug fix was not possible. Of the last 45 bug fixes, 20 of them could have been fixed by someone other than the original developer. Since the developer was almost always waiting until the end of the day to deal with bug fixes, it was always at least a two-day bug fix. If one of the developers from the specific area was able to work on the bug fix immediately, it might improve the number of one-day bug fixes.

Cameron suggested that it wouldn't work because the developers from the different areas would still need to learn the system and contact the developer since they were the only ones who knew the code and could quickly hypothesize the correct issue. Irwin thought that the developers from different areas could do it—but only if the code was well documented by the original developers, but it was not. While documentation had gotten better, developers by and large still did not document their code very well.

The team agreed that some modifications to the process, such as contacting the area developer before contacting the original developer might work. Cameron volunteered to work with the developers and the area developers to work through an improvement in the process.

The team agreed that although these changes might modify the numbers even more, the results gotten already were good enough to report to the management council. A meeting was scheduled for the following Thursday.

Second Presentation to Management Council: Results

The Electrons were second on the management council's agenda. Both Jan and Kim attended the meeting. Once again, Janka gave most of the presentation, although Robbie reviewed the results portion of the IDMM.

Following the presentation, Kim complimented the team members on their dramatic results. What was incredible, Kim thought, was that while the service reps were obtaining more information from customers and staying on the phone longer, no additional reps had to be hired! Could it be that they did not have to handle as many complaint calls?

Jan surprised everyone, especially Kim, by displaying overhead transparencies of three emails received from customers, thanking JTS for its very professional approach to ascertaining the area of the problem, followed by prompt and reliable bug fixes. Jan had to admit that increased sales could not be traced directly to the improved service yet, but it seemed to be a likely result in the near future. The summary measures for the Balanced Scorecard and the key indicators continued to show marked improvement. Jan thought that it was only a matter of time until the financial portion of the scorecard would begin to improve. Before sitting back down, Jan said, "You're certainly making a believer out of me!" Kim and Alex exchanged glances and nodded their approval.

Drew also expressed admiration and then asked a blunt question. "How do we move the numbers further? Your target's a good one but we're not there yet. Where do we go from here? How do we increase the number of bugs fixed in one day?"

Irwin spoke for the team. Irwin said that they had instituted a combination of the four proposed solutions and that implementing some of the others might result in further improvements. However, the team had concluded that it might not be possible to achieve the target 95% of the time without a real breakthrough.

Janka remarked that the team had already begun thinking about replicating the new process for other types of support calls, the next step in the IDMM. Janka said the team hoped to present its IDMM to the other JTS service centers.

Drew said that as far as other centers were concerned, the sooner they began using the new process the better! Whether they used it was not an option on their part!

Jordon thanked the team for its presentation and looked forward to hearing how the replication proceeded. Jan restated the intention to examine the other ideas and said that Jordon would meet with the management council when all the information was prepared. Jordon reminded everyone that it would be many months before another idea could be implemented, so the replication efforts needed to proceed.

Kim and Alex invited the team members to dinner at the Rusty Pelican on Key Biscayne as a way of celebrating their accomplishments to date. The team's work was far from done. Replication was not as easy as it sounded.

Standardize the Process

At the next team meeting, Janka again thanked the team members for their help in making the presentation. While Janka and Robbie made the actual presentation, the others had helped prepare the overheads and handouts and participated in the rehearsals.

Integrated Case Study ■ 205

The next item on the agenda was to standardize the new process for handling bug fixes. By documenting and describing the process, the team could be virtually certain that its efforts would continue to pay dividends. From their training, the team members knew that improvements were often short-lived without a process to assure standardization. Once the process was standardized and the IDMM control system was in place, the team could consider replication.

The standardization process began with revising the process flow diagram, or Flowchart, to accurately describe the new process. In Step 4, a Flowchart was developed to show the new process. The revised Flowchart is presented in Figure 7.19.

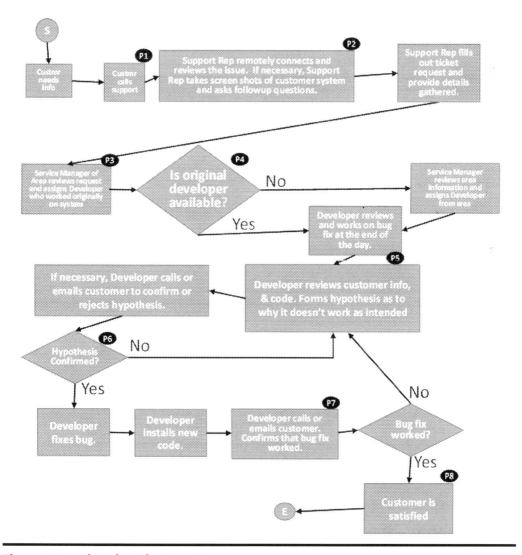

Figure 7.19 Flowchart for New Process.

Through the IDMM control system, the measuring points were designated, the formulas for calculating the measurements were noted, and the appropriate persons were designated to make the ongoing measurements.

Once the Flowchart was revised, the team completed the rest of the control system. By tracking data on a Statistical Control Chart, the process owners will know whether their process has remained stable and predictable (i.e., in statistical control) or not.

Because Cameron had just completed KWB's process management course which covered these topics, Cameron volunteered to prepare the first draft of the control system. Chris offered to help in the data collection and analysis to be used in constructing the Statistical Control Charts.

Prior to the team meeting, Taylor and Chris reviewed the control system with the service reps to verify that the Flowchart accurately depicted the new process. Actually, the reps had already improved upon the process by putting the service center computer on the JTS network. This enabled them to know instantly which developer worked on the original project. They also planned to create a new file to track service work for each customer, thus maintaining a permanent "life history" of each system a customer owned. They thought it might be useful to sell support maintenance contracts and to send reminders to customers that their systems should be upgraded.

The team marveled at Cameron and Chris' control system and formally adopted it for the IDMM. Janka said that not only would the control system assure that the process would continue to be used, but it would also be instrumental in the replication process, in addition to being a training tool for new employees.

Standardization: Replication—Other Support Calls

With the IDMM control system finished, Janka said that the team needed to create similar systems for other support calls. This included User Interface requests to find info, permission changes, hardware repair, etc. While the approach was to be the same as for bug fixes (i.e., asking better questions when a customer calls), the questions would have to relate to each specific type of support call. Also, because it seemed very helpful for the service reps to know something about how the systems functioned, some additional training would need to be scheduled.

Each team member agreed to work on one or more types of support calls to develop a specialized service process, incorporating input from the service reps and developers. Fortunately, some support calls, such as permissioning changes, were simpler to fix than bug fixes. It was discovered, for example, that with a few minor tweaks, customers could set their own permissioning instead of requiring them to call into the service center to set the permissions when a new employee came on board. And better video training decreased the number of User Interface issues, shortening both the amount of time support reps needed to spend with customers and the number of User Interface calls that came it. It was also determined that two of the manufacturers the company used for the hardware had higher repair needs than the others. The company stopped ordering from those manufacturers and the number of repairs required went down.

Janka announced to the team that the first stage of replication had been completed.

Standardization: Replication—Other Locations

Although Drew, vice president of service, plus Jan and Kim were solidly behind applying the Electrons' new process at other service centers, there was a lot more involved than simply copying and distributing the IDMM.

This became evident at the first presentation at the San Jose center. The developers and service reps politely listened to Robbie's presentation, but asked no questions. Drew was determined to gauge their reaction and probed further. But it was not a simple response. The San Jose group didn't think their customers were bothered by bug fixes because there had not been many complaints. Also, San Jose was different from Dade County and had different conditions, or so they said. It also appeared that the next logical step was to eliminate some of the support service rep jobs. Why should they shoot themselves in the foot?

Following the presentation, an exasperated Drew sat down with Georgie Mills, the San Jose service manager. Georgie was more than willing to try the Electrons' approach, but admitted that it would be tough getting everyone's cooperation. Georgie reminded Drew that it wasn't like the old days when anyone who wore the wrong color shirt could be fired. Georgie said management influence had even decreased since Jan and Kim had implemented all these new programs, including "all that empowerment stuff." Georgie had been through some of the training and it made sense, but hardly anybody else knew much about the program, although they knew just enough to sabotage any attempts at management.

Georgie agreed to think of ways to generate more enthusiasm among the San Jose service staff. Drew acknowledged that ramming the new process down their throats would be worse than doing nothing. Perhaps San Jose would prove to be the exception.

The following week, Cameron made a presentation at the Chicago service center. The developers and support reps weren't so polite. They interrupted Cameron often and called the approach ridiculous. The general attitude was that the Chicago center was doing just fine and that it didn't need a bunch of people from Miami telling them how to do their jobs. Drew's meeting with James Brown, the service manager at Chicago, didn't fare any better than the meeting in San Jose.

Drew canceled the rest of the presentations scheduled for the month and suggested a meeting with Jan and Kim, plus Janka and Alex.

They all agreed that their replication plans may have been naive. It would be hard to expect the San Jose or Chicago staffs to have any buy-in or much sense of ownership. Maybe the Electrons should have kept the other service centers informed while they were progressing through the IDMM, even inviting their input. Also, they admitted that they had not tuned into the staffs' favorite website, WIIFM.com, or "What's In It For Me?" Why should anyone on those staffs want to do things differently? If anything, it sounded as if they might lose their jobs if efficiency improved.

Kim was really dismayed over a fundamental issue. The real power of having a team solve a problem is the ability to reproduce the solution in other places, but how do you do that without stepping on toes? Everybody looked to Alex for the answers. Perhaps Alex had run into this situation with other clients.

"I see several underlying issues here," Alex began. "First of all, you have the natural human tendency to resent somebody else telling you how to do your work, even if they happen to be right. Second, it sounds as if the San Jose and Chicago people don't see any need to change, or they're not sure how the change is related to solving any problems they may have. Surely, they must get some complaints! Also, maybe they resent the Electrons team. All the service people at JTS went through the training together but only the Electrons have made any real progress. The Chicago team spent six months trying to decide which change management system works best, and then they disbanded the team. Finally, you've got the security issue. Many people associate Florida Power & Light's layoffs with its winning a big quality prize. High quality means fewer jobs in some people's eyes!"

"That's a pretty good summary," Jan remarked, "but how are we going to deal with this thing? Just let everybody solve their own problems and keep the solutions to themselves? Our old military style of leadership, as you called it, doesn't sound so bad now! At least I didn't have to worry about hurting people's feeling when I told them to do something! And to think we've invested all this time and money …." Kim was sinking lower and lower.

Alex was getting a little red in the face. "Jan, you hired me to help you through this transition. You remember we cautioned at our first meeting that changing cultures and management style would not be a piece of cake. I strongly recommended that we engage full-time facilitators for all your teams, but you vetoed the idea. Let me give you another recommendation, one I was going to suggest next month."

"Alex, anything you have on your mind, please say it," a pained Kim said quietly.

"OK. This has worked for some companies. I didn't think we were quite there yet, but the idea is to have an annual Chairperson's Cup coupled with a service exposition or Expo. The concept is to have selected service staff, including all team leaders, facilitators, and service managers, attend a daylong series of presentations by ten teams which we have identified as having the best IDMMs. The next day would be devoted to having Expos, with display booths set up for all teams to display and talk about their IDMMs."

"Also, every three months, team leaders and facilitators would meet at Quality Forums, or retreats, to discuss quality issues and share any progress they have made. At all of these events, both you and Kim should participate to show your support and to add to the recognition."

Jan was growing a little impatient. After thanking Alex for what seemed like "a nice idea," Jan tried to get Alex to explain how it would help solve their current problem. Drew and Kim also failed to see the connection.

"Everything I just said doesn't directly help our current problem, but there is some relationship. Teams put out a lot of effort in solving problems. Just ask Janka. The Chairperson's Cup and the Expos are a way to recognize those efforts. The recognition comes in two doses, one from management and the other from peers."

"Coupled with the quarterly meetings, a lot of good information will be shared and publicized. As the meetings occur and teams tell others what they're working on, you'll find that groups like San Jose or Chicago will be asking for details about how problems were solved. They'll be begging teams like the Electrons to make presentations. It's really just simple psychology, letting the idea to replicate come from the other service centers."

"Another idea is to put your IDMMs on the computer network, linked to a database. When a team is assigned or selects a problem, the first thing it should do is check whether another team has already solved the same problem. If so, then they would contact the other team for more information. Instead of feeling resentment from being told how to do something, they may be grateful for saving them some time."

"Publish a newsletter that talks about results. Whet people's appetite for more information! Even if the service department thinks it can live with a certain level of customer headaches, office general managers may have a different perspective. Their bonuses now depend on customer satisfaction, don't they?"

"Yes, it probably was wishful thinking that we could stand there and tell other service centers about our great new process in Dade and expect them to do handstands. In retrospect, it would have been better to have publicized the Electrons' efforts and the improvements in productivity and customer satisfaction. Perhaps the office or service managers at San Jose and Chicago would have wanted to achieve the same results in order to meet their financial objectives. Maybe they would have contacted Janka for more details and requested a presentation. The approach makes all the difference in the world!"

"Jan and Kim, in my opinion, you need to do two more things. I'll tell you and then I'll shut up. When an IDMM is considered for replication, other areas have got to be free to modify it for their own circumstances. I understand that the biggest concern among San Jose customers is not bug fixes, but permissioning. Who knows, maybe they will study the Electrons' process and find a way to improve it."

"The other thing is, and I know this may sting, but I think it is essential that you go on record that no one will ever lose their job at JTS because of the quality initiative. There's just too much skepticism among the employees that they're working themselves out of jobs. And, Jan and Kim, if you're really committed to your quality plan, and truly believe in it, you should expect to be hiring, not firing, people. I don't see how such a promise could hurt you. Enough said."

No one said anything for a few minutes. Kim finally broke the silence by clarifying the understanding that Alex was recommending that the Electrons make no more presentations unless requested to do so. Alex said that was correct, but reiterated the point that there had to be some method of publicizing the Electrons' efforts.

Jan reluctantly went along and asked Kim to develop some of the publicity and recognition ideas Alex had suggested.

As it turned out, Alex was right on target. Within three months of publication of the first "Quality Newsletter," in which the story of the Electrons' IDMM was featured, the new process, with minor modifications, was in place at all but two of the JTS service centers.

Janka was pleased to report that the replication at other locations had virtually been completed and that the team could proceed to the end of its IDMM. While it was not an official step, it was an important one nonetheless.

Self-Assessment and Future Activities

Janka reviewed the last step with the team. Janka said that the team needed to PDCA its own activities (i.e., what lessons did they learn that would benefit their future IDMMs). Next, they needed to consider what, if anything, should be done regarding the new process.

Janka asked each team member to state something that the team did very well and something that might be done differently the next time.

The list summarizing the things that went well included:

- After the earlier blow-up involving Chris, the team began to function more like a team and everybody was more at ease and willing to listen to others' ideas.
- The team members frequently volunteered to do assignments, with everybody sharing.
- Used service reps' input and adopted it when feasible, assuring their buy-in.
- Very customer focused.
- Followed IDMM process well and didn't get off track.
- Employed data well. Really made a big difference.
- Support from Jan, Kim, and Alex was crucial.

The list of things that could be improved included:

- Attendance at meetings was high (97%), but two members always had to be reminded that the meetings were starting. They should attend without prompting.
- Meetings frequently ran over the allotted time.
- Perhaps Harper should have been kept better informed early on.

- Replication among other service centers should be handled differently.
- Janka should not have done all the management council presentations.

Regarding future activities, the team agreed that for the next six months it would monitor the results of replicating the new process to other appliances and at the other locations.

The team agreed that Janka would be the team's liaison to Jan regarding the future system changes. One idea to follow up on was offering just-in-time training using the new software to customers for a monthly fee. A survey of customers was currently underway to learn if they would pay a monthly subscription fee and whether they perceived a benefit.

Final Presentation to Management Council

The very last event was the team's presentation of its entire IDMM to the management council. The meeting was attended by both Jan and Kim.

Chris and Cameron handled the presentation. Once again, in addition to describing their IDMM, the Electrons' presentation linked their results to improvements in the broader picture, the Balanced Scorecard, and measurement of key activities. Questions were very limited, as the presentation was largely a vehicle for recognition.

Chris stated that the Electrons had been selected as one of the top ten teams to make a presentation at the first Chairperson's Cup the following month.

Following the presentation, Jan and Kim took the team members and Alex to lunch at Jan's private club in Coconut Grove. Each member was presented with an acrylic paperweight inscribed with his or her name, with the JTS quality logo etched around it.

On behalf of the Electrons, Janka thanked Jan and Kim and promised to surprise them about their next IDMM.

Summary Chapter 7 Questions

- What kind of data did the JTS executive leaders look at?
- What kind of data did the sub-teams working the Ten-Step Ideal Decision Making Model utilize?
- What kind of obstacles did the team face?
- How did they overcome those obstacles?
- How realistic do you think this case study is?

References

1980. "Strategic Management in Corrections Tool Workbook, Management and Behavioral Science Center." May 1980.
2021a. "Analytics." Accessed March 7, 2021. https://www.lexico.com/definition/analytics.
2021b. "Analytics." Accessed March 7, 2021. https://www.techopedia.com/definition/30296/analytics.
2021c. "Analytics." Accessed March 7, 2021. https://www.dictionary.com/browse/analytics.
2021d. "Analytics." Cambridge Dictionary. Accessed March 7, 2021. https://dictionary.cambridge.org/us/dictionary/english/analytics.
2021e. "Analytics." Accessed March 7, 2021. https://www.merriam-webster.com/dictionary/analytic.
2021f. "Positioning Technology Players within a Specific Market." In *Research Methodologies*. Gartner Group.
Ackoff, Russell L. 1971. "Toward a System of Systems Concepts." *Management Science* 3(11).
Ackoff, Russell L. 1974. *Redesigning the Future*. New York: Wiley.
Ackoff, Russell L. 1975. "Does Quality of Life Have to Be Quantified?" *General Systems* 20.
Ackoff, Russell L. 1978. *The Art of Problem Solving*. New York: Wiley.
Ackoff, Russell L. 1981. *Creating the Corporate Future*. New York: Wiley.
Ackoff, Russell L. 1994. *The Democratic Corporation*. Oxford: The Oxford University Press.
Ackoff, Russell L. and Fred Emery. 1972. *On Purposeful Systems*. New York: Aldine Atherton.
Ackoff, Russell L. and Elsa Vergara. 1981. "Creativity in Problem Solving and Planning: A Review." *European Journal of Operations Research* 7:4.
Adams, James. 1974. *Conceptual Blockbusting*. San Francisco, CA: W.H. Freeman.
Aguayo, Rafael. 1990. *Dr. Deming: The American Who Taught the Japanese about Quality*. Vol. 1st. Secaucus, NJ: Carol Publishing Group.

Amudavia, David M. and Nelson Mango. 2003. "Enhancing Community Based Research: The Case of a Participatory Action Research Experience in a Rural Community in Kenya." *ALARM 6th and PAR 10th World Congress in University of Pretoria*, South Africa on 21–24 September 2003, Pretoria, South Africa.

Andersen, Barry. 1980. *The Complete Thinker*. Englewood Cliffs, NJ: Prentice-Hall.

Bożek, Agnieszka. 2020. "Subjective and Contextual Determinants of Engagement in Actions beyond Basic Professional Duties." *Polish Psychological Bulletin* 51(4):249–259. doi: 10.24425/ppb.2020.135457.

Chems, Albert and Louis Davis. 1975. *The Quality of Working Life*. London: Collier Macmillan.

Churchman, West. 1968. *The Systems Approach*. New York: Delacorte Press.

Collins, James C. and Jerry I. Porras. 1994. *Built to Last: Successful Habits of Visionary Companies*. Vol. 1st. New York: HarperBusiness.

Cutterbuck, David. 1979. "The Future of Work." August 1979.

DeBono, Edward. 1971. *Lateral Thinking for Management*. England: American Manufacturing Association.

Dickson, John. 1969. *Systems Thinking*. Harmondsworth, England: Penguin Books.

Dickson, John. 1977. "The Plight of Middle Management." December 1977.

Drucker, Peter F. 1987. *The Frontiers of Management: Where Tomorrow's Decisions Are Being Shaped Today*. Vol. 1st Perennial Library. New York: Perennial Library.

Drucker, Peter F. 2001. *The Essential Drucker: Selections from the Management Works of Peter F. Drucker*. Vol. 1st. New York: HarperBusiness.

Durmaine, Brian. 1994. "Why Do We Work?", December 26.

Elliot, Roland. 1990. "The Challenge of Managing Change." March 1990.

Emerson, Harrington. 1979. *Efficiency as a Basis for Operation and Wages, History of Management Thought*. New York: Arno Press.

Emery, Fred. 1995. "Participative Design: Effective, Flexible, and Successful, Now!", January/February 1995.

Emery, Fred and Einar Thorsrud. 1976. *Democracy at Work*. Leiden: Martinus Nijhoff Social Sciences Division.

Ewing, D. 1977. "Discover Your Problem-Solving Style." December 1977.

Faller, Ally. 2020. "What is Natural Language Processing and Why is it Hard?" Last Modified February 7, 2020. Accessed March 28, 2021. https://www.colorado.edu/earthlab/2020/02/07/what-natural-language-processing-and-why-it-hard.

Fenwick, P. and E. Lawler. 1978. "What You Really Want from Your Job." May 1978.

Gantt, Henry Laurence. 2007. *Organizing for Work*. 2007 ed. Bellingham, WA: Enna Products.

Garbers, Yvonne and Udo Konradt. 2014. "The Effect of Financial Incentives on Performance: A Quantitative Review of Individual and Team-Based Financial Incentives." *Journal of Occupational & Organizational Psychology* 87(1):102–137. doi: 10.1111/joop.12039.

Garvin, David A. 1987. "Competing on the Eight Dimensions of Quality." *Harvard Business Review*, November.

George, Claude. 1968. *The History of Management Thought*. Englewood Cliffs, NJ: Prentice-Hall.

Gharajedaghi, Jamshid. 1984. "On the Nature of Development." *Human Systems Management* 4.

Gilbreth, Frank Bunker and Harrington Emerson. 1993. *Motion Study: A Method for Increasing the Efficiency of the Workman, Classics in Management*. London: Routledge/Thoemmes Press.

Gilbreth, Frank Bunker and Lillian Moller Gilbreth. 1973. *Applied Motion Study: A Collection of Papers on the Efficient Method to Industrial Preparedness*, Hive Management History Series, no 28. Easton, PA: Hive Pub. Co.

Guiliano, Vincent. 1982. "The Mechanization of Office Work." September 1982.

Gunn, Thomas. 1982. "The Mechanization of Design and Manufacturing." September 1982.

Hackman, J. Richard and J. Lloyd Suttle. 1977. *Improving Life at Work*. Santa Monica, CA: Goodyear Publishing.

Hayes, John. 1981. *The Complete Problem Solver*. Philadelphia, PA: Franklin Institute Press.

Jackson, K. F. 1975. *The Art of Solving Problems*. New York: St. Martin's Press.

Kaplan, R. S. and D. P. Norton 1992. "The Balanced Scorecard—Measures that Drive Performance." January–February 1992.

Koberg, Daniel and Jim Bagnall. 1974. *The Universal Traveler: A Soft Systems Guide to Creativity, Problem Solving, and the Process of Reaching Goals*. Los Altos, CA: William Kauffman.

Lewin, K., R. Lippit, and R. K. White. 1939. "Patterns of Aggressive Behavior in Experimentally Created Social Climates." *Journal of Social Psychology* 10(1):271–301.

Lynch, Robert F., Thomas J. Werner, and Livia C. Lynch. 1992. *Continuous Improvement: Teams & Tools*. Atlanta, GA: QualTeam.

Main, Jeremy. 1994. *Quality Wars*. New York: The Free Press.

Maslow, Abraham. 1954. *Motivation and Personality*. New York: Harper and Row.

Mink, Oscar G., Rosemary Morrow, and Thomas J. Shindell. 1990. "A Critical Review of Current Thought on Guaranteed Employment Practices." *Human Resource Development Quarterly* 1(2):153–165. doi: 10.1002/hrdq.3920010206.

Newell, A. and Simon, H. 1972. *Human Problem Solving*. Englewood Cliffs, NJ: Prentice-Hall.

Osborn, Alex F. 1964. *How to Become More Creative: 101 Rewarding Ways to Develop Your Potential Talent*. New York: Scribner.

Ouchi, William. 1981. *Theory Z: How American Business Can Meet the Japanese Challenge*. Reading, MA: Addison-Wesley.

Poots, Alan J. and Thomas Woodcock. 2012. "Statistical Process Control for Data without Inherent Order." *BMC Medical Informatics and Decision Making* 12:86–86. doi: 10.1186/1472-6947-12-86.

Randel, Amy E., Benjamin M. Galvin, Lynn M. Shore, Karen Holcombe Ehrhart, Beth G. Chung, Michelle A. Dean, and Uma Kedharnath. 2018. "Inclusive Leadership: Realizing Positive Outcomes through Belongingness and Being Valued for Uniqueness." *Human Resource Management Review* 28(2):190–203. doi: 10.1016/j.hrmr.2017.07.002.

Rhoads, C. J. 2005. *Lies, Damn Lies, and Statistics*. Unitof1.

Rhoads, C. J. 2008. "Do Small Entrepreneurial Firms Use Technology More Effectively?" *The Journal of Business Management & Change* 3(2):35–52.

Rodgers, Bryan, Jiju Antony, Rick Edgeman, and Elizabeth A. Cudney. 2021. "Lean Six Sigma in the Public Sector: Yesterday, Today and Tomorrow." *Total Quality Management & Business Excellence* 32(5/6):528–540. doi: 10.1080/14783363.2019.1599714.

Roth, William. 1982. *Comparing the Effects of Cooperation, Competition, and Conflict on the Speed with Which Different Personality Types and Personality Type Pairs Can Generate Useful Solutions to Problem*. Dissertation, University of Pennsylvania.

Roth, William. 1989a. "Get Training Out of the Classroom." May 1989.

Roth, William. 1989b. "Try Some Quality Progress Glue." December 1989.

Roth, William. 1989c. *Work and Rewards: Redefining Our Worklife Reality*. New York: Praeger.

Roth, William. 1991. *A Systems Approach to Quality Improvement*. New York: Praeger.

Roth, William. 1993a. *The Dangerous Ploy of Downsizing*. Los Angeles, CA: California State University.

Roth, William. 1993b. *The Evolution of Management Theory: Past, Present, Future*. Delray Beach, FL: St. Lucie Press.

Roth, William and Douglas Ferguson. 1991. "How to Play the Teambuilding Game." August 1991.

Roth, William F. 2010. *Comprehensive Healthcare for the US: An Idealized Model*. New York: CRC Press, Taylor & Francis Group.

Rubach, Laura. 1995. "Downsizing: How Quality Is Affected as Companies Shrink." April 1995.

Ryder, J. A. Jr. Unpublished. *Improving and Measuring Corporate Performance with the Balanced Scorecard*.

Schon, Donald. 1971. *Beyond the Stable State*. London: Temple Smith.

Shostack, G. Lynn. 1984. "Designing Services that Deliver." *Harvard Business Review* 1984(January).

Stayer, Ralph. 1990. "How I Learned to Let My Workers Lead." November-December 1990.

Taylor, Frederick. 1911. *The Principles of Scientific Management*. New York: Harper.

Townsend, Patrick and Joan Gebhardt. 1992. "Measurement: Neither a Religion nor a Weapon." October 1992.

Townsend, Patrick L. and Joan E. Gebhardt. 1986. *Commit to Quality*. New York: Wiley.

Tribus, Myron. 1975. *The Three Faces of Technology and the Challenge to Engineering Education, R P Davis Lecture on the Practice of Engineering*. Morgantown, WV: College of Engineering, West Virginia University.

Trist, Eric. 1980. *The Evolution of Socio-Technical Systems*. 2 vols, *Issues in the Quality of Working Life*. ON: Ontario Ministry of Labor.

Trist, Eric, G. W. Higgins, H. Murray, and A. B. Pollock. 1963. *Organizational Choice*. London: Tavistock Publications.

Tuckman, Bruce W. and Mary Ann C. Jensen. 1977. "Stages of Small-Group Development Revisited." *Group & Organization Studies* 2(4):419–427. doi: 10.1177/105960117700200404.

van Droffelaar, Boy and Maarten Jacobs. 2018. "Nature-Based Training Program Fosters Authentic Leadership." *Journal of Leadership Studies* 12(3):7–18. doi: 10.1002/jls.21569.

Von Bertalanffy, Ludwig. 1962. "General Systems Theory: A Critical Review." *General Systems* 7.

Wilkerson, James L. 1995. "Merit Pay Reviews: They Just Don't Work!", June 1995.

Zorn, Michelle L., Patricia M. Norman, Frank C. Butler, and Manjot S. Bhussar. 2017. "Cure or Curse: Does Downsizing Increase the Likelihood of Bankruptcy?" *Journal of Business Research* 76:24–33. doi: 10.1016/j.jbusres.2017.03.006.

Zwicky, F. 1969. *Discovery, Invention, Research through the Morphological Approach*. 1st American ed. New York: Macmillan.

Index

4W1H, 68, 136

accessibility of data, 99–100
accuracy of data, 99–101
Ackoff, Russell, 15, 16, 17, 42, 69
analysis of variance, 111
analytical fields of data, 99–101
analytics
 business, 88
 software, 97
analyze data step of IDMM, 132
Aristotle, 85
Ask Why At Least Five Times, 40
Attribute Analogy System, 41
autonomous work groups, 27, 28

Bagnall, Jim, 36, 38
Balanced Scorecard, 147–148, 150, 151, 157, 196, 201, 204, 212
big data, 88–90, 100
 benefits and pitfalls, 88
 conspiracy theories, 90
 dirty data, 96
 sources, 99
 speed of technology, 91
 use in IDMM, 136
 wrong impression, 100
binary logistical regression analysis, 111–112
binary variable, 102, *See* dummy variable
Brainstorming, 45–48, 121, 154,
Breaking The Ice, 61, 64, 77, 120
buggy model, 94
Business Intelligence, 87, *See* analytics:software

categorical data, 105
Cause And Effect Diagram. *See* Fishbone Diagram
causes category of IDMM, 132
characteristic model, 94
charter, 125–126, 127, 156
Check Sheet, 78–79, 157
Churchman, West, 57, *See* Dialectic
cleaning of data, 102
collect data on causes step of IDMM, 134
collect initial data step of IDMM, 128
Collins, Jim, 18
Competitive Analysis. *See* analytics:software
consider possible options step of IDMM, 132
consistency of data, 99–101
corrective action plan, 136
correlation, 110
Cost-Benefit, 182
CRM (Customer Relationship Management), 90, 99
CSV (comma separated variable), 100

dashboard, 149–150
data visualization, 105, 106
DeBono, Edward, 33, *See* Lateral Thinking
decision category of IDMM, 132
decision step of IDMM, 132
Definition of Grouping Similarities, 34
Delbecq, Andre, 52, *See* Nominal Group
Deming, W. Edwards, 15, 143
descriptive analytics, 105, 111
descriptive statistics, 105, 106
diagnostic analytics, 104

Index

diagram the process step of IDMM, 130
diagramming the causes and effects step of IDMM, 132
Dialectic, 56
Drucker, Peter, 15
dummy variable, 110

Eight Dimensions of Quality, 132
Emerson, Harrington, 21
Emery, Fred, 64, 74 *See* Search Conference
ERP (Enterprise Resource Planning), 90, 99, 101
establish performance measures step of IDMM, 131
Expert Consultant, 37, 39, 68

Fishbone Diagram, 50, 54–55, 60, 82, 134, 154, 172
Flowchart, 61, 62, 75, 77, 131, 165, 205
Force Field Analysis, 61, 66, 67–69, 190–195
Forced Connections, 33–34

Gantt, Henry, 21
Garvin, David, 132
GIGO (Garbage In Garbage Out), 88, 96–97
Gilbreth, Frank, 21
Gordon, William, 41, 46, *See* Synectics
granularity, 89
granularity of data, 99–101
group differences, 105, 110–111

hedgehog concept. *See* Collins, Jim
Hierarchy of Needs
    Belongingness, 8–9
    Esteem, 9–10
    physiological needs, 6
    Safety, 78
    Self-Actualization, 10
Histogram, 78, 80, 134
holistic approach, 23, 40
hyperactive, 17, *See* problem-solving attitude

Ideal Decision Making Model, 125
Idealized Design, 61, 66, 68, 69–71, 178
IDMM (Ideal Decision Making Model), 125
inactive, 15, *See* problem-solving attitude

inferential statistics, 105, 111
Interaction Associates Checklist, 37
interactive. *See* problem-solving attitude
interval data, 105
Ishikawa, Kaoru, 54, *See* Fishbone Diagram

Just In Time training, 117

Kaplan, Robert S., 147, 148, *See* Balanced Scorecard
Kawakita, Jiro, 50, *See* TKJ
knowledge engineer, 92
knowledge management, 92
knowledge representation, 92
Koberg, Daniel, 36, 38, 41

Lateral Thinking, 33
Lewin, Kurt, 67, *See* Force Field Analysis
Lynch, Bob, 127

machine learning, 92
macro perspective, 118
management,
    decentralized, 2
    systems, 1
    technology, impact on, 2
    telecommuting, impact on, 2
Manipulative Verbs Technique, 38
Maslow, Abraham, 5
Matrix, 34
Mcleod, Saul, 6
measure success or failure step of IDMM, 167–168
mission measures, 132
Modified Delphi, 55–56, 57
Modified Idealized Design, 61, 72–73
Morphological Analysis, 34
Morphological Forced Connection, 34, 36, 41
multivariate analysis, 105, 111

natural language processing, 92, 94
neural networks, 92
Nominal Group, 50, 52, 55
Norton, David P., 147–148, 151, *See* Balanced Scorecard
numbers category of IDMM, 126

Ohno, Taichi, 40, *See* Ask Why At Least Five Times
OLTP (On Line Transaction Processing), 90, 99
Operational Creativity, 46
ordinal data, 105, 110
Osborn Checklist, 37
Osborn, Alex, 37–38, 45, *See* Osborn Checklist

Pareto Diagram, 80–81, 134, 154, 159
Parnes, S.J., 34, *See* Sliding Column Method
PDCA (Plan-Do-Check-Act), 137, 177
preactive, 17, *See* problem-solving attitude
predictive analytics, 104, 111, *See* inferential statistics
preprocessing of data, 102
prescriptive analytics, 104
privacy of data, 99
Problem Setting, 48–49
Problems-Within-Problems, 37
Process Function Deployment, 66, 75, 77, 134
process output measures, 132
process variable measures, 132

quality improvement teams, 25, 26, 27

reactive, 16, *See* problem-solving attitude
regression analysis, 82, 103, 105–106, 110, 111
Relationship Analogies, 40
relevancy of data, 99–101
reliability of data, 99–101
reward system, 4
richness of data, 99–101
Ryder Jr., James A., 148, *See* Balanced Scorecard

Scatter Diagram, 78, 81, 122, 176
SCM (Supply Chain Management), 90, 99, 101
scope step of IDMM, 157
Search Conference, 61, 64, 66, 74
Search Engines, 90
Seek-the-Larger-Network, 37

Service Blueprinting, 76, 77, 134
Shewhart Chart. *See* Statistical Control Chart
Shewhart, Walter, 79, *See* Statistical Control Chart
Shostack, G. Lynn, 76, *See* Service Blueprinting
Six Sigma, 9
Sliding Column Method, 34–35
social media, 87, 90, 99, 101, 104
social system, 21
sociotechnical systems, 21
Solution Preference Identification, 34
standardization, 137
Statistical Control Chart, 78, 79, 122
Storyboard, 45, 47–48, 57, 68, 154, 157, 165, 167, 177, 195
stratification, 134
stratified sample, 103
Swapping, 58, 59
Synectics, 41, 42

task force, 17, 25–27
Taylor, Frederick, 2, 21
technical systems, 21–22
timeliness of data, 99–101
TKJ, 50–51, 55, 57, 68, 83, 136, 144
Townsend, Pat, 63, *See* Two Words
TQM (Total Quality Management), 9
Training Just In Time, 117
transformation of data, 89
Tribus, Myron, 75, *See* Process Function Deployment
Two Words, 63, 77

validity of data, 99–101
Van De Ven, Andres. *See* Nominal Group
Van De Ven, Andrew, 52
Vergara, Elsa, 42
visual recognition, 92
VLDBS (Very Large Data Base), 91, *See* big data

Word Manipulation, 32

Zwicky, F., 35, *See* Morphological Analysis